Economic Stabilization

OBJECTIVES, RULES, AND MECHANISMS

PUBLISHED WITH AID FROM

THE CHARLES PHELPS TAFT MEMORIAL FUND

UNIVERSITY OF CINCINNATI

Economic Stabilization

OBJECTIVES,
RULES,
AND
MECHANISMS

BY
WALTER P. EGLE

PRINCETON UNIVERSITY PRESS
FOR
UNIVERSITY OF CINCINNATI

1952

Printed in the United States of America
by Princeton University Press, Princeton, New Jersey

FOREWORD

....

THE purpose of this study is to explore some areas of the problem of economic stabilization which appear to have been somewhat neglected in the current literature on stabilization. The reader, therefore, must not expect to find a detailed treatment of all the problems which have arisen in connection with business fluctuations and efforts to overcome them. The selection of problems follows from the author's tendency to examine the possibilities of economic stabilization within the framework of an essentially private system of enterprise. In the choice of this method of attack he was guided by the belief that very large and influential sections of the American public still feel a strong respect for private ownership and control of economic resources.

The student of economics undoubtedly will appreciate the peculiar difficulties surrounding stabilization efforts in such an environment. On the other hand, there can be no denying the fact that the problem of how to banish fluctuations of total economic activity is singularly meaningful from the viewpoint of an economy which is to retain capitalist institutions. However little we know about the causes of business fluctuations, it is certain that these spurts and slumps are peculiar to, and fundamentally conditioned by, the fact that the power of decision-making about the use of economic resources in capitalism is in the hands of a multitude of private individuals. In a collectivized system the problem of instability is bound to appear in a sense substantially different from that of the cycle.

The study has a central theme which by its nature can be developed only in stages. This theme is the subjection of stabilizing efforts of the government to a clearly defined and binding objective (guarantee). It involves questions of both ends and means which—in the interest of orderly and systematic presentation—have been dealt with separately, as much as this is possible. Also, since the theme is by no means an original contribution of this writer, it was found advisable to present it in already known versions and to proceed from there to demonstrate inherent possibilities of development into currently more appealing versions, i.e., as regards the issue of the proper *goal* of a stabilizing program. Therefore the careful student should read the book as a whole before reaching conclusions about the merit of the theme, despite the fact that the method of partial development and later expansion involves a certain inevitable amount of repetition.

In enlarging upon an already known and by no means generally popular theme, the writer has been fully aware of the dangers involved in the venture. Those members of the economic profession who account for the introduction of the proposal to adopt a mandatory objective of stabilization procedure may feel that the variations and enlargements presented in this study lead to such distortions of their thought as to amount to heresy. The large remainder of the profession, on the other hand, may not take any more kindly to the idea of binding objectives, despite the writer's effort to adapt it to modern thinking as regards the substantive goals of national economic policy. Yet it would be unwise to drop the subject in the face of such possible dangers. Perhaps it will be possible to convince at least some of those who are opposed to binding stabilization objectives that loosely defined goals, pursued on a mere policy basis rather than on the basis of a firm governmental commitment, are the greatest obstacle in a nation's effort to break with the tradition of economic instability. The factor of political expediency which so overwhelmingly appears to be on the side of loose standards of stabilization and of improvisation as to stabilizing means should not be permitted forever to obstruct progress in the discussion of countercyclical programs. On the other hand it is to be hoped that the originators of the notion of a mandatory goal can be convinced that the soundness of their basic line of reasoning does not depend upon the selection of the particular objective (guaranteed stable money) which they favor. The general logic of their theory is that the achievement of a stable system of *private* enterprise necessitates the adoption of a rigorously binding objective which, after years of determined and successful enforcement by the government, may eventually become increasingly self-sustaining in the sense that the actions of private enterprise will be such as to dampen economic fluctuations. This important idea should not be tied up with a rather narrowly reasoned, and theoretically untenable, philosophy concerning the proper division of responsibilities between government and private enterprise, such as is exemplified by the claim that the legitimate part which the government is to play in stabilization begins and ends with taking exclusive control of the supply of money for the purpose of guaranteeing a stable level of prices. Stable money cannot be achieved in a vacuum, so to speak. Effective measures designed to stabilize the value of money must inevitably proceed through channels which affect total employment, output, and national income. This is not saying, of course, that a stable money would give us precisely the same degree of general economic stability as, for example, stabilization of output or income. If the latter types of objectives actually offered a more satisfactory standard for countercyclical procedure and carried more public appeal than stable money alone, there should be strong reasons for the proponents of a stable-money rule to adapt their general idea of binding targets to these circumstances.

The author is strongly indebted to his colleagues at the University of Cincinnati, Professor William W. Hewett and Messrs. Myron J. Spencer and Robert Wessel, who have given helpful criticism and suggestions for improvement at various stages of the work. Also, he expresses his gratitude to Mr. Gerhard Colm, economist on the staff of the Council of Economic Advisers to the President of the United States, for his judicious advice preceding the revision of the manuscript. Finally, this book could not have been written without the numerous discussions which the author had with Mr. Aaron Director, University of Chicago, on the basic prerequisites of stabilization procedure which would be compatible with an attempt to preserve a predominantly private system of enterprise. The author's gratitude, however, is not matched by his confidence of having written something with which Professor Director would be in complete agreement; he takes full responsibility for the ideas and proposals which are presented in this study.

Valuable comments and suggestions on major parts of the book were made by Professor Albert G. Hart, Columbia University.

W. P. E.

Cincinnati 1951

CONTENTS

[ix]

PART III

THE METHOD OF BINDING TARGETS

PART IV

THE MEANS OF STABILIZATION

PART I

SOME GENERAL ISSUES CONCERNING STABILIZATION

PART I

SOME ... PROBLEMS ...
... ...

CHAPTER 1

PSEUDOSTABILIZATION PROBLEMS

....

The Obscuring Influence of the Stagnation Doctrine

A GREAT deal of contemporary economic discussion in the United States as well as elsewhere passes for discussion of economic stabilization although it has really nothing to do with the problem of instability and with methods designed to achieve overall stability of the economy.

Let us bear in mind that the phenomenon which gave rise to the problem of instability is the succession of violent ups and downs of total economic activity which characterizes the history of the private-enterprise system. It is to this problem that the discussion has to be brought back. Whether or not the succession of ups and downs is aptly referred to as business cycles is a matter of secondary importance. Those who feel that this term is too suggestive of the elements of periodicity and regularity may discard it. For them the term business fluctuations would seem to answer the purpose. For those among us, however, who are accustomed to using the word cycle in a less technical sense—merely to refer to the succession of booms and slumps—cycle will continue to serve as a convenient abbreviation, as well as will the adjectives counter-cyclical and anticyclical. There appears to be little danger of harm involved in the use of these terms.

As long as we do no more than try to reach an agreement on what is meant by instability, it matters very little what are the causes of this instability. The frequent distinctions of endogenous and exogenous causes, and of causes which are controllable within the framework of capitalism as against causes which are uncontrollable, are important when it comes to de-

[3]

signing stabilization procedure. But these controversial issues should not be allowed to obscure the fact that there is a problem of instability. Nor does the obsolescence of certain types of cycle theories prove anything against the relevance of the cycle problem itself. It may be true that the prevalence of the gold standard prior to World War I was of some importance for the business fluctuations in the nineteenth and early twentieth centuries, but the disappearance of the gold standard should not give rise to the suggestion that the cycle problem has virtually ceased to exist for this reason (Hawtrey). Clearly, the interwar period was marked by booms and depressions, and this is what counts.

However, the chief obscuring factor in the general discussion of instability and stabilization today is the stagnation doctrine. Many writers fail to separate clearly the problem of chronic unemployment from that of the cycle. The cycle problem is, so to speak, drowned in the flood of stagnation, and in proposals designed to make our economy operate at the full employment level. This is unfortunate. Stagnation has very little to do with short-run instability. In fact, if we think of stagnation in terms of a chronic underemployment equilibrium it is obvious that we are dealing with something that is distinctly stable. Of course, not every stagnationist thinks of stagnation in terms of equilibrium. Most specialists in this field, including Keynes and Hansen, seem to have in mind an economy in which cyclical upswings are short and weak in comparison to the slumps. Here stagnation is not presented in terms of an underemployment equilibrium but rather in terms of a tendency toward a level of activity involving a permanent though somewhat varying float of unemployed resources, both human and material. But even in this version there is not much left to say about cycles. Whatever fluctuations of activity these stagnationists consider likely, or possible, could hardly give rise to major concern. What counts in these circumstances is the alarming size of the float of unemployment over the average of years.

Countercyclical and counterstagnation programs involve different solutions not only as regards ends but also means. Effective countercyclical machinery must satisfy, first of all, the need for quick action. The lag between the recognition of the need for action and between the taking of action and its effects on the economy must be as short as possible (the ideal would be action based on forecasting of needs). In contrast to counterstagnation policy, countercyclical policy and machinery must be quickly reversible. Not only downswings but also upswings must be checked before they become untractable. Speedy changes from income-supporting to curbing measures are necessary. In addition to flexibility and reversibility, a countercyclical program must facilitate action of great strength and stamina, to deal with possibly stubborn destabilizing forces. Yet the aspect of strength and stamina of controls is not as characteristic of countercyclical machinery as that of flexibility. On the other hand, a program designed to meet secular stagnation involves primarily ability to embark upon continuous and presumably powerful income-supporting operations. Although the intensity of such operations may have to vary somewhat through time—depending on whether the total of private activity showed some degree of fluctuations—flexibility here is clearly secondary to stamina of means. Especially if the goal is to be no less than full employment, action would be in the direction of supporting the economy (particularly if we start from a low point) rather than putting the brakes on private investment and privately generated income. The only exception to this rule would be provided by instances in which the government might have overestimated the necessary amount of support and hence would have to correct its mistake through temporary curbing action.

There exists a strong presumption that machinery designed

[5]

to cope with a cyclically unstable economy is not adequate to meet secular stagnation. But it is also fair to say that a counter-stagnation program may fail to offer any solutions in the face of a cyclically dynamic economy. Such a program, based as it is on the assumption of fairly steady and persistent drags on activity, relies on relatively unwieldy devices for supporting total activity.

These points are so obvious that it is difficult to see how there could be any confusion between the problems of cycles and stagnation. In fact, it takes additional elements to explain why the student of current economic literature cannot obtain a clear impression as to what is meant to refer to cyclical fluctuations, and what to chronic depression.

One of these elements is the almost universal acceptance of the full-employment objective. Inasmuch as the economy of the nineteenth and beginning twentieth century, despite its dynamic character, was not able to achieve full employment even in good times, it would seem that countercyclical programs which aim at the full-employment mark are bound to become involved in continuous income-supporting operations. Even a somewhat less ambitious goal may leave a certain residual of this program. The problem itself is serious for any specialist on countercyclical action since there exists no factually observable level at which a cyclically dynamic economy is in equilibrium.

There is another reason why countercyclical discussion is so often mixed with plans purporting to cope with stagnation. One may not subscribe to the stagnation doctrine in its graver version (Keynes, Hansen) but still speak of a problem of chronic underemployment, and hence become involved in something which closely resembles counterstagnation plans.

A clarification of the complications caused by the full-employment goal would anticipate too much of what has to be said later and hence will be postponed. But the second point can be dealt with immediately.

Two Versions of the Stagnation Doctrine

There are at least two different meanings of the term stagnation. For want of a better word, we shall call one version the doctrine of uncontrollable stagnation and the other the doctrine of controllable stagnation.

Proponents of the first hold the fatalistic view that certain conditions under which the private-enterprise system was able to perform satisfactorily have definitively disappeared. According to this view capitalism was able to render a most important service to men as long as there existed an abundance of resources to be exploited and a rapidly growing supply of labor to be employed. In the last few decades, it is argued, these conditions have changed in such a way as to mark the end of capitalism's usefulness. Utilized natural resources are said to be no longer abundant; the frontier, revolutionary technological advance, rapid population growth are held to be a matter of the past. In short, certain types of opportunities for profitable investment of funds and of entrepreneurial effort are regarded as having measurably disappeared, and along with them the chances of expansion of the type necessary to cyclical upsurges. Nor is it considered possible, in this version, that the community could do very much about these problems as long as it insisted upon maintaining a system of private enterprise.

Let us now look at the second version of the stagnation problem according to which chronic underemployment does not result from forces which are uncontrollable within the institutional framework of capitalism. By and large the expounders of this view are eager to point out that the causes of chronic depression are fundamentally alien to capitalism.[1] They claim that capitalism—in the sense of a system based on private property, competition, freedom of individual economic motivation and

[1] See, for example, Howard S. Ellis in B. M. Anderson, J. M. Clark, et al., *Financing American Prosperity: A Symposium of Economists*, New York: Twentieth Century Fund, 1945, pp. 126-196.

venturesomeness, the profit motive and consumer's choice—has never been fully tried, and in the last few decades less so than before. A wave of regulatory legislation and an excessive emphasis on individual and group security fostered, in part, by government are said to be responsible for the questionable performance of the system we have. The loss of dynamic qualities, i.e., the inability of the system to furnish investment outlets for savings commensurable with the savings activity of the public and banking facilities, is linked with the anomaly of monopoly (in the widest sense of the word, including policies of pressure groups involving restrictive results) and with the increasing tendency to avoid risk-taking.

Ambiguity of the Term Antistagnation Procedure

Both groups of stagnationists speak of the necessity of adopting antistagnation measures. The term antistagnation procedure, however, is ambiguous. It may mean several different things. For instance, it may mean a direct onslaught on the alleged forces of stagnation, an attempt to banish them from the scene of private enterprise. This is known as reactivation or rejuvenation of capitalism—terms which are suggestive of the view that stagnation is controllable.

Since the end of World War II a variety of rejuvenation proposals have appeared in American economic literature. Broadly speaking, their purpose is to strengthen private venturesomeness and risk-taking. In some proposals the need for tax reform is greatly stressed. Most elaborate suggestions have been made to the effect that income from security-investment be taxed more heavily than income derived from risk-investment. In the same category belongs the suggestion (which is not new) that money hoards be subjected to a special levy. To foster new and small enterprise, some specialists recommend an extension of the current provisions for the tax treatment of operating losses and capital losses. In some instances it has been suggested that the provisions be carried to the extreme of complete loss-sharing on the part of the fiscal agent (Hansen). In addition, there are proposals designed to encourage competition through reform of patent law, through removal of government support of monopoly in all respects (tariffs, price-maintenance clauses, agricultural crop support, etc.), through governmentally financed research to be made freely available to industry (especially with an eye on the needs of small enterprise incapable of carrying on extended technological research) and, of course, through a more vigorous application of antitrust procedure. Last but not least, the banking system is to be revitalized through reform purporting to diminish bank income from government bonds, thereby forcing our commercial banks to reemphasize loans to private business as a source of income.

There is hardly any part of the economy that is not covered by this campaign for the reestablishment of pioneering investment and risk-taking. The fruit of such efforts, presumably, would be a return to the dynamic pattern of the previous century.[2]

On the other hand, antistagnation procedure may mean an attempt to offset, or compensate for, the factors or tendencies which are said to make for chronic depression. The terms offsetting or compensating can be given different interpretations, primarily in the sense of various degrees of political and economic radicalism. For example, one might conceivably go so far as to call the resort to rigorous central planning and coercive forms of resource allocation (with or without transition to public ownership) an offsetting or compensating procedure. But this is not in line with the usual thinking on the subject, at least not in the United States. There prevails a tendency to have the government abstain from action which would abolish the working rules and organizational characteristics

---

[2] In the already mentioned study, *Financing American Prosperity*, at least half of the contributors follow an amazingly similar pattern of thought along the above lines. In addition to Ellis, see also the contributions of Hansen and Slichter.

of the economic area whose unsatisfactory performance gives rise to the desire for compensating action, i.e., the area of private enterprise. This may mean but one thing: an attempt to build up, side by side with private enterprise, an area of governmental enterprise (a mixed or dual economy). In this fashion a fuller utilization of available resources is to be secured.

This compensatory version of antistagnation procedure appears to be associated with the doctrine of uncontrollable stagnation. The historical relationship is indeed close. But we must hasten to add that the compensatory method now enjoys wider application. Not only does the method dominate the current debate on cycle control—a fact which must be considered in detail later—but it has also been proposed for purposes of *reactivating* private enterprise. In this latter sense, compensatory action is to perform a twofold function: (1) to lift the level of activity through increased governmental investment and publicly generated income; and (2) to create additional investment opportunities for private enterprise. This dual purpose is indicated by the popular concept of compensatory-developmental policy.

Moreover, the boundary line between uncontrollable and controllable stagnation is not sharp. Lately the campaign for reactivating private enterprise for purposes of full employment has been joined by economists who, some ten years ago, presented the stagnation problem primarily in its graver version. A conspicuous example is furnished by Professor Hansen, who has vigorously joined the campaign, perhaps to the point of making original suggestions along the previously mentioned lines of antitrust action, tax reform, and other measures aiming at greater risk-taking.[3] However this does not mean that this important writer has forever discarded the relevance of that more ominous set of obstructions to private investment

---

[3] See particularly his contribution in *Financing American Prosperity*, pp. 199-264.

and employment (retardation of basic technological progress, population growth, private resource development) with which his name is associated. One may safely conclude that his appraisal of capitalism—even in the event of successful attempts to stimulate private investment—would still be in the direction of sluggishness and that it takes, in addition to such attempts, a mixture of compensatory public investment and private investment over many years to come in order to secure a high and rising level of income.

Reactivation of Private Enterprise Is Not Stabilization Procedure

At this point let us return to the subject of the relationship between antistagnation and stabilization procedure. The reactivation approach, however important and valuable from the standpoint of preserving the system of private enterprise, is not in itself short-run stabilization. On the contrary, it is the very opposite, at least as long as the drive toward venturesomeness and risk-taking is carried on with *single-mindedness* of purpose, that is to say, without concomitant action designed to cope with general booms and slumps. If it is true that the so-called tendency of savings to be in excess of private investment is merely the result of monopoly and an increasing preference for security investment, then a determined and far-reaching program designed to foster risk-taking and pioneering investment might generate business fluctuations such as we have never seen before, unless such a program could be accompanied by an effective program of countercyclical action. Particularly aggravating is the suggestion that the banks should be forced back on the path of greater aggressiveness in lending policy (see, for example, Ellis).[4] From the standpoint of short-run stabilization, such a suggestion should not be made without attempting to show whether, or to what extent, an aggressive lending policy of private banks is compatible with

[4] *Financing American Prosperity*, pp. 148-153.

effective central banking control aiming at damped fluctuations. So far there hardly exists a genuine countercyclical plan which favors establishment of aggressive private banking on the basis of liberal requirements as to liquidity. Stabilization experts are most unanimously of the opinion that a relatively unrestrained system of private banking has failed in providing a monetary framework suited for a system of private competitive enterprise, and that it cannot provide such a framework. Hence the widely expressed desire for banking reform which aims at stronger control of the lending policies of private banks, both as to the quantity and quality of loans. It does not matter, at this point, how far (from the standpoint of cycle control) the regulation of banks should go. In other words, it does not matter whether banking reform should go to the extreme of enforcing something in the nature of a 100 per cent reserve plan, or stop short of such radical curbing of banking power.

To be compatible with short-run stabilization, the campaign for reactivation must proceed with some moderation. However important the principle of competition and risk-taking from the viewpoint of resource utilization, it would be unwise to rely completely on this principle. Let us not make a one-sided issue of aggressive banking. Limitations on measures designed to foster profit motives and risk-taking suggest themselves quite generally from the standpoint of curbing business swings. For example, a program of tax abatement for income from risk-investment might, in the interest of greater stability, have to be accompanied by a set of rules according to which the tax abatement on business profits, dividends, and high personal incomes could be varied in accordance with the phase of the cycle. The degree to which such income is to be favored taxwise might have to depend on the depth of the slumps, and tax incentives might have to give way to a policy of discriminating against such incomes in times of speculative booms. This, of course, is far from being a novel idea, and it is mentioned here merely for the sake of showing what kind of measures might reconcile reactivation of private enterprise with short-run stability of the economy.

The Compensatory Approach to Antistagnation Policy and the Problem of Stabilization

We may now turn to the compensatory version of antistagnation procedure which, to repeat, is closely related to the conviction that chronic underemployment cannot be remedied simply by an attack on monopoly and the atrophy of private venturesomeness. Our interest in this alarming theory is, again, limited to the question of the logical relationship between the proposed type of antistagnation measures and the subject of short-run stabilization.

The average propounder of the doctrine of uncontrollable stagnation is not primarily concerned with methods to overcome business swings. If there be any doubt on this score, it is only because he is not satisfied with merely raising total activity to the full-employment mark but also tries to see to it that this level, once reached, subsequently is maintained. In this latter respect he invites for himself, perhaps, a problem of instability. But it is of a new kind, not the sort of problem with which cycle theory has been grappling. Let us contrast these two types of problems as sharply as possible.

Only a short time ago, when it was still fashionable for economists to apply their minds to the riddle of the business cycle, there came to some prominence the theory that intermittent spurts and slumps were caused by almost irresistible movements of private investment, in conjunction with the so-called wavelike character of innovation (Schumpeter), or the wavelike character of business psychology (Pigou). As long as this, or a similar, view of autonomous investment cycles prevailed, attention was focused entirely on instabilities in the economy per se.

In the hands of the stagnationist, the problem of instability tends to undergo a major change of meaning. Instead of being a problem of spurts and slumps of private investment, it becomes a problem of the stamina of governmental income-supporting machinery. The proposal for continuous and possibly large loan-financed central income-supporting measures accounts for an unmistakable tendency to be preoccupied with the question a growing national debt. In a country like the United States, such preoccupation is highly understandable, considering the widespread public anxiety and skepticism concerning controls which involve a possibly steep rise of public debt or a stiff increase in taxation to balance a conspicuously large government budget. In the writings of Professor Hansen and other stagnationists, distinct and elaborate efforts are made to prove that after some decades of consistent and determined deficit financing the government budget would eventually tend to become balanced at reasonable taxes to service the public debt. The growth of the national debt would come to a halt; an allegedly higher and higher level of private investment, induced by the government's promotional investment and by simultaneous reactivation programs indicated earlier, would account for this fortunate event.

Now it is true, of course, that the worry about the stamina of governmental income-supporting machinery stems, in part, from factors operating within the area of private enterprise. But it is not any longer fear of the volatile character of private investment which troubles the mind. This fear is replaced by the fear of slow and inadequate response of private investment activity to deficit financing. Slow response is perfectly consistent with the drive for orderly and precalculated expansionary action by government, but it makes uncomfortably large demands on the size of the government's budget. The issue is reflected in a change of terminology about budgetary controls. As long as the view of volatile (autonomous) private investment prevailed, budgetary operations appeared in the modest role of pump-priming. A cyclically dynamic economy, so we were told, moves on its own momentum when it expands. It may have to be "shoved off dead center, so to speak, in order to resume the normal movement from crisis and depression to revival and recovery."[5] But the volume of governmental spending involved in pump-priming bears no precalculated quantitative relationship to the recovery effect which is expected. The leverage effect is totally out of proportion to the effort, quite in contrast to the compensatory-developmental operations which fit the case of a stagnant economy. In fact, the role of government, vis-à-vis such an autonomous expansionary process, is supposed to shift quickly from pump-priming to curbing action, on the theory that spasmodic breakdowns of activity are the result of excessive speed of expansion.

It would be an exaggeration to say that the assumption of unstable private investment patterns has totally disappeared in the thinking and writing of stagnationists. Here and there, proposals to lift activity from a lower to a higher level contain elements of thought which genuinely belong in the theory of cycle control. After its voyage from the bottom to the top, the economy might acquire some instabilities which it did not possess before. If this should be the case, intended compensatory action (based on the assumption of a constant multiplier effect) admittedly might turn out to have unintended pump-priming effects. The response of private enterprise might also be worse than expected. By and large, however, the proponents of perpetual antistagnation procedure have done little to avoid the impression that they postulate an economy which, as far as private investment response is concerned (and also the consumption function), is now fairly well suited for precalculable expansionary action by government. The economy, in their opinion, has reached a point where central budgeting for full employment—including limited forecasts of private investment activity—is not beyond the hope of reasonable attain-

[5] Alvin H. Hansen, *Fiscal Policy and Business Cycles*, W. W. Norton and Company, Inc., New York, 1941. p. 262.

ment. They tend to think in terms of fairly stable relationships among the main components of national income (income-consumption relationship, income-investment relationship, etc.).[6]

Continued Interest in Cycle Problem Is No Detriment to Theory of Stagnation

The purpose of this discussion is not to discredit the doctrine of stagnation. Rather, the inference to be drawn is merely that the issue of business swings and their remedy should be kept strictly apart from that of secular stagnation. Only in this fashion can clear, unequivocal results be obtained in both areas of economic analysis. The advantages of separate discussion remain even if, in a treatment of specifically countercyclical problems, one decides to keep the subject of *continuous* income-supporting measures within hailing distance. For this, one need not subscribe to the stagnation doctrine in its graver

[6] In one form or another, the influence of this hypothesis of a docile economy underlies most of the full-employment models and the policy inferences drawn from them. The crucial point is not that these models are essentially static, i.e., a series of equilibrium positions of systems of static relationships. Equilibrium models can be set up and have been set up by economists who do not reckon with a tendency toward a chronic underemployment level of activity. Such models, after all, can serve purposes other than policy proposals. The influence of the stagnation doctrine is more nearly felt in the postulate that—as one critic points out—"the major components of the national product are determined by the scale and character of the government's fiscal operations—in a setting, of course, of relationships among the components, expressing other economic forces." (Albert G. Hart, "Model Building and Fiscal Policy," *The American Economic Review*, September 1945, pp. 531-532.) More precisely, the influence is felt in the assumption that federal budgetary magnitudes—government expenditures, revenues of various taxes, and "other magnitudes which may be thought of as directly controllable by government"—are the active variables of the economic system. The components of the national product (investment, consumption) are passive variables. The same goes for the components of national income (wages, profits, etc.) as well as for the components of disposable income (individual savings, consumers' spending).

This procedure is really meaningful only in respect to an economy which promises fairly reliable responses to central budgetary operations. It would hardly make sense in an economy loaded with forces which tend to generate violent fluctuations of private investment.

version. All that is necessary is to assume (as this writer does) that monopolistic restrictions and undue concern with security account for chronic underemployment. As will be shown later, removal of this underemployment had better be entrusted to a gradual attack on monopoly rather than to monetary-fiscal expansionary controls, which, after all, may produce inflationary leakages rather than full employment as long as these restrictive barriers are allowed to exist.

As its title indicates, this study is devoted to cyclical fluctuations and their control. To single out this topic implies, of course, a belief as to the practical importance of this subject. This belief is not farfetched. The unusually prolonged postwar prosperity does not prove that cycles are gone. In part, this phenomenon may be attributable to the unusual circumstances of the war and its aftermath. Let us also bear in mind that some progress has been made in cycle control. Both the government and influential private groups are not only keenly aware of the possibility of a slump but appear to be willing to do more nearly the right things to avoid disaster than was true in the twenties and before. On the other hand, these improvements do not appear to be sufficient to let the matter rest. We are still far from having accepted, as a nation, a program which entitles us to be at ease. Anything can happen still.

As to stagnation, it goes without saying that an essentially capitalistic nation should have some plan of action to meet such a contingency if and when it should arise.

CHAPTER 2

TWO SCHOOLS OF THOUGHT ON COUNTERCYCLICAL ACTION

....

An Attack on Underlying Causes versus Compensatory Cycle Control

THE campaign for economic stabilization has arisen from the experience of cyclical instability in the private-enterprise system. As long as the community thinks in terms of this type of economic organization, and clings to it, all efforts at stabilization must be shown to be compatible with the maintenance of at least a predominantly private character of enterprise. Subsequent to stabilization, scale and composition of national product must continue to be determined, primarily, by the forces of the market. In other words, the achievement of stability has to proceed in the form of an effort to create an essentially *self-sustaining* equilibrium.

For a long time—in the United States as well as in other countries adhering to private enterprise—the discussion of stabilization actually proceeded in such terms. Economists reared in the classical tradition were engaged in an effort to detect the causes of violent ups and downs and, after having reached some conclusions about the nature of these forces, suggested means and ways of eliminating them from the scene.

In the last two decades, however, this approach has quite perceptibly faded into the background. The reasons for this are not entirely clear. One contributing factor might have been the fact that some noted specialists arrived at conclusions about the character and significance of the destabilizers which discourage the idea of a direct onslaught on causes. We need not think here of the extreme hypothesis that the causes are entirely beyond human control (as in the case of the theory of crop variations and their alleged responsibility for overall fluctuations in economic activity). More influential, perhaps, has been the theory of some well-known specialists (notably Schumpeter and Robertson) which associates cyclical instability with technological progress and secular growth. Cycles are said to be caused by a wavelike pattern of major innovations which supposedly establishes an *inherently* unstable pattern of economic development. Persuasive arguments in favor of tolerating swings have emerged from this quarter. They center in the proposition that depressions normally fail to destroy as much as periods of prosperity add to industrial technology and material wealth so that, on balance, the secular tendency is one of growth—and a fairly rapid rate at that. To be sure, this view does not altogether preclude efforts to control swings. But the aim would have to be modest.

It is doubtful to what extent this theory has contributed to the current deemphasis on cause removal. The theory is by no means widely accepted, at least not in the ambitious form in which it was developed by Schumpeter. There have been many specialists who adhere to some form of monetary explanation of cycles (Hawtrey, Wicksell, Hayek, Fisher, Simons, and others). Without needing to go into any detail, it may be said here that the monetary cycle theory permits fairly optimistic conclusions about the merit as well as the feasibility of cycle control through an attack on causes. One of the inferences which may be drawn is that cycles are devoid of constructive meaning and hence should be exterminated. In particular, cycles do not appear as a symptom and form of secular growth. Therefore any tolerance of a wide leeway for swings on behalf of efficiency and growth is not indicated. In the words of these writers, the primary destabilizing factor—periodic expansions and contractions in the total volume of bank loans initiated, or at least made possible, by a system of private competitive commercial banking—amounts to a perversion in our economy. Far from endangering the basic long-range objectives of progress and growth, and far from attacking a vitally necessary institution of capitalism, a program embodying the removal of this alleged destabilizing factor is said to free the private-enterprise system from something which should never have been allowed to enter.[1]

This theory, too, is far from being generally accepted. The same holds true of all the remaining cycle theories, be it one of the many versions of the underconsumption theory, or the overinvestment theory, or the so-called psychological theories. In fact, it is safe to say that the deemphasis on cause removal is not so much due to the influence of any particular theory which claims that the destabilizing forces are either desirable or, as the case may be, uncontrollable within the framework of capitalism. Rather it appears to be the result of the simultaneous presence of so many conflicting theories. This phenomenon clearly indicates that we possess as yet no trustworthy knowledge about cycle causation. True, there prevails considerable agreement as regards the nature of the forces and processes which account for *cumulative* tendencies, once the economy has started to move from depression to upturn, or from boom to depression. But the causes of the turning points, and the degree of influence which these initial forces exercise upon the ensuing processes of expansion or contraction, remain in the dark.

It is understandable that the impatient eye of those interested in workable programs of checking swings has begun to look for alternative methods of stabilization. As in the case of the stagnation theory, the answer appears to be the com-

---

[1] At this point the reader cannot fail to notice a certain parallelism between the previously discussed stagnation doctrine and the theory of cycles. In each case there appear grave versions embodying underlying causes which cannot be removed without jeopardizing the institutional framework of capitalism or its vitality, and other versions pointing toward causes which, by contrast, cry for removal in order to establish a well-functioning system of private enterprise.

pensatory approach. Rather than trying to isolate and remove the underlying causes, this approach amounts to an attempt merely to offset them with the aid of a system of variable income-supporting or, as the case may be, income-depressing central operations. Government is to furnish the flexible balance wheel, largely through countercyclically varying budgets and monetary policies. The attempted goal is no longer a self-sustaining equilibrium of total private investment and privately generated income. In fact, the notion of overall stability in terms of a self-sustaining balance meets with profound skepticism. If there is to be such a thing as a stable level of activity it must, according to prevailing opinion, be a matter of *continuous* stabilizing operations on the part of government. Nor is this all. In addition to being continuous, the operations are described as having to be heavy most of the time. Thus stabilization of total activity presents itself as a stabilization of the *sum* of private and governmentally determined activity. At no time, therefore, would there be such a thing as a self-sustaining balance of private enterprise per se, unless the term were meant to refer merely to the possibility of some self-containing private sector of the (mixed) economy.

As applied to a cyclically active economy, the compensatory method is subject to much greater difficulty than in the event of a stagnant system. The assumption of precalculable responses and of fairly stable relationships between the major components of national income or disposable income can no longer be made. If the method is to be applied, it must be presented in a different light. As will be shown later in detail, the hope rests on the ability of government to make fast decisions on the basis of current experience (as indicated by sensitive indexes), and on marked flexibility and reversibility of compensatory devices. Even so, the method has very frequently been the object of sharp criticism, some of which must be dealt with here.

The upholders of the tradition of cause removal claim that

the compensatory method is, at best, remedial rather than preventive. Merely to offset swings of private income and employment through a variable layer of governmentally determined activity is said to be superficial. Even if this offsetting procedure should be successful in the sense of leading to a stable sum of private and public activity, it would fail to make any contributions to the problem of how to secure greater inherent stability of private enterprise—the very heart of the stabilization issue.

This is merely one of several types of criticism.[2] Frequently the attack consists of expressions of doubt that compensatory efforts can achieve a stable aggregate of private and public activity. Thus it has often been argued that central income-supporting measures may aggravate rather than reduce unemployment in private industry and, hence, exhaust themselves in a race against unfavorable business reaction. It is also claimed that compensatory efforts are normally doomed to failure on account of insurmountable difficulties of proper timing, as well as proper determination of the order of magnitude of government action. Proper timing is said to depend either on correct forecasting of coming events in the private sector or, at a minimum, on incredibly fast and flexible action of government on the basis of the current situation. In view of past records, neither forecasting nor administrative alertness and flexibility of governmental policy are said to warrant optimism as to the potentialities of the method. Again on the basis of past experience—and with particular reference to the domestic scene—skepticism has arisen about the possibility of giving any compensatory program the necessary degree of political acceptance and assuredness, in terms of a clear-cut legal arrangement embodying unequivocal authority and responsibility on the part of government to practice compensa-

[2] Since the above as well as the following attacks on the compensatory approach are spread broadly through the entire current literature and public debate on stabilization, the writer has found it unnecessary to cite particular sources on the subject in question.

tory controls in pursuit of a defined goal. In the absence of such an arrangement, the compensatory method is said to suffer from a fatal lack of stamina, i.e., from inability or unwillingness of the officials at the administrative center to keep counteracting swings when the going becomes rough and demands offsetting measures of considerable magnitude and duration. Also, in the absence of such an arrangement, it is claimed that compensatory programs are bound to be left to the mercy of legislative log-rolling, to the pursuit of special interests rather than of general economic stabilization.

Finally, there prevails widespread fear concerning the future status of private enterprise in the event that the compensatory method should very definitively become the core of our stabilization program. Depending on the creed or temperament of the critics, this anxiety centers either around the subject of increasing economic inefficiency, or around the specter of ruthless dictatorship involving the loss of traditional economic and, perhaps, even cultural freedoms.

All of these objections and misgivings (some of which prevail even among advocates of the compensatory method) deserve our most careful attention, especially in view of this writer's conviction that the compensatory method is an indispensable part of any hopeful program of countercyclical control. Only some of these attacks, however, lend themselves to an appraisal prior to the positive contributions to the stabilization problem which this study hopes to make. The remainder of the issues will be taken up as the analysis progresses and permits a sharper focus.

The Inevitable Compromise between Compensatory Action and an Attack on Underlying Causes

Unfortunately, the term compensatory or offsetting action suggests such narrow limitations as to the nature of what is to be achieved that the champions of this method invite for themselves unnecessary criticism. In point of fact there can be no such thing as a stable, or even nearly stable, aggregate of private and public employment or product without the achievement of some stabilizing effects in the private sector of the economy. If somebody is willing to go so far as to admit that a program of countercyclical budgetary and monetary operations of the government may succeed in stabilizing the "Nation's Economic Budget" at, or near, some premeditated level, then he cannot justly argue that the method is devoid of any attack on the underlying causes of swings. It is hopeless to claim that if in times of falling private production the government succeeds in bolstering total effective demand (income), this compensatory action has no steadying influence, for the time being, on private business expectations and, hence, on private production and employment. Let us grant that the factors which initiate the downturn of private activity are unknown. Let us even grant that these initial forces go unchecked as far as the ensuing compensatory action is concerned. All this does not matter for the issue on hand. What does matter is the fact that successful compensatory action is certain to interfere with the cumulative forces and processes which normally aggravate a downswing if given a chance to develop. These cumulative forces, and these cumulative processes, constitute the really serious part of the cycle problem. Therefore any method which promises to interfere with these forces can claim for itself that it makes a vital contribution to cause removal.

Without going into any detail about cumulative forces, two more or less obvious points can be made. Cycle theorists agree that cumulative spirals are caused, among other things, by unstable business expectations (waves of optimism and pessimism). An upswing is likely to be sustained and accelerated by the anticipation of further rising markets and prices; a downswing is likely to be accelerated by the expectation of falling demand and deflationary price tendencies. To break into this pattern of expectations is tantamount to laying a basis for reduced fluctuations. This is one concrete contribution which a system of consistent income-regulating measures of the compensatory type can make. Secondly, aside from exercising a steadying influence on business psychology, a successful compensatory program can claim for itself a steadying influence on the supply of credit. Here again we are concerned with a factor which primarily belongs in the category of cumulative forces. Whereas there is no conclusive evidence in support of the claim of monetary cycle theorists that turning points are *initiated* by changes in banking policy, there has been very little challenge of the hypothesis that in the past rapid expansions and contractions in bank loans are a *deepening* factor for business fluctuations. Compensatory fiscal controls, especially if combined with a closer cooperation with central banking policy, involve a firmer grip over the movements of the supply of credit and money.

For anyone who does not insist on strict even-keel performance of private enterprise, successful interference with cumulative forces and processes must be of great importance. If compensatory action can achieve the latter, he should come out in favor of this method. The promised results gain in stature if independent reasons can be established in favor of the view that it is undesirable to seek strict even-keel operations. This will be done in a later part of the study.

Nor is there any necessity for assuming that a compensatory program must stand by itself, i.e., that it cannot be combined with other measures designed to give us a more balanced economy. In particular, the approach is perfectly compatible with reform aiming at a better inter-industry balance and greater mobility of factors. In short, it is compatible with efforts to reduce monopolistic barriers. Insufficient emphasis on this point by some advocates of compensatory devices has given rise to unnecessary misgivings on this score.

So far the drift of our argument has been that the compensatory method is capable of working on certain underlying causes of fluctuations. It will actually attack such causes if it achieves what it is primarily supposed to achieve, namely, to produce a stable aggregate of private and public employment (income). Now we must turn around and look at the other side of the medal, i.e., the fact that there can be no stabilization program built *exclusively* on cause removal, free from any elements of planning and compensatory procedure. No matter how much a particular program stresses cause removal and the attainment of an essentially self-sustaining equilibrium of private enterprise, there will always have to be a certain irreducible minimum of premeditated action (planning) and central regulation of the scale of activity. The element of planning arises initially over the determination of the level at which the economy is to operate. Furthermore, it arises over the fact that this premeditated level has to be reached and defended with the aid of central compensatory action.

These facts can be demonstrated with the aid of an example, taken from the school of monetary cycle causation. According to this type of theory, the road to the elimination of business cycles is reform purporting to secure firm regulation of the money supply in accordance with some objective which, if reached and maintained, indicates the absence of monetary disturbances. Usually, the objective is a stable level of prices measured by some broad and truly representative index of commodity prices.

Let us begin by showing that planning actually lies behind this endeavor and that this planning can be concealed or minimized, but not avoided. The planning consists, first of all, of an essentially arbitrary decision at the inception of the program, namely, the arbitrary choice of the level at which prices in general are to be kept stable.

In some instances, the proposal for stable money has been made in the form of the suggestion that prices in general should be stabilized at a particular historical level which is chosen on the grounds that everything was well, from the standpoint of national income and employment, during the time at which this particular level prevailed. Depending on what has happened to prices since that time, the proposal involves either an initial reflation or deflation prior to stabilization. For example, proposals made during the depression of the thirties refer to some price scale of the twenties as the proper mark for stabilization and, hence, invariably embody an initial reflationary policy. Recent proposals, on the other hand, suggest stabilization after some deflation from current prices.[3]

The desire for restoration of some historical scale of prices is always indicative of the type of thinking which operates with the concept of normal business in the sense that the economy, at such prices, tended to show a relatively high degree of stability. But quite aside from the fact that some particular price level of the past becomes increasingly insignificant the more remote it is from the present, and the more pronounced the inflationary or deflationary movements since that normal state of affairs, the notion of a factually observable normal is in itself misleading. Any period of the past refers to some phase of the cycle. If there is something in the nature of an equilibrium level through which activity passed in its way from depression to boom, and vice versa, such a level could not be ascertained, at least not with our present state of knowledge. Nor can the problem be solved through the choice of arithmetic averages, such as the average between high and low points in the time series. Such averages cannot be considered equilibrium levels "unless some independent reasoning establishes them as such."[4] It would be naïve to use some average level between booms and slumps for purposes of establishing the secular trend and to identify this trend with stability. Although there are trend forces which are distinct from the

[3] See, for example, George L. Bach, "Monetary-Fiscal Policy, Debt Policy, and the Price Level," *The American Economic Review*, May 1947, p. 231.

[4] William Fellner, *Monetary Policies and Full Employment* (University of California Press, Berkeley, California, 1946), p. 16.

forces producing intermittent ups and downs of activity, we cannot simply take arithmetic averages obtained from factual material and regard them as a measure of these trend forces. There exists an interaction between trend forces and cyclical forces. "If the trend were different, the fluctuations would be different; and in the absence of the forces producing the fluctuations, the long-run drift of the time series would undoubtedly be quite different from anything actually observable. This is another way of saying that 'normal' or 'equilibrium' cannot be observed in statistical material."[5]

Not every proponent of stable money goes through the trouble of trying to find some normal or equilibrium position for purposes of establishing the mark at which the value of money is to be stabilized. Often the schemes are devoid of economic analysis. The period which is selected for setting a standard is then chosen, quite naïvely, because it spelled prosperity. Innocence of language and a typical understatement of the means which it takes to do the job cannot conceal the fact that we are being presented cases of genuine and unadulterated planning in terms of premeditated and, from the standpoint of the properties of a private economy, arbitrary levels of activity.

The planning aspects of the stable money scheme are least apparent if the case for price level stabilization is presented on the abstract grounds that money, in order to furnish a suitable standard of value, must be stable (Fisher, Simons). To tolerate a money with fluctuating and, as far as the future is concerned, uncertain purchasing power is said to amount to an incongruous situation. A basic principle of money is violated. It must not be violated any longer. Reform is long overdue. It must come in the form of decisive action which will terminate the past era of halfhearted measures devoid of the promise of success. The necessity of such action, according to this view, must not be confused with any reasons which may speak for stabilization

[5] *Ibid.*, p. 19.

of the money value at any *particular* historical level. They are regarded as being entirely of secondary importance, and the more the campaign for stable money is kept free of them, the better. The principle of stable money stands by itself and can be attained at any level of prices. It is axiomatic. Any price level, including the one which happens to exist at the time of inception, is suitable. Action should not be delayed on account of prevailing conditions and should not be preceded by initial inflationary or deflationary corrections. So the argument runs.

In appraising this argument, several points must be kept in mind. In the first place, when an abstract proposition is translated into policy it inevitably acquires something which it did not seem to have before. It is all very well to argue the case for stable money without reference to any factual level of prices. But when it comes to an actual stabilization of money the community must commit itself to some specific price level. The fact that some economic theorist may show no preference for a price level which is either higher or lower than the one which prevails at the inception of the scheme, and that he may not favor either a reflationary or deflationary interim prior to stabilization, does not relieve him, or anybody connected with policy-making, from the necessity of singling out some factual scale of prices and making it the mark of stabilization efforts. He has to break into the economic process in basically the same arbitrary way as the sponsors of a program who exercise a strong preference for the particular scale of prices at which the value of money is to be stabilized. The price scale which happens to prevail at the inception cannot be expected to be an equilibrium price level. To choose it as a starting point for monetary stabilization is tantamount to changing the course of prevailing cyclical tendencies.

Moreover—and this point is especially important—the value of money cannot be stabilized in a vacuum. It cannot be established apart from the objectives which are favored by those who openly adhere to the method of central planning, i.e., stable employment, or output, or income. The channels through which monetary stabilization proceeds are the same channels through which the stabilization of employment or income travels. If we stabilize the level of prices, we stabilize, *pari passu*, the level of employment. Let us not be deceived by the fact that the two types of objectives are not quite coextensive, or by the fact that proposals for monetary stabilization often refer to old-fashioned techniques of control relatively free from public suspicion of central planning and regulation. If these techniques—open market operations, changes in the terms of lending by banks—should prove to be sufficient to give us stable money, they would prove tolerably effective in giving us stable employment or income. If, on the other hand, they are ineffectual in the latter respect, they are so in the former also. It is true that as against the criterion of employment, the criterion of the price level seems to offer, in the long view, certain advantages of simplicity. Whereas we could not choose the employment criterion without having to make specific *ex ante* allowance for the growth of the working population, a once-selected price scale could always be left the same (except for occasional revision in the weighting of the index itself following changes in the commercial importance of individual commodities). But the advantage of simplicity is not as great as it appears on the surface. Properly timed price level stabilization, too, will have to make *ex ante* allowance for economic growth, to avoid deflationary friction. The only difference is that such allowance does not show up in the objective itself.

Let us now broaden the argument that there can be no exclusive reliance on cause removal.

First of all, such an attempt would be severely handicapped, at the present time, by the lack of trustworthy knowledge concerning the nature and degree of severity of the factors which account for crises and recoveries. If tried, the attempt could easily prove to be a costly failure. Instead of giving us stability, it might lead to a series of new disturbances, perhaps to stagnation. At a minimum, the venture might suffer from unwarranted one-sidedness or—in the case of a multiple attack—from misjudgment of the importance of this or that causal element.

Secondly, even if our knowledge of causes should substantially improve within the visible future, exclusive reliance on cause removal would still be of problematic value. Conceivably, the results might be gratifying. This is to say, the level of activity might settle above the mean average of booms and depressions. In addition, the secular rate of progress and growth might be faster than in the past. But there is no assurance that this would happen, and no nation which hitherto enjoyed a reasonably high degree of resource utilization over the average of years, and a fairly rapid increase in productivity and living levels, may be inclined to take a chance.

Thirdly, since in the absence of forces producing fluctuations the level of activity as well as the long-run drift of productivity would be different from anything observable in the past, it is more than likely that society would refuse to endorse any program of stabilization unless *premeditated* objectives were embodied in the program. To satisfy the need for public appeal, these objectives would have to be fairly ambitious. Viewed over time, the stabilization program would have to be presented in terms of balanced growth at, or near, the full employment mark. Premeditated objectives are alien to an approach which relies on nothing but cause removal and seeks to establish a natural level of activity and a natural rate of growth. They are a logical part of compensatory procedure.

Given such planned objectives, the case for cause removal is, however, by no means closed. But it must inevitably become a limited affair. It must be pursued hand in hand with offsetting techniques. The most promising area for cause removal is that of cumulative forces. As was pointed out, an attack on these forces is implied in the type of controls which usually are referred to as compensatory devices. But it may well be that in addition the need for a direct attack on certain destabilizers is indicated, provided it is possible to isolate them.

To sum up this discussion: no matter at which of the two rival methods we look, there are strong grounds for arguing that neither method can do the entire work. The two must be combined. But no general rules can be established in advance as to how much burden should be placed on each. The more we remain in the dark about the nature of the forces making for instability, the greater must be the emphasis on the compensatory method. The same holds true if the forces should become known but should prove to be unremovable except at the risk of jeopardizing the institutions or virility of capitalism. In this extreme case the compensatory measures would actually become nothing but offsetting measures, devoid of any implicit powers of cause removal. Needless to say, in these circumstances the economy would have to undergo great changes in the allocation of resources and the composition of national product in connection with offsetting policy. To overcome a slump, unemployed resources would have to be shifted into channels which are isolated from the troubled private industries. Large layers of make-work would have to be established and, as the tide turned, abandoned. Fortunately, this uninspiring picture can be dismissed from the mind. Pure offsetting rests on highly unrealistic assumptions. One would have to assume, for example, that the government fights a slump with the aid of increased public outlay on roads, dams, bridges, etc., without being able to exercise at least *some* steadying influence on private production of cement, steel, and so forth. Public and private enterprise do not come in watertight compartments. Sustained income-supporting measures originating in the former seep into the latter, via direct government purchases from private sources as well as via the disbursement of publicly created income in private markets, be it for consumption or for investment (secondary, tertiary, etc., effects).

The Crucial Problem of a Workable Cooperation between Business and Government

So far our appraisal of the compensatory method has proceeded on the supposition that the authority and responsibility of government for cycle control is firmly established. This assumption cannot be made in the United States. True, our national government has become a factor in economic stabilization, but whatever it has done in the interest of greater stability of our economic life did not spring from clearly defined responsibilities and actions. A strong element of political uncertainty has been throwing its shadow on central countercyclical policy. As one critic points out, stabilization is a relative newcomer among the goals of governmental policy.[6] Moreover:

"The problem of integrating public policies toward economic stability is made difficult by the relation of private group interests to governmental policy. Under pressure from numerous organized groups, governmental programs tend to run off in all directions. For example, each dollar of expenditures or taxes reflects an uneasy political equilibrium between advocates and opponents of some governmental program. This political equilibrium might be upset to some group's disadvantage if the program were obliged to contribute to economic stability. The total effect of many such policies may outweigh other activities directed toward achieving stability. These conflicting policies dictated by powerful group interests may prove to be an insuperable obstacle to achieving a stable economy."[7]

[6] Roy Blough, "Political and Administrative Requisites for Achieving Economic Stability," *The American Economic Review*, Papers and Proceedings, May 1950, p. 168.
[7] *Ibid.*

The situation has been such that private enterprise could not afford any longer to disregard central government policy in matters concerning the overall tendencies of markets and jobs—without, however, being able to form any reliable impressions as to what to expect from government. The scene has been blurred. A wide margin for shifting the emphasis of economic initiative and control from the private to the public sector—or vice versa—seems to be left, partly in accordance with the prevailing political trends and the influence of partisan politics, and partly with reference to the pressure of circumstances. There has always been a danger of too late or too little, of legislative improvisation and opportunism about means as well as goals.

If there prevails any doubt about when, to what extent, and how long the government will act to offset any actual or anticipated swing, most serious obstacles to stabilization are present. Given a certain tradition of central stabilizing efforts, our producers, investors, and trade unions will look toward the administrative center trying to anticipate government policies that may be adopted. In a given downswing Congress may, at some stage, begin to consider certain income-supporting measures. Suppose that by the nature of the bills introduced in Congress, or by the initial tone of the Congressional debate, the public is led to believe that a measure of substantial proportions will be forthcoming. The effect might be that the downswing tends to come to a temporary halt. If so, the liquidation of bank loans diminishes, price cuts proceed more slowly, the rate of discharge of workers declines, a certain revision of inventory policy takes place—all due to a certain amount of optimism aroused by Congress. Suppose, then, that the debate drags on or that the measures which are finally adopted turn out to be disappointingly weak. The response might be a precipitous decline of activity. Possibly, the maneuver repeats itself several times, involving a series of setbacks and a deepening of the slump. Each time new methods might be tried. One by one, the methods might fall into disrepute, not so much, perhaps, because of inherent inefficiencies but rather because of halfhearted and inconsistent application.

Generally speaking, the situation referred to is best characterized as one of mutual uncertainty between government and private business. Each side is looking at the other for guidance. While private enterprise is casting its eyes upon the government to anticipate central policies that might be adopted —and hence is trying to adapt its own decision-making to what the government does—the government itself may be attempting to obtain guidance for its policy-making by trying to anticipate probable business behavior. Neither side qualifies as an independent agent around which to build an effective stabilization program. The result might be inaction, at least at certain crucial moments. Inaction is bound to result when neither side is able to reach any tangible conclusion as to what the other side may do. More than likely, economic conditions deteriorate during those moments. To avoid this, one of the two sides would have to be able to make very fast decisions. For obvious reasons the community would regard the government as the agency which should come forth with prompt decisions and actions. But without the background of firmly established procedures and objectives, the notion of government as a flexible balance wheel is difficult to translate into action.

Possible Roads toward a Solution of the Problem

There is no easy way of establishing a workable cooperation between government and private enterprise in pursuit of greater economic stability. This holds true, at any rate, for a community characterized, on the balance of political opinion, by conservative instincts as regards the type of economic organization. Surely it would be superficial merely to refer to a mixed economy and to let it go at that. As it is, the term mixed economy is sufficiently vague to be amenable to various interpretations. It can be used, for example, simply to characterize what we now have. This is not particularly revealing, since the present admixture is bound to be the fruit of many circumstances and forces, and not just that of any systematic drive toward arrangements motivated by desire for stability. An admixture of private enterprise and government can be achieved in different forms and with different dividing lines, all of which, presumably, are compatible with the term mixed economy, at least within wide limits. The term can be, and has been, construed to apply to an arrangement which is the fruit of deliberate efforts to prevent any (premature) radical change in the organizational character of our economy, either in the direction of outright collectivism or, for that matter, unbridled capitalism. Let us grant that this is a plausible rationale of a mixed economy. Let us grant, also, that the achievement of greater economic stability is one of the factors which are instrumental in preventing a wave of revolutionary enthusiasm for a radical change in the type of economic organization. Even so, strong concern must arise over the fact that as yet we do not have definite working rules for such a mixed system. The countercyclical debate must progress beyond the stage of mere slogans and produce the blueprint of an admixture of government and private enterprise which convincingly demonstrates the possibility of checking swings. To be politically acceptable, the solution must be free from the danger of a broad attack on private property and enterprise. Also excluded from consideration are arrangements which would leave the institution of private ownership formally intact but a mere shadow of its former self. While strong demands will have to be made on private economic parties to cooperate with the government in the effort to curb swings—otherwise no arrangement will be a success—it is nevertheless clear that the decisive improvements will have to come on the side of government. The government's share in the effort will have to be shaped into a pattern which makes it meaningful for private parties to cooperate with the government in mitigating slumps.

In the judgment of this writer, there exist two logically distinct ways of improving the pattern of the government's role in stabilization. One concentrates on the nature and mode of application of compensatory *means*. By contrast, the second approaches the subject of improvement via the *goals* of the government's action. This is to say, either the means or the ends can be examined from the viewpoint of how to minimize the present uncertainty of private parties as to when, how much, and in what form the government will act to support or curb total economic activity.

In the United States the first of these possibilities seems to have received more attention among specialists than the second. Although we shall have occasion to evaluate various specific proposals for the improvement of means, the main characteristics of the attempted solution may be briefly indicated at this point.

Broadly speaking, the aim is to entrust compensatory procedure as much as possible to a set of permanently installed and fully routinized compensatory devices which mechanically start to operate countercyclically as the economy begins to go off balance. If the economy were equipped with a set of potent devices of this sort, cycle control would no longer be dependent on the work of Congress. Stabilization would be removed from the continuous process of formulating policy and legislation about objectives and means. It would also be removed from administrative discretion. All in all, the expedient of permanently installed and routinized stabilizers is designed to free stabilization from most of the obstacles of the past: conflicting policies about objectives and means, legislative delays in providing the executive branch with a basis for action, administrative delays in taking action as well as politically biased interpretation of legislative instructions. Needless to say, strong reliance on built-in stabilizers would also facilitate less emphasis on attempts at action based on forecasting. Provided a program of this sort were adopted, the proponents of this method could claim that the countercyclical influence of the devices would gradually become sufficiently familiar to producers, workers, and consumers to furnish a fairly reliable measure of the role which the government can be expected to play in regard to meeting future swings. If so, the result will be the creation of a basis for intelligent private action and planning. Depending on the strength of the installed devices, something in the nature of a floor and ceiling for swings might develop. In this event there would be a tangible basis for steadying private expectations concerning markets, job opportunities, prices, etc. Such steadying influence on private expectations would greatly benefit the effectiveness of the central stabilizers.

Now a word about the second possibility, i.e., an attempt to improve the government's role through reform concerning the objective of central compensatory operations. It has already been pointed out that one of the main obstacles to effective cycle control lies in uncertainty about the degree of determination with which government is ready to pursue a given objective. Such uncertainty will not be removed simply by a clarification of, and general agreement about, the nature of the target. It is not enough for a community to decide in principle that its stabilization program should be dedicated to, let us say, stable full employment. As long as this, or any other, goal is pursued merely on a policy basis—in the sense that the government is expected to pursue it as well as it can but without any guarantee of success—there will always be room for public doubt about the validity of the goal.

Here we stand at the threshold of the proposition that it might be necessary for a community to dedicate itself to a relatively modest objective but, at the same time, to subject its government to a binding responsibility for reaching and defending this goal. This type of procedure would recommend itself especially in the event that no satisfactory degree of stabilization could be obtained with the first method, i.e., the resort to built-in stabilizers. As will be shown later, a guaranteed objective does not go well with complete reliance on such stabilizers. If the government is to be able to hold a binding target, allowance must be made for discretionary administrative powers as regards the timing and order of magnitude of compensatory operations (within broadly defined rules laid down by legislation). In addition, it might be necessary to resort to fresh legislation from time to time about suitable means to meet unusually tenacious disturbances. But the goal itself should stand and must not become the subject of subsequent legislative or administrative revisions under normal (peacetime) conditions.

The adoption of a binding target could hardly mean that total activity will not fluctuate any longer. The situation is not as simple as that. The purpose of a binding target is merely to make sure that the government would have to work faster and more consistently than heretofore, if and when the economy goes off balance. Continuous maintenance of the goal would be possible only if the government could act on the basis of correct forecasting of future trends. Short of this very distant possibility, compensatory action has to take its signals from sensitive indexes. This fact, together with lags between the taking of action and its effects on total demand, supports the view that deviations of total activity from the adopted norm can take place.

A binding target merely lessens the danger of confusion between government and private parties; it does not altogether remove it. Basically, each side would still look at the other for guidance in making decisions about the future. But private enterprise would at least know that the government is forced to come forth with countervening action if deviations of activity from the adopted mark persist for any length of time. Repeated experience with determined governmental action would eventually teach private interests that it pays to speculate against the continuation of incipient swings. In these circumstances the initiative in countercyclical procedure will shift more and more toward private enterprise. This enviable result does not lose its attractiveness because of the fact that private countercyclical decisions would always be motivated, in the last analysis, by the threat of intervening government action and the loss of opportunities for making speculative gains, once activity, prices, and so forth are restored by government.

For the moment this may suffice to substantiate our general assertion that certain possibilities for improving the stabilizing potentialities of a mixed system do exist. Our next task will be to inquire in detail how much each of these two procedures is actually worth. We shall begin with the method of built-in stabilizers.

PART II

THE BUILT-IN STABILIZERS

CHAPTER 3

THE THEORY OF BUILT-IN STABILIZERS

....

Automatic Management

BUILT-IN STABILIZERS are usually referred to as automatic stabilizers. From the viewpoint of traditional economic theory this is a strange and problematic use of the term automatic. For a long time the concept of economic automatism was associated with the so-called forces of the market. These forces were to see to it that society enjoyed an unhampered allocation of its resources commensurable with consumers' choice, to the point of equal marginal returns on factors of production in all branches of industry. The underlying assumption, of course, was that of free competition making for smooth readjustment of factor allocation to changes in demand and costs of production. In this picture of competitive interindustry balance, the impersonal law of supply and demand reigned. This picture possesses all the essential elements of economic automatism. The absence of monopolistic (and monopsonistic) influences accounts for the absence of discretionary power over prices, etc., on the part of individuals or groups. Prices, profits, the allocation of resources—in short, the entire economy—is regulated by the anonymous, impersonal, nondiscretionary, nonpolitical, and, in principle, predictable mode of operation of the law of supply and demand behind which, of course, stands the motive power of personal self-interest forced into constructive and socially beneficial channels. All this is familiar and need not detain us here. Among economists and competent men of public affairs it is now commonly recognized that the envisaged state of affairs can under no circumstances be regarded as something which comes and remains by itself.

[43]

The presence of a large crowd of competitors in the various industries, devoid of economic organization and collective action, is nothing natural. If and when we have such an arrangement, or even merely an approximation thereof, we have it only because the community deliberately and firmly arranges matters in this fashion and resorts to rules of binding force.

In the last analysis, automatism is the fruit of precise, commonly known, understood, and valid laws. This determines the role of government in the economic life of a nation, both positively and negatively. The positive aspect is the establishment and enforcement of laws defining the limits within which the economic process is to be entrusted to ordinary commercial motives. Negatively, the government is to refrain (with certain exceptions) from entering into the economic life as a producer or buyer, or from interfering with the process of pricing and distribution, either actively or simply by allowing itself to become the tool of pressure groups seeking to harness the power of government for their own purposes.

The so-called automatic central stabilizers do not fit into this traditional concept of economic automatism. In all of these devices the government is very much in evidence as a producer, or buyer, or redistributor of income. The government is to influence the scale, and perhaps even the composition, of national product. The only link with automatism lies in the fact that these stabilizers are to be handled on the basis of minutely prescribed rules of operation, to exclude all elements of administrative discretion as well as the resort to fresh legislation.

If this procedure qualifies as economic automatism, it can do so only in the sense of automatic management of governmental economic controls. This concept concerns only the form of government procedure, but it is inarticulate as regards the extent to which government participates in the economic life of a nation. A socialistic government, although fully in possession and control of economic resources, could be envisaged as fitting the bill. If automatic management is to go hand in hand with a policy of minimizing government in industry, a separate case must be made for this—with independent arguments.

Now it must be granted that such a case can be made with relative ease, namely from a practical point of view. Considering the complexity of the forces and contingencies with which a stabilization program has to cope, one is driven to the conclusion that the technique of fully routinized stabilizers can be applied with success only in isolated instances. It can be applied where the criteria for operation are sufficiently simple and unequivocal to permit complete reliance on a set of formalized procedural rules. In an authoritarian environment there might be a good many instances of this sort, simply because the public can be made to accept procedural shortcuts in defining situations to be covered by rigorous rules. Here the entire job of economic stabilization might be left to a set of streamlined central devices, provided, of course, such a government were at all willing to adhere to any specified and lasting rules. Be that as it may, the case is different in an individualistically inclined community. By the very nature of its political, social, and economic philosophy such a community creates and tolerates complexities that are detrimental to routine solution. Impossible demands on the method of prescribed rules would be made if on every occasion distinct weight were to be given to such elements as specific fact finding, allowance for novel or extenuating circumstances, expression of self-interest of the private parties involved, rights of appeal to courts—and to all of the remaining amenities of the democratic process.

In fact there is no room here for central management of controls which would satisfy rigorous tests of automatism. Normally, routine is mixed with elements of discretionary judgment of those entrusted with execution of controls. Even such a device as unemployment compensation—surrounded as it is by detailed legislative instruction—involves situations which call for use of good judgment. If this holds true of this proverbial example of an automatic stabilizer, how much more must it apply to other more complex devices such as the personal income tax, the corporate income taxes, and our system of farm price supports—all of which are widely acknowledged as automatic stabilizers. There is no escape from the conclusion that if in these instances we wish to speak of automatic devices we must resort to more liberal tests of automatism without, however, going so far as to render the term meaningless. This can be done. A valid set of requisites is that a stabilizing arrangement is (1) permanently installed, (2) well defined in its main provisions and purposes, and (3) reliably linked to cyclically sensitive criteria (indexes) in the sense that the device starts to operate countercyclically as soon as these criteria indicate the need for action. If a stabilizing arrangement satisfies these requisites it possesses the major characteristic of automatism, namely, predictability of action. Although such predictability is the fruit of adherence to a constant framework of rules it does not require pedantic insistence that every minor detail of management be reduced to the "level of a bank teller rather than that of a bank president." Provided the basic framework stands firmly, the public can feel assured that, given certain contingencies, a certain type of action designed to counteract such contingencies will be forthcoming. To obtain such assurance is what counts. It is the economically as well as psychologically significant part of automatic management, whereas the insistence on perfect standards of nondiscretion has very little practical significance. One could even afford to make some concessions as regards the requisite of permanency. A stabilizing scheme need not stand unchanged forever. But it must stand unchanged sufficiently long to become a factor which can be integrated reliably into short-run private planning. No uniform answer can be given as to the minimum time that is required for such purpose. If an arrangement lasts through a fiscal year without being subjected to significant change, then one is entitled to assume that it does enter, intelligently, into short-run business planning.

In this sense, then, one may safely regard the aforementioned stabilizers as true examples of automatic management. The basic framework of our personal income tax, the corporation taxes, social security, and even farm price supports, appears to be sufficiently stable to satisfy the tests of automatic stabilizers.

The Nature of the Countercyclical Work

All of the existing as well as proposed built-in stabilizers are either fiscal or monetary. Therefore the nature of the counter-cyclical tendencies can be described very aptly in the manner of Professor Hart, according to whom a fiscal automatic stabilizer will push the government's budget toward deficit in case of a slump and toward surplus as business improves, while either a fiscal or a monetary automatic stabilizer will expand the public's stock of cash in a slump and reduce it in high prosperity, or tend to reduce the public's demand for cash in a slump and increase it in high prosperity.[1]

Stabilizers which involve automatic budgetary deficits and surpluses counteract business swings more effectively than those which merely vary the money stock or the demand for cash. This is due to the fact that government deficits and surpluses have a more direct bearing on total income (and total effective demand) than do mere variations in the quantity of available money. A deficit caused by, let us say, an increase in unemployment benefits constitutes disposable income on the part of those who receive the benefits, and this support of personal income is bound to translate itself quickly into effective demand. The same directness of effect attaches to deficits produced by loan-financed public outlay on goods

[1] Albert G. Hart, *Money, Debt and Economic Activity* (New York: Prentice-Hall, Inc., 1948), p. 475.

and services. In all cases of budgetary deficits or surpluses, variations in the money stock may also be involved, but this phenomenon is almost of secondary interest, behind the additions to, or subtractions from, total income.

It so happens that all of the automatic stabilizers now in force in the United States operate very close to income. Since the abandonment of the automatic gold standard there is not one automatic stabilizer which produces mere variations in the stock of money. A theoretical example of such a stabilizer would be a system of automatic management of open-market operations according to which cash would be injected or withdrawn under the guidance of some price index or a similar cyclically sensitive index. At present, open-market operations as well as all the other central banking controls are handled on a discretionary basis. The recently proposed commodity reserve currency system (Graham proposal) would operate primarily through the income stream, as will be shown later.

The Test of Adequacy of Automatic Stabilizers

The greater the compensatory burden to be placed on automatic stabilizers, the more urgent becomes the question "How far can this method reasonably be extended?" There are several possible attitudes on this subject.

One is that the schemes should be of modest scope. They should be of such kind that they merely work in the right direction without, however, being charged with the full burden of restoring activity quickly around some premeditated mark, or furnish something in the nature of *dependable* limits beyond which fluctuations cannot go. In the process of counteracting a swing, the absolute order of magnitude of their compensatory work might grow as the economy goes more and more off balance, but if the schemes wear out prematurely in a sustained swing nothing should be done about it. Behind this view stands either the conviction that cyclical movements should merely be somewhat retarded so as to create opportunities for private business to catch its breath—to rally against a prevailing shrinkage of markets and prices through a combination of readjustments and income-supporting measures based on a strengthening of confidence—or the conviction that the bulk of the compensatory work should be entrusted to discretionary controls.

Neither of these views permits a thorough examination of the adequacy of automatic stabilizers. Such examination should be carried out under the assumption of exclusive reliance on built-in devices in a determined drive toward cycle control. Only in this fashion can distinct results about adequacy be obtained. If the results should prove to be negative, there still remains the possibility of using automatic stabilizers in conjunction with discretionary procedure.

The test of adequacy should not be made unreasonably hard. There are numerous reasons which speak against a transition to strict even-keel performance of the economy.[2] Consequently one should not become disturbed by the fact that automatic stabilizers are inherently incapable of forestalling swings (they presuppose the actual occurrence of business fluctuations before they start their countercyclical work). Rather, the test should concentrate on the question of ability to create dependable limits for cycles which are in keeping with the notion of a margin of tolerable fluctuations.[3] However vague this stipulation may sound, it must suffice at this point. But one thing is certain: the test of a tolerable margin of swings implies much more than mere retardation in the

[2] See Chapter 11, p. 144.
[3] This notion appears to receive increasing recognition in current stabilization literature. It can be found, for example, in the recent study of J. R. Hicks, *A Contribution to the Theory of the Trade Cycle,* Oxford: Clarenden Press, 1950, especially on pp. 164-165. The same is true of M. Friedman's recent article entitled "A Monetary and Fiscal Framework for Economic Stability," *The American Economic Review,* June 1948, p. 264. See also A. G. Hart, *Money, Debt, and Economic Activity,* New York: Prentice-Hall, Inc., 1948, pp. 487-488.

rate of deterioration in output and employment. If automatic stabilizers were only capable of a parachute effect, the economy might still have to land on the rock-bottom of a severe depression, such as the depression of the thirties. Barring the possibility of extraneous recovery forces (such as the adoption of a specific government recovery program, wars or threats of war, or major technological developments), there might be no timely point during a downswing at which business psychology receives encouragement to rally effectively against a prevailing deterioration of market conditions. To give such encouragement, the built-in machinery must be strong enough to create confidence in a floor at which national income is still high enough to preclude catastrophic low levels of morale, employment, and investment.

In the following chapters we shall appraise the strength of the currently existing stabilizers, and also of some proposed novel devices, from the viewpoint of this particular test. We shall begin with a quantitative estimate of the strength of the schemes now in force. The next step will be to examine some schemes which have been suggested in recent years. We shall have to introduce the distinction between two different types of built-in schemes which, for want of better terms, shall be referred to as fixed schemes and flexible schemes. The first type is an arrangement which operates against cycles although the features which account for this influence remain absolutely unchanged throughout the cycle. Stabilizers which operate on the revenue side of the government's budget usually refer to stable tax rates and stable levels of exemption. On the side of public expenditures, the type is exemplified by unemployment compensation and relief, provided the allowances per individual or family do not vary. In other words, the government must pay the same amount per unit of time to all comers who qualify on stated terms, irrespective of the phase of the cycle. Despite their inflexible provisions, these schemes permit, of course, a change in the total amount of their income-supporting or curbing operations. To illustrate: as the number of unemployed persons keeps rising during a slump, the total amount of compensation per week or per month keeps growing. Or, as the aggregate personal income keeps falling, the absolute size of the government's deficit keeps rising with constant tax rates (provided total government outlay is not curtailed).

The flexible type covers stabilizers which embody a deliberate effort to adapt the countercyclical features to the prevailing degree of economic fluctuations, i.e., on the basis of prescribed rules of countercyclical adaptation. The case may be illustrated by a tax scheme which involves mechanical countercyclical rate changes commensurate with the degree of intensity of business swings. The faster the drop in activity, the greater the rate of tax abatement.

At present, no flexible automatic schemes are in force.

C H A P T E R 4

THE EFFECTIVENESS OF EXISTING
STABILIZERS

·

....

A Quantitative Estimate of the
Countercyclical Strength

In his recent study on *Money, Debt, and Economic Activity*
Professor Hart has attempted what he calls a crude estimate
of the countercyclical strength of automatic stabilizers now in
existence in the United States. After asking how much, with
a drop of $10 billion in national income, the government's
budget would be shifted in the direction of a deficit on account
of the automatic stabilizers, his answer is as follows:

". . . a crude over-all estimate of all the automatic stabilizers
would be that they increase the budget deficit (or reduce the
budget surplus) of federal, state, and local governments by
about a third of any drop in income.

"In terms of monetary theory, this means that if a drop in
investment and consumption lowers the annual rate of national
income by $10 billion, these stabilizers create an 'offset to
saving' of the order of $3 to $4 billion per annum. Investment
may, therefore, drop $3 to $4 billion per annum relative to
saving without carrying national income down by more than
$10 billion."[1]

It is of interest to know how these findings were arrived at.
Involved are separate estimates of the effects of corporate
income taxes, personal income tax, social security contributions, unemployment compensation, and indirect taxes. For
each of these items Hart estimated what he calls the "swing"

[1] *Op.cit.*, p. 479.

in connection with a change in national income, expressed in terms of a percentage of national income.

Of the corporate income taxes, Hart says that the swing would be about 4 per cent of any change in national income if corporate profits varied in proportion to national income (corporate profits are estimated at about 10 per cent of national income in prosperity, and he assumes that these profits are taxed at roughly 40 per cent). However, he arrives at the conclusion that the swing must be nearer to 6 or 8 per cent of the change in income, for the following reasons: (1) profits change more, proportionately, than national income (even after correcting both series for fictitious profits and losses from revaluation of inventories), and (2) fictitious inventory profits and losses count as profits or losses from the standpoint of taxation.

The swing of the personal income tax is said to be no less than 12 per cent of national income, and may exceed 15 per cent. At the rates and exemptions which prevailed at the time of his writing Hart estimated personal income tax as running about 10 per cent of national income in prosperity. But again allowance must be made for the fact that taxable income fluctuates more than national income, whereas income exempt from tax, of course, is more stable than national income.

Social security contributions are considered by Hart as varying roughly in proportion to national income. The swing is said to be about 2.5 to 3 per cent (figuring on a 3 per cent level for prosperity).

For unemployment compensation he estimated a fluctuation of from 2 to 5 per cent. In leaving such a wide difference he allowed for the fact that the rise in unemployment compensation with a $10 billion fall in national income depends very much on the composition of the drop in income.

Indirect taxes (other than property taxes), estimated to have been about 8 per cent of national income in the postwar years, are assumed by Hart to have a rather low income-elasticity. He ventures an estimate of the swing from 3 to 5 per cent.

Added together, these figures suggest to Hart a total swing of from 25 per cent to 35 per cent of national income or, in terms of a $10 billion fall of national income, an automatic increase in the budget deficit, or reduction of the budget surplus, of about $3 to $4 billion.[2]

This finding, according to Hart, does not encourage hope that these stabilizers create a satisfactory defense against slumps. Primary reliance on automatic devices (even with some improvement of the devices) might work in a world in which governments would not have to face irregular military outlays, export financing, etc.—in short, if government expenditures were predictable and stable. In these circumstances "we are not likely to see the bottom drop out of economic life as it did after 1929."[3] But his subsequent search for possible improvements in automatic stabilizers—and even more his preference for some combination of automatic and discretionary procedure—clearly indicates the presence of doubt on his part that the floor which the present devices may establish would prove to be high enough to be acceptable to the public. The only conclusion to which one is reasonably entitled is even more alarming. The prevailing devices may merely be sufficient to exercise a retarding effect on business fluctuations.

To this conclusion one is led not so much by the above estimate but by reasoning about the character of the devices. To promise a floor, they would have to be able to intensify their countercyclical influence as the economy goes more and more off-balance. But this is not the case. To illustrate the point, let us consider the tax schemes. Although the size of the deficit automatically grows as taxable income shrinks, the rate of growth of the deficit (fall of tax revenues) will not be intensified in the course of economic contraction. On the contrary, because of the probability that many of the corporate

[2] *Ibid.*, pp. 478-79. [3] *Ibid.*, p. 479.

profits and high personal incomes are particularly sensitive to a reversal of general economic activity from boom to depression, the most serious inroads on tax revenues are bound to be made in the relatively early stages of the downswing. As these incomes vanish, the progressive structure of taxes loses a good part of its sting on government revenues. Therefore, if the drop of tax revenues does not do the trick of stopping downswings in their early stages, it is not likely to do so in the more advanced stages. To obtain accelerating compensatory effects on the tax side of the budget, the rates of taxation would have to be lowered during downswings. Under present arrangements this would require, in each instance, special legislation. The process would not be automatic.

Suggested Improvements in Existing Stabilizers

It is not easy to draw a sharp line between suggested improvements in existing stabilizers and proposals for the adoption of novel stabilizers. Take, for example, the not infrequent proposal to increase the progressiveness of our income taxes for purposes of strengthening the automatic countercyclical effects of these taxes. Inasmuch as we do have a progressive income tax, and inasmuch as compensatory reactions do evolve from it in conjunction with fluctuations in incomes, a change toward a more progressive structure would seem to amount to no more than an improvement in existing schemes. On the other hand, whatever progressiveness we now have is not the fruit of specifically countercyclical policy. Therefore it may be argued that we would indeed have a novel arrangement if the tax became more progressive for countercyclical reasons. The same difficulty of distinction arises over any other stabilizer which, so far, has been merely an incidental countercyclical device.

Perhaps the easiest thing to do is to ignore the fact that most of our existing stabilizers owe their existence to other than countercyclical reasons and to treat proposed changes simply in terms of improvements of their countercyclical effectiveness. This does not preclude the possibility of appraising the suggested reforms also on other grounds (for example, standards of equitable taxation).

Let us begin, at random, with the notion of increasing the progressiveness of our personal and corporate income taxes, to a point at which these taxes promise to function as a truly powerful automatic stabilizer. The question is how far such tax reform could go before it comes into conflict with values other than short-run stabilization. If we agree that the basic long-range values in our economic life are efficiency, secular progress, and equality of opportunity, it follows that only one of these values—equality of opportunity—is clearly in harmony with a system of stiffly progressive taxation. The potential conflict between equalitarian ideals, on the one hand, and those of efficiency and progress on the other suggests a compromise which precludes a drastic increase in progressiveness over currently prevailing standards. This holds true, at any rate, for policy designed to make capitalism work.

Short of drastic increases in the progressiveness in our direct taxes, the pursuit of improvements in existing stabilizers is not likely to lead to measures of great importance. To consider the tax system as a whole, there exists the possibility of a reduction or elimination of such taxes as the excises on various commodities (tobacco, alcoholic beverages, theater admissions, imports), with a correspondingly heavier emphasis on income taxes. While such preference for direct taxes usually stems from considerations of tax equity, it can also be defended on the basis of the relative inefficiency of excises as stabilizers. Here the limitations are primarily of a practical kind. As long as the government's budget remains relatively large, the excises could not be dropped without a very marked increase in income tax rates or decrease in the level of exemptions, or both. On theoretical grounds the method of bringing more citizens within the income tax paying brackets is sound. But the political and administrative odds are against such a change, and in a discussion of tax reform for actual policy purposes nobody can afford to disregard this fact. The writer agrees with the view that proposals for abolition or serious reduction of excises will have a chance for success only in the event of a reduction in the size of the federal budget, so that the loss of revenue from these taxes would not have to be offset by more extensive or intensive income taxation.

A minor chance for countercyclical tax improvement refers to the familiar idea of allowing tax payers with varying incomes to average their income between tax years so that the average tax which they owe for several years is proportioned to their average income over a stretch of years. This idea can be brought in line with the desire for better automatic stabilizing reactions of the personal income tax. If a tax payer's income in a certain year should fall below his recent average, and if some provision were made to the effect that this person becomes entitled to a refund to equalize his tax position with that of a tax payer with a level of income of the same size, the countercyclical influence of the income tax would be increased, provided the timing of the refund is right. The timing is right if the refund comes in the year during which the person's income is low. The chances are that the incomes of many persons will fall below their recent average during a downswing so that automatic refunding operations could take place on a wide scale.[4] The principle of averaging the income of several years, combined with prompt refunding, also improves the stabilizing effects of corporate income taxation.

Again, in the interest of proper countercyclical timing of refunding operations, it has been suggested that everybody might be made to pay income tax on the full amount of his income, with no personal exemption for himself and his dependents. The equivalent of the exemption should then be given to everybody through weekly or monthly family-allow-

[4] Hart, *op.cit.*, p. 481.

ance checks, on a routine basis. This system is to show its merits in times of cyclical unemployment. The tax collection would stop at once, but not the refunds. The per-capita exemption equivalent would keep coming in, and its effect would be to dampen the fall in consumer spending.[5]

The search for countercyclical improvements of existing tax stabilizers might lead to still other suggestions, but it is doubtful whether these suggestions would yield quantitatively important propositions. Unless the implied reforms justify themselves on the grounds of basic principles of taxation, or would constitute a significant simplification in tax administration and collection, they tend to be merely indicative of a rather strained preoccupation with the subject of built-in countercyclical gadgets. There remains, however, one tax proposal which embodies such a far-reaching change from established budgetary practice that it cannot very well be regarded as a mere improvement in our existing tax stabilizers. The change in question is the proposed establishment of a premeditated high level of employment combined with the principle of setting tax rates in such a way as to balance the budget at this level of employment. This proposal will be dealt with later, in a chapter dealing with novel stabilizers.

On the expenditure side of the government's budget, the area of social security has frequently been singled out for suggestions of improved countercyclical arrangements. There is no doubt that an extension of the system of unemployment compensation for groups not yet covered would make some contribution to automatic compensatory action. The same goes for the resort to higher standards of benefit payments per person or per family (and contributions to the compensation fund), as well as the possibility of a guaranteed government allowance to unemployed persons still without a job after having exhausted the period of benefit payments from unemployment compensation proper, or to families lacking a bread-

[5] *Ibid.*

winner. Although we are referring here to actual tendencies in the United States, the scene is not ripe for attempting quantitative estimates of countercyclical effects. But the result of such changes would most likely fall short of establishing a floor. Since the total amount of income-supporting operations from these sources is strictly determined by the extent to which employment actually deteriorates, and since the allowances will have to keep themselves well below rates of pay for employment, all that can be expected with some degree of certainty is that downswings would be somewhat more retarded than otherwise.

The area of government outlay on goods and services is by and large still devoid of automatic countercyclical devices. The method of public works, in particular, is handled on a legislatively flexible basis. Only in our agricultural policy do we have something which approximates a built-in stabilizer. The automatic aspects of the agricultural program could be considerably strengthened by a transition from the present price support system to a full-fledged automatic commodity standard of money (Graham proposal), according to which the dollar would be legally defined in terms of a composite commodity unit consisting of a set of important raw materials. In fairness to the originators of this proposal, one must acknowledge the fact that this scheme, as it stands now, would cover a much wider area than agriculture. Moreover, in contrast to the present price support program, it does not embody the feature of stabilizing individual prices but—in accordance with the tenets of a stable money scheme—stabilization of an average of prices. All in all, it is an entirely new device, and will be treated as such in this study.

To bring this discussion to a close, it can be said that the inventory of the ways in which existing automatic devices might be improved does not lead to optimistic conclusions. In each case there are limitations for reform which forbid thinking in terms of enlarging the devices to such an extent that a tolerable margin of instability could be established in this fashion. Complete reliance on somewhat improved types of existing stabilizers is self-defeating in a nation which has come to think in terms of banishing major slumps from the scene. The result can only be a lasting blow to the theory and practice of built-in devices. It remains to be seen whether some entirely new schemes hold greater promise, or whether any existing device can be surrounded by rules of counter-cyclical adaptation which permit it to become *temporarily* more powerful without involving a permanent upward revision in the size of the government's budget (taxes, etc.).

CHAPTER 5

PROPOSED CONSTANT STABILIZERS

....

The Agreed-High-Level Balance of the Budget[1]

SINCE the compensatory reactions of budgetary stabilizers consist of automatic deficits and surpluses, all fiscal reform aiming at better stabilizers of this type must consist of measures designed to make fluctuations in national income bring about deficits and surpluses of such magnitude that truly powerful countercyclical tendencies can be expected. One way of attempting this is to plan a budget which would balance at an agreed high-level of national income. Actual deviations of income from the planned level would then result in automatic deficits or surpluses which promise to be attuned in size to the prevailing degree of off-balance, measured by the extent to which actual income deviates from the planned level of income.

This involves the following steps. First, the community must agree on a level of income at which it would like to see its economy operate. Presumably this would be some reasonable approximation of full utilization of resources. Secondly, the tax rates and levels of exemption would have to be set in the light of expected yield at a level of income corresponding to such reasonably full employment. Once set, these tax rates and exemption levels would have to be kept unchanged, unless there were some major change in national economic policy or condition of national economic life (for example, rearmament). Thirdly, this tax policy would have to be accompanied by a

[1] Beardsley Ruml and H. Chr. Sonne, *Fiscal and Monetary Policy*, Washington: National Planning Association, 1944. Also see the study of the Committee for Economic Development, *Taxes and the Budget*, New York: Committee for Economic Development, 1947.

government expenditure policy embodying the following features: equalization of public outlay with the expected total tax revenue at the planned level of income (a planned balanced budget), and deliberate abstinence from countercyclical revisions on the expenditure side of the budget. The latter feature implies that the community must refrain from increasing total public outlay on goods and services in the course of downswings or, as the case may be, from reducing such outlay during upswings. It further implies that the conditions and terms under which public transfer payments will be made shall not be altered countercyclically. This amounts to a policy of short-run stability in total public expenditures, except for one obvious qualification: the absolute amount of public outlay for transfer payments will vary automatically through the cycle.

The proposed plan involves the keeping of two budgets for the government, a hypothetical budget which is balanced, and an actual budget which would be automatically unbalanced in the event that actual income deviates from the planned income level. Thus the traditional principle of balancing actual receipts and outlays is given up in favor of the idea of merely balancing planned receipts with (actual) outlay.

In the long view, the scheme appears to come closer to a balancing of actual receipts and outlay. Yet there is no certainty that deficits and surpluses will average out over a stretch of years. The scheme lacks adjustment machinery for such averaging out (in contrast to the so-called Swedish budgets which are supposed to avoid long-run deficits or surpluses).[2] A preponderance of bad years would lead to a long-run deficit, and a preponderance of good years to a surplus. Lack of symmetry between booms and depressions, however, is not the major reason why surpluses and deficits might fail to average out in the long view. Much depends, in addition, on how high the hypothetical income level is set. If it is set ambitiously

[2] Hart, *op.cit.*, p. 466.

high—well above the degree of resource utilization that private enterprise could *consistently* achieve—there might be a tendency toward cumulative deficits and a rising public debt.

According to Professor Milton Friedman's systematic and concise presentation of the scheme, the adoption of an agreed high-level budget should go hand in hand with certain additional reforms. Among these the most prominent is the abolition of fractional reserves for private commercial banks, both to remove a potential destabilizer and to make sure that the regulation of the money supply is deprived of all discretionary features. The power to create or destroy money is to be concentrated in the hands of government which would regulate the amount of money in circulation in strictly automatic fashion, i.e., via budgetary deficits and surpluses.[3]

How effective would this scheme be? Unfortunately, a fair appraisal could be made only if the proposal were specific about the size of the budget in relation to the world of private transactions. But the propounders of the plan are not specific on this score. If the budget is relatively small, fluctuations in income will give rise to only small deficits or surpluses, and hence to only small income supporting or curbing operations. On the other hand, nobody will deny that a very large budget relative to the volume of private transactions offers considerable promise that compensatory influences will be powerful. At the same time, the occasion for cyclical fluctuations might then be small considering that a substantial portion of the community's resources would be under direct governmental control.

From the general nature of the plan, it may be surmised, however, that a large budget is not contemplated. Traditionally, the search for built-in stabilizers has always gone hand in hand with the desire for as little government as possible. If the above plan were not meant to follow this tradition, it

[3] Milton Friedman, "A Monetary and Fiscal Framework for Economic Stability," *The American Economic Review*, June 1948, p. 245.

would be a distinct surprise. A specialist is not likely to go through the trouble of designing permanently installed devices without being motivated by the hope that stabilization can be bought with a minimum of governmental effort. He is apt to believe that—on a dollar-for-dollar basis of compensatory action—more can be achieved with a permanently installed device ' than with action predicated on fresh legislation as emergencies arrive, simply because a permanently installed device is meant to minimize the elements of uncertainty and surprise for business and therefore to create a better chance for favorable private response. Also, he cannot help being aware that the very permanency of built-in schemes suggests caution as to how far government is to be integrated into the economic process. In each instance these schemes draw final boundary lines between business and government. When unnecessarily large central stabilizers are installed, the error is particularly costly from the standpoint of policy designed to maximize the area of private enterprise. By contrast, stabilizing procedure predicated on *ad hoc* legislation (of limited duration) can afford an occasional deep thrust by government, since it does not attempt to draw any final dividing line between the area that is to be government and the private area. Periods of heavy emphasis on government can give way to a set of lightly implemented controls as the need for central stabilizing action diminishes.

Lack of concreteness about the relative size of the budget is only one of the reasons which make it difficult to appraise the plan. A further complication arises over the fact that in its most tightly reasoned form (Friedman), the plan is to go hand in hand with the abolition of fractional bank reserves. Were it not for this abstract feature, some pertinent factual criticism about the effectiveness of budgetary surpluses and deficits could be made, i.e., with reference to an economy in which deficits and surpluses arose at a time characterized by stable tax rates and exemption levels. It could be stated, for example, that the huge cash surpluses of the Treasury in the first half of 1948, running at the rate of $12 billion, apparently had only a moderate anti-inflationary effect. Equally, the budget deficit in 1949 seems to have had no noticeable antideflationary influence. But these recent experiences cannot establish conclusive evidence against the plan, since the budgetary surpluses and deficits may have been counteracted by changes in the volume of private borrowing from banks, in the sense that bank credit expanded when the government ran a surplus and contracted when a deficit occurred. Another mitigating factor against the surplus of 1948 might have been the still enormous backlog of private demand combined with unusually high private liquid balances carried over from the war.

Given a 100 per cent reserve system, automatic deficits and surpluses might be operating on more fertile ground. Instead of being potentially antagonistic forces, the budget and the money supply might cooperate in counteracting business swings. The monetary factor itself might amount to more than merely creating the right kind of background for budgetary deficits and surpluses to regulate total effective demand. It might become an active corrective itself. As prices in general began to fall during a slump, and as the quantity of available money would rise rather than shrink (in contrast to prevailing tendencies), the real value of the money stock would go up. This increase in the real value of the money stock (and certain fixed assets such as bonds) might eventually increase the consumption function.[4] Spending might be encouraged. But unfortunately there is no certainty about this. The rise in the real value of cash balances becomes a dependable cause of increased spending only in the event that a price floor is in sight. As long as prices are expected to keep falling, the public's

[4] This, according to Friedman, is the main corrective embodied in the plan. It would exist even if the quantity of money remained merely constant. The government's contributions to the money stock through automatic deficits merely reinforce the feature in question (op.cit., p. 259).

[65]

desire to wait for still better bargains may outweigh the incentive to save less because of the rise in the real value of liquid assets. In the event of a modest budget, the combination of a rising money stock and the additions to the income stream provided by deficits is not, in itself, a guarantee of a floor. It is merely possible that a floor might be established. Fundamentally the plan belongs in the category of mere retarding arrangements, although it might very well prove to be a better retarding device than our existing stabilizers.

Regrettably, this pessimistic conclusion will have to stand despite certain additional ingenious arguments in favor of the plan. According to Friedman, the automatic reactions of the budget are supposed to have a quicker impact on aggregate demand than discretionary procedure. The total lag between the need for action and the effect of such action on demand is said to be shorter than in the event of discretionary procedure.[5] The crucial factor here is that part of the total lag which lies between the need for action and the recognition of this need. For a firmly installed mechanical device, such as the one in question, this lag would be negligible. For discretionary procedure devoid of forecasting, much valuable time might elapse between the moment of need and the taking of tangible cognizance of such need.

Yet all this does not prove that the scheme would succeed in reducing cyclical fluctuations to tolerable proportions.[6] The forces making for swings may be so stubborn that nowhere along the line can reliable limits for swings be established with the aid of the adaptive machinery, since this machinery is too rigid to permit spurts of intensifying income-supporting operations which exceed the strength of downward pressures. Rigidity in the face of disappointing results creates a dilemma for the advocate of automatic stabilizers. The desire for transition to a larger planned budget comes into conflict with re-

[5] *Ibid.*, p. 255.
[6] This point is admitted by Friedman himself on page 264 of his study.

liance on automatic procedure. At least a new budget would have to stand for a considerable length of time. Frequent revision in the size of the planned budget would surely destroy the heart of the plan. The work of stabilization would be taken over by the revisions rather than by the automatic deficits and surpluses at each planned level of the budget. A lasting transition to a budget large enough to satisfy all contingencies would be a risky affair from the standpoint of private enterprise. It would involve permanently stiff rates of taxation. In comparison with this, the conservative gesture of setting up an intentionally balanced budget might impress the public very little. Moreover, let us bear in mind that the actual budget would be balanced only if total income happened to stay near the planned level to which the planned budget is geared taxwise. Therefore, if it ever came to the adoption of the proposed device in a country like the United States, the chances are that the agreed high-level budget would not be large enough to satisfy all contingencies.

The Commodity Reserve Currency Plan

Of the remaining field of proposals for centrally installed stabilizers we shall consider only the multiple commodity money standard commonly referred to as the commodity reserve currency plan or simply Graham proposal.[7] As it was originally designed, the composite commodity unit in terms of which the dollar is to be defined legally would include several grains, fats, metals, textile fibers, tobacco, hides, rubber, petroleum, and some foodstuffs (altogether, some 23 basic raw materials).[8] This selection had been made to meet two conflicting requirements: the commodity aggregate "must be comprehensive and nondiscriminatory; but at the same time

[7] The standard was advocated almost simultaneously by two different economists bearing the name of Graham, namely Benjamin Graham and Frank D. Graham.

[8] Benjamin Graham, *Storage and Stability*, New York: McGraw-Hill, 1937, p. 53.

it must not be overwhelmed by the sheer number of the items with which it deals."[9] Fortunately, according to the scheme's originator, there exist two criteria which aid in the choice of the components. One is that the commodities included must be dealt in on recognized commodity exchanges; and the other that the "exchanges must be prepared to assume part of the burden of storage, including the task of maintaining the stored products in merchantable condition by appropriate rotation."[10] The first factor is regarded as immensely simplifying the practical execution of the scheme. The commodity units purchased by the monetary authority[11] would be acquired in the form of ordinary purchases on the commodity exchanges, and deliveries against contracts made on the exchanges would be effected by means of warehouse receipts. There would be no need for the monetary authority directly to handle the reserve goods. Both the collection of the required assortment of warehouse receipts and the actual storage of the commodities could be safely left to private initiative.

The products selected are goods in which futures-trading is being carried on at various commodity exchanges. They form only a part of the products in which such trading takes place. The remainder (mostly foodstuffs) was not included in the composite unit for technical reasons, such as the need for cold-storage service.

A wider group of reserve goods was favored by the late Professor Frank D. Graham.[12] In commenting on Benjamin Graham's original selection of twenty-three products, he suggests that "there is no reason, other than perhaps a superior administrative convenience, for limiting the number of com-

---

[9] *Ibid.*, p. 51.   [10] *Ibid.*

[11] In the original version of the plan by Benjamin Graham (Storage and Stability) this authority was to be the federal government. In his revised scheme (*World Commodities and World Currency*; New York: McGraw-Hill, 1944) the authority is to be an international agency, in keeping with his recent desire to make the scheme adoptable on an international scale.

[12] *Social Goals and Economic Institutions*, Princeton University Press, 1942, p. 102.

modities in the commodity unit and, as experience warranted, the number should no doubt be increased until it included all readily storable goods of a non-specialized character."[13] This might include not only iron ore but also pig iron and standard steel plates; not only fibers but also certain standard textiles, and so forth. This suggestion stands in contrast to revisions of the proposal which have appeared since the appearance of Benjamin Graham's first book on the subject. These revisions show a tendency toward making the selection of reserve commodities smaller than in the original version. Perhaps under the influence of the critical comments of Hayek,[14] and other economists who react favorably to the basic idea of the plan, Benjamin Graham has narrowed the commodity basis to fifteen products.[15] This development appears to result from an effort to make the commodity standard more suitable for adoption on an international scale. Only commodities important for their place in world production and in international trade are chosen.[16]

It is apparent that there exists as yet no final agreement on the precise form of the proposed standard. But certain points are definitively agreed upon. It is agreed that not the individual prices of the components, but merely their aggregate price, should be stabilized. In other words, the individual prices are to be allowed to fluctuate in accordance with changes

[13] *Ibid.*

[14] F. A. Hayek, *"A Commodity Reserve Currency,"* The Economic Journal, June-September 1943, p. 182.

[15] *World Commodities and World Currency*, pp. 43-45.

[16] Broadly speaking, the more one tries to adjust the composite unit for the purpose of satisfying a group of industrial and agricultural countries, the more difficult the selection is bound to become. If each prospective member were to insist that its national peculiarities as a *producer* be considered—so that the scheme could function, among other ways, as a powerful domestic compensatory device—discussion might at first run in the direction of adding more and more items to the list, until finally, as a compromise, it might run in the opposite direction: only a few basic raw materials, produced in all countries, might be suggested. The narrower the unit, the greater the similarity to the gold standard from the standpoint of breadth, and the greater its shortcomings as a domestic compensatory device in each member nation.

in relative demand and operating costs (competitive price mechanism), without any interference from the monetary authority. Nevertheless, since the authority is to buy or sell the monetized commodities only in terms of the entire composite unit, such operations might cause the market price of this or that component to be substantially higher or lower than it would be without the proposed arrangement. In connection with the authority's buying operations, this would be the case if there existed a temporary shortage of any one commodity included in the unit. To meet this difficulty it is agreed that the authority should be empowered to substitute "futures" for the present commodities whenever the current price rises by more than a fixed percentage over the future price (this being the reason for selecting goods in which trading in futures is organized). Furthermore, it is agreed that the plan demands a proper weighting of the different commodities which are to be included. Presumably a proper weighting would not present a great difficulty since the technique has been worked out in the formulation of familiar index numbers. It is also realized by all friends of the plan that from time to time the weighting would have to be revised in accordance with changes in the relative commercial importance of the commodities. Finally, the proponents of the standard point out that the level at which the plan is begun is a matter of some significance. At one time, Benjamin Graham suggested that the aggregate minting price should be based on the aggregate market price of the decade 1921-1930 (average), a suggestion which by now has become outmoded, even in his own view. Hayek confines himself to the general observation that the plan is most easily put into operation when a fall of market price threatens.[17] From this remark it may be inferred that the minting price should be fixed at, or slightly below, some prosperity level, and that the logical moment for inception is the beginning of a depression.

[17] *Op.cit.*, p. 180.

The mechanics of the plan are visualized as corresponding very closely to those of the automatic gold standard. The basic idea is that the monetary authority would mechanically issue currency in exchange for a fixed combination of warehouse receipts covering the complete unit, or for any multiple thereof. Equally, currency would be mechanically redeemed in terms of the complete unit whenever the market had an incentive to purchase from the monetary agency.[18] The currency issued would closely correspond to the gold certificate; it would be fully backed by reserves.

It is expected that warehouse receipts would be presented to the agency as soon as the aggregate market price of the composite unit fell ever so little below the minting price. Conversely, the agency would have occasion to contract the volume of money in circulation as soon as the market price rose over the minting price. The buying and selling offers are to be announced by the agency at frequent intervals, and the market watched for chances to buy and sell on stated terms rather than relying completely on the initiative of private traders.[19] The effect would be that the aggregate market price could never seriously rise above, or fall below, the minting price. The difference between the prices at which the agency buys and sells units would be determined by the cost of physi-

[18] According to Benjamin Graham, in *World Commodities and World Currency*, the aggregate unit of warehouse certificates bought and sold might run in terms of $100 per unit, but for practical reasons it might be preferable, according to him, to resort to a considerably larger trading unit, let us say $100,000. For the benefit of the reader, let us reproduce an example of what Graham would include in a $100 unit of commodities: 12 bushels of wheat, 12.5 bushels of corn, 87 pounds of cotton, 25 pounds of wool, 24 pounds of rubber, 34 pounds of coffee, 9.25 pounds of tea, 300 pounds of sugar, 16.3 pounds of tobacco, 6.3 barrels of petroleum, 7,480 pounds of coal, 204 pounds of wood-pulp, 506 pounds of pig-iron, 35 pounds of copper, and 4 pounds of tin (*op.cit.*, p. 45).

[19] This feature is favored by Benjamin Graham but not, apparently, by Hayek, who would like to see the initiative concentrated in the hands of private traders, leaving the monetary agency in a purely passive role except for the announcement of buying and selling offers.

cal storage, plus the cost of withdrawing and selling units or assembling them for deposit in the reserve.[20]

In the version of Professor Frank D. Graham, the adoption of the plan should go hand in hand with a gradual resort to a 100 per cent reserve system for banks. In this event the proposed standard would gradually become the exclusive, and fully automatic, regulator of the nation's (or world's) supply of money.

In the highly optimistic account of Frank D. Graham, the scheme appears to be a cure-all of major economic ailments.[21]

[20] It is of interest to note that the proponents of the standard do not avail themselves of the opportunity to inflict a heavy and possibly rising carrying charge on the money itself, as a method of reducing the ability of money to satisfy the desire for liquidity. Thus they by-pass an aspect which caused Keynes to show considerable interest in a commodity standard (other than gold). He was inclined to argue that variations in the money stock affect total effective demand only through the medium of changes in interest rates. He also argued that with our present form of money even a substantial increase in the quantity of money relative to other forms of wealth will fail to cause the money rate of interest to fall below a certain minimum. In this connection, the present negligible carrying costs of money (plus certain other "characteristics of our monetary system") are said to play an essential part. For "if the carrying costs were material, they would offset the effect of expectations as to the prospective value at future dates. The readiness of the public to increase their stock of money in response to a comparatively small stimulus is due to the advantages of liquidity (real or supposed) having no offset to contend with in the shape of carrying-costs mounting steeply with the lapse of time." (*General Theory of Employment, Interest, and Money*, New York: Harcourt, Brace, 1936, p. 230.)

[21] "1. Stabilization within narrow limits of the average price of the group of commodities composing the commodity unit.

"2. Provision of a 'sound' (that is, solidly backed) dollar of substantially constant purchasing power. . . .

"3. Elimination of the paradox of 'poverty in the midst of plenty' by preventing destruction of the purchasing power of private producers, and their employees, such as now occurs in depressions.

"4. Promotion of equity as between debtors and creditors, employers and employees, and the parties to all contracts involving the elements of time and money.

"5. Assistance in stabilizing business and economic conditions generally.

"6. Provision of an alternative superior to expenditures on public works and other such inept means of providing employment in times of depression.

"7. Creation of a reserve of primary commodities which might be of

Not only would it serve to stabilize employment and prices in the industries covered by the composite unit, but it would also indirectly reduce the amplitude of employment and price swings in the industries which are not included. Because of its quality as a permanently installed device, free from political uncertainty and wrangling, it is claimed to be far superior in its general leverage effects on income to the inept alternative of variable public outlay on dams, bridges, etc.

A reformer is at liberty to present his plan in the best possible light. Perhaps his readers will understand that he is deliberately exaggerating the merits of his scheme for the sake of making it clear what kind of problems he has in mind when he sets out to find a solution. He wishes to show the full range of his attack, and he does so by crediting his scheme with successful performance all along the line. The less pleasant part of showing the limitations and qualifications of the solution comes later, and it does come in the case of Frank D. Graham, as we shall see presently.

To be sure, certain performances of the standard can be taken for granted; in fact, in some respects the scheme may be clearly superior to all the formerly existing automatic commodity standards, including the gold standard. In the case of mono-metallic or bi-metallic standards, the stabilizing influence of the monetized commodity amounted to merely a slow

---

vital importance in some great emergency such as drought, pestilence, or war.

"8. Advancement in the scale of living, through production at maximum levels, with maximum employment, along with facilitation of adjustments necessitated by technological progress.

"9. Checking of inflationary booms by the withdrawal from the reserve of important raw materials and the consequent redemption and cancellation of the equivalent currency.

"10. Improvements of the facilities for foreign trade and finance by providing a means of payment, in tangible goods, of sums due on foreign debts, or for our exports, without any depression of our markets. There could be no competitive depreciation of exchange since the dollar value of foreign currencies would be automatically correlated with the foreign currency price of the composite of commodities in the unit." (*Social Goals and Economic Institutions, op.cit.*, p. 96.)

tendency of the money supply to check a downward or upward movement of prices in general. Critics of the gold standard have commented on the proverbial sluggishness with which the supply of newly mined gold rose in times of deflation, and fell during inflation. Moreover, gold was never more than a fractional reserve; it supported a superstructure of nationally limited currencies. Hence its function as a mechanical compensatory device depended on the cooperation of banking policy, in the sense of mechanical changes in the bank rate of interest along with increases or decreases in a nation's gold reserves. Strict adherence to the mechanical bank rules of the automatic gold standard was a rare thing, even in the days when the gold standard was firmly accepted. Furthermore, as a regularizer of domestic production, the gold commodity figured heavily only in those few countries in which gold mining was a major industry. The rest of the countries depended for compensatory effects on international gold flows resulting from discrepancies of price-level movements. For them the gold standard was merely a device to regulate the money stock, whereas the primary significance of the proposed multiple commodity standard is that of regulating the income stream. At least it was the intention of the originators to design a powerful income-supporting device.

But is it adequate to establish dependable limits for business fluctuations? In answer to this question, it is of interest to note that Frank D. Graham was not willing to see the standard exposed to a severe test. He proposed to have it relieved of the burden of counteracting severe deflationary forces through supplementing it by the public works' method.[22]

[22] "If there is a persistent disposition to hoard money . . . even when the prospect of profits in general was stabilized and interests had been adjusted thereto, the volume of commodities in the 'reserve' would steadily accumulate. This would be no great disaster but, should the reserve ever become unwieldy and unlikely under any circumstances to be exhausted, a leaf might be taken from the book of our present monetary and banking policies. The reserve would then be permitted to fall somewhat below 100 per cent through the issue of unbacked notes, in

This suggestion of supplementary public works must come as a distinct surprise to his readers. An alleged bulwark against discretionary methods is to be rescued by the very discretionary methods which it is to ward off.[23] This unfortunate impression is not removed by the contention that "the real danger, however, probably lies not in excessive accumulation of goods but in the opposite direction, that of an inadequate reserve, especially if issues of money be not confined to, or solely regulated by, the proposed warehouse receipts."[24] It is commonly assumed that the real test for a stabilizing device is ability to cope with deflation rather than inflation. Few reformers, if any, have felt that the potential weakness of their scheme lay on the anti-inflationary side. In fact, if stabilization were but a matter of stopping a cyclical price rise, most experts would be satisfied with central banking controls.

It is not difficult to discover the source of Graham's apprehension about the adequacy of the standard in the face of tenacious destabilizing forces. As compared with a program of deficit finance implemented by a combination of tax reduc-

---

payment of current government charges or expenditures on newly initiated public works, until prices rose sufficiently to lead to drafts on the reserve." (*Op.cit.*, pp. 102-103.)

[23] The public works' method had been condemned by Mr. Graham only a few pages previous to this suggestion. There the stimulus of public works is said to be "by definition, ephemeral, and this leads to fears of what might happen when it is withdrawn" (p. 88). This type of criticism arises from the consideration of spending based on *ad hoc* legislation. But, then, Graham goes on to say that "even persistence of pump-priming is . . . of little avail without *assurance* of its indefinite continuation." The reason for this, allegedly, is that only the consumers' goods industries are bound to be benefited by fiscal deficits. No effort is made to prove this point. Finally, in considering the case of "indefinite continuation with or without assurance thereof," Graham speaks of still another shortcoming of public works, namely, that the government gets "no *quid pro quo* whatever" (as in expenditures for straight relief) or gets a *quid pro quo* in a nonsalable form (roads, bridges, parks, and so on).

This attack, although justified in respect to the shortcomings of insecurely established programs of public outlay on work projects, is unusually severe for someone who is willing to resort to loan-financed public works in times of severe depression.

[24] *Op.cit.*, p. 103.

tion and loan-financed additional outlay on public works as well as various types of transfer payments, there is a certain narrowness in the impact of the standard's compensatory operations. Large segments of the economy are not covered by it, whereas a program of reduced taxes and increased public expenditures can be made to support employment and income in all segments of the economy. The standard does not, and cannot, make allowance for flexibility in the choice of industrial and geographic areas in which, at particular times, the need for tax incentives and public buying is greatest. The stabilization of the markets outside the composite commodity unit must forever rely on a chain of communicated stimuli. The readiness of the monetary agency to maintain an infinitely elastic demand for the reserve commodities might easily give rise to one-sided leverage effects in the insured industries in the sense that profits made in these industries, as well as loanable funds from elsewhere, are invested where the risk is least. The result is mal-allocation of resources and increased sales pressure through unduly enlarged capacity. The accumulation of reserves without adequate income-supporting effects outside the insured markets could easily provoke mounting fears that the minting price will have to be lowered or that the agency's purchases might be rationed. If so, the producers of the reserve commodities might be tempted to limit their output in an effort to prolong the life of the standard. But the standard's income-supporting potentialities might then be drastically lowered. To prevent this, the advocates appear determined to make the initial selection as well as subsequent membership of industries dependent upon the acceptance of competitive principles. Suppose that efforts of this sort were crowned by success. In this case, equally bad alternatives emerge. The combination of insured markets and competitive supply practices will necessitate either a public policy of permanent removal of "excess" reserves through destruction or will lead to a continuous piling up of reserves to the point of eventual disaster in the form of government unloading in the market for whatever price can be obtained. The choice, therefore, is between tremendous economic waste or a breakdown of the standard.

Considering these difficulties, one might be tempted (like Frank D. Graham) to suggest a further widening of the scheme, to bring as many industries as possible under its wings. However, the thought of doing so is sufficiently forbidding, both technically as well as politically, to make serious consideration unnecessary. An attempt to make the composite unit so broad as to cover the bulk of national production would make the proposal as absurd as the similar suggestion pertaining to the previously discussed novelty, namely to establish adequate compensatory reactions of an agreed high-level budget through making the budget very large. In either case the government would become the employer of the community's resources. Little comfort could be derived from the fact that the government would be subjected to a set of fixed rules minimizing the vesting of discretionary powers in the central agency entrusted with the execution of the schemes.

C H A P T E R 6 ·

RULES OF ADAPTATION OF FLEXIBLE STABILIZERS
TO VARIOUS DEGREES OF OFF-BALANCE

....

The General Nature of the Approach

THE stabilizers considered so far fail to inspire confidence in a stabilization program exclusively based on automatic machinery. Still pursuing the subject of automatic compensatory devices, we must now inquire into the possibility of a different species of automatic stabilizer. The possibility concerns the case of prescribed rules of countercyclical adaptation attached to certain compensatory controls, in accordance with various degrees of economic off-balance. The controls themselves may be of various kinds, provided they are sufficiently broad to affect the economy at large. They may be taxes, government outlay on goods and services, or central banking controls. Any one of these controls might be applied on the basis of prescribed rules which determine the degree of intensity of use in accordance with the prevailing extent of cyclical disturbance.

As a preliminary step, this procedure necessitates the selection of some index which is indicative of the overall performance of the economy. Once such an index has been chosen and accepted by the public, it becomes the guide for cycle control. The countercyclical devices are to be geared to this particular guide through a set of rules according to which a certain rate of change of the index must evoke a certain rate of change in the intensity (or direction) of the compensatory work of the devices in question.

To illustrate the principle, let us use an example from tax management. Suppose total income is chosen for purposes of an index. Suppose also that a broad type of tax—such as the personal income tax—is to furnish the compensatory device. To begin with, the tax rates must be set with reference to some desirable level of total income (employment), in the sense that total tax revenues promise to balance government expenditures at this particular level of income. As income began to deviate from this mark, the income tax rates would change in a predetermined fashion. For instance, a one per cent drop in income during a certain period of time, such as a month, might be met by a one per cent decrease in tax rates for the same period. Conceivably, the rate of change in the tax rates might be made to be progressive: whereas a one per cent drop in income might be met by merely a one per cent decrease in tax rates, a five per cent fall in income (for the same period of time) might be countered by, let us say, a twenty per cent cut in taxes. The purpose of such a progressive pattern would be to secure a high floor under income. But whether merely proportionate or progressive, the tax-rate changes must follow a prescribed mode in order to establish automatic procedure. The rules of adaptation must also permit reversible action.

The fondest hope that could be entertained is that total employment or income would tend merely to oscillate around the premeditated mark. Whether there is any basis for such hope depends on several factors which must be briefly examined.

Some Important Factors

The question of the best possible index is of only secondary importance. All that is necessary in this respect is that the selected index, or a combination of indexes, must be representative of general economic performance and fairly sensitive to swings. In the above example we have spoken of an employment index. But we might as well have used some other aggregate, such as gross national product, or net product, or total personal income, or perhaps some broad price index. Although these aggregates are not coextensive, any of them might do. The choice might be made dependent on some technical considerations. One is the speed with which the statistical data can be assembled and computed. Furthermore, since the procedure is to be absolutely devoid of forecasting, the index should not be sluggish. A sluggish index, or an index which understates the order of magnitude of cyclical processes, should be avoided even if it offers certain advantages in other respects, such as distinct public appeal or ease of assembling factual data.

Much more important than these matters are those which relate to the controls. A control must in itself be sufficiently elastic and pliable to permit countercyclical adaptation along prescribed rules. While this question of flexibility also arises in connection with discretionary procedure, it comes up here with greater urgency. Where rates of change in the intensity of countercyclical use of controls are to follow a predetermined pattern, there is little or nothing that can be done in the way of making allowance for the inherent limitations of a control. A certain control may be potentially powerful but also unwieldy in the sense that it requires much time and planning to be put into operation, or in the sense that it tends to have a momentum of its own after it has been set in motion. The proverbial example of such an unwieldy control is that of heavy public works. Even with a shelf of blue-printed and authorized projects, some time will normally have to elapse before work can actually be started. Moreover, it may not be feasible to expand or contract the volume of such activity in accordance with some prescribed formula of adaptation. By contrast, discretionary use of the public works' method enjoys relatively greater freedom in the way in which it employs this particular control. It can confine its use to offset severe and stubborn fluctuations and select more handy controls to fight minor swings. Generally speaking, it can hope to make the best possible use of this device by predicating action, in each concrete case, on as much information about the nature and strength of the prevailing unsettling factors as can be obtained. In the event of uncertainty about the factors, discretion suggests cautious restraint in the use of the method of heavy public investment projects, in favor of other more pliable devices.

Unfortunately there exists a presumption that those controls which are most pliable and, for this reason, lend themselves most easily to rules of change are also those which tend to be wanting in effectiveness, while those controls which tend to have a fairly reliable impact on total economic activity may not be amenable to automatic management. The present writer does not stand alone in the belief that there exists an adverse relationship between the inherent degree of short-run variability of a control, on the one hand, and the reliability of impact of the control, on the other.[1] Considering the elements which make for variability, and those which decide over reliability of private response, this is not strange. Administrative variability of controls—in a nation which believes in a workable maximum of *private* decision-making over the use of economic resources—tends to grow in proportion to the *indirectness* of the controls. The criterion for indirectness is the absence of governmental directives to specific individuals, or specific groups. It is also the absence of coercion in the sense that the public is left with a good deal of choice as to how it responds. If this is the correct meaning of the concept of indirect controls, then the natural field for such controls is still the regulation of the money stock, i.e., the regulation of the terms under which private persons may avail themselves of loans or liquid balances. More concretely speaking, the natural field is that of discount policy and open market operations. This is also the logical field for prescribed rules of countercyclical adaptation in the use of controls.

By the above standards, the criterion of directness is the

[1] See, for example, Milton Friedman, "A Monetary and Fiscal Framework for Economic Stability," p. 256.

presence of specific central directives involving some degree of coercion. The term clearly indicates direct interference with the allocation of resources, the structure of the price system, the wage structure, and the distribution of income in general. While the distinction of direct and indirect controls can easily be exaggerated, and while the two principles often overlap, it is nevertheless possible to characterize certain controls as direct or indirect. Certain highly specific and coercive controls, such as individual price and wage controls, most assuredly are direct. But they have not been acceptable in peacetime in the United States and need not be brought into this discussion. Certain other controls appear to stand on the borderline between the two categories and also appear closer to peacetime choice of controls. All the budgetary controls seem to fit this case. They involve central directives as far as the distribution of income and the allocation of resources are concerned.

We shall briefly examine these controls for inherent possibilities of automatic countercyclical variation. If there are distinct possibilities of this sort, the case for described rules of adaptation must be taken seriously. But if there are only remote chances, the method in question has only very limited significance since budgetary controls are the main stabilizing weapons.

On the expenditure side of the budget, the method of heavy public construction has already been characterized as unsuitable for the purposes on hand. Reversals in the direction of this control are hard to handle. A mechanical change from a rising to a falling rate of public investment activity would be apt to lead to unfinished projects and, hence, to possible waste and criticism. What might be meaningful is to make the total amount of funds available for works projects subject to prescribed rules of change, but to leave the actual disposition of the funds to administrative discretion. This might mean a broad and permissive delegation of powers to some agency enabling it to determine the starting point of time-consuming projects, or to abstain from starting such projects in favor of incidental work projects involving less time for completion and leaving greater leeway for starts and stops. In addition, discretionary judgment would be called upon to avoid bottlenecks, friction between private and governmental policy in the labor market, and between private and public investment interests.

By comparison, government outlay to farmers offers greater opportuntity for prescribed rules of adaptation. In a sense the so-called Brannan Plan appears to fit the bill. According to this plan, the farmers are encouraged to sell for whatever price they can get in the market, with the understanding that they will be reimbursed for any gap between market price and a legislatively set support price. The reimbursement per unit of sale would mechanically vary as the market prices indicated larger or smaller deviations from the support price. It must be kept in mind, however, that this scheme is apt to go hand in hand with some government control of agricultural output, and here we strike upon an element which is bound to require fresh legislation from time to time. Crop controls are designed to narrow the gap between market price and support price, and to hold the size of reimbursements within manageable limits. If the planning of output does not follow any prescribed rule of adaptation (for example, a steady rate of increase in permissible output commensurable with population growth), but instead becomes a matter of short-run policy-making that allows for all sorts of contingencies, the scheme remains essentially discretionary. As compared with the central feature of crop control, the proposal to vary reimbursements in accordance with the size of the gap seems almost of secondary importance. Moreover, the support price itself might easily come in for frequent revisions under the influence of log-rolling tactics, so that further inroads are made into the principle of lasting prescribed rules. Among other things, a true scheme of countercyclical adaptation of agricultural aid along the lines of predetermined rules would require either fixity of the support price or, at a minimum, a system of revisions of this hypothetical price which follows a mechanical formula (such as a parity formula devoid of benevolent interpretation on the part of the farm bloc). Analogous reasoning holds for any other type of subsidization.

It is also questionable whether government transfer payments can be burdened with countercyclical adaptation. Changes in relief standards during swings would have to keep themselves within narrow limits. On the downswing, a liberalization of allowances would have to keep itself within the limits of maintaining the incentive to seek employment and of avoiding inequity between relief groups and those who earn their wages through work. On the upswing it would contradict humanitarian principles to reduce the size of family allowances, or to tighten the standards of eligibility, considering that the costs of living tend to be high and perhaps keep rising. On the whole, changes in relief standards are a matter of long-range economic policy.

From the standpoint of the federal budget, there is one particular type of expenditure which appears to be clearly amenable to mechanical countercyclical variation. This is the system of federal grants-in-aid to state and local governments. It has been proposed that the federal government extend grants for state and local public works which vary percentage-wise in accord with economic conditions.[2] But it will be noted that the distinct possibilities of mechanical variation which exist in this case are due to the fact that the arrangement stays, so to speak, in the financial sphere. Except for possible psychological effects, the impact on effective demand must await the use of these funds by the state and local governments, and in this respect the problems are the same as in the case of direct federal works programs. On the whole this example supports our general assertion that the natural field for mechanical

[2] For example in the Report of the Joint Committee on the January 1949 Economic Report of the President, March 1, 1949.

rules of countercyclical change in the handling of controls is that of regulating the amount of available balances.

On the tax side, variability in accordance with predetermined rules appears to be limited also. Frequent changes in personal income tax rates, or in exemption levels, present formidable administrative and economic problems, not only for the government but also for the tax payers. Changes in exemption levels (Simons) would be especially annoying. Millions of tax payers might be thrown in, and out of, the tax-paying income brackets. Variability of corporate income taxes is also limited. The prospect of continuously varying tax rates might play havoc with business expectations and calculations. If effective and constructive changes in business tax rates are to be made, they should be made for known intervals of sufficient length so as to permit intelligent business reaction. On the other hand, there might be a certain opportunity for varying excises and sales taxes in accord with economic conditions, on the basis of prescribed rules. If necessary, these rules could provide that changes will be made only within certain limits as to frequency (for example, only once for every six months), and also as to degree. While it is not intended here to go into any detail, attention must be drawn to the fact that suggestions of countercyclical variations in indirect taxes become impressive only on the assumption of a closer coordination of federal and state tax policies.

The Crux of the Problem of Mechanical Rules of Change

The foregoing observations about the limitations of variability in budgetary controls may not be generally accepted. But they are not of decisive importance. The chief obstacle lies somewhere else. It is the difficulty of having to decide in advance, and for all relevant situations, how much acceleration or deceleration in the use of the controls it might take to meet future contingencies. Even a community which is firmly resolved to stabilize its economic life, and is not afraid of innovation in stabilizing procedure, might easily shrink back at this point, questioning the wisdom of making such a decision. Even some experimentation prior to the inception of rules would not yield a reliable basis for making up one's mind. To say otherwise would be tantamount to making the untenable assumption that the forces which account for swings are always of the same strength. While the severity of a swing will eventually be fully registered by a suitable index, it cannot be claimed that a certain rate of change of the index, at a certain phase of the cycle, is a reliable guide for measuring the strength of the underlying destabilizing forces. Several slumps may start in a similar fashion, showing the same rate of fall in the index. Nevertheless, a marked difference may show up later. In one case the disturbance may prove to be minor whereas in others the contraction goes on and gains momentum.[3] A uniform mode of acceleration in the use of controls might mean costly delay and damage in some cases.

At this point it might be objected that this discussion operates with an intolerably narrow concept of rules of countercyclical change in tax rates, expenditure programs, and central banking controls. It might be argued that the purpose of such rules is not to reduce the handling of such controls to sheer routine but to make certain that the control will be used to fight swings. The meaning of a rule, in this view, is merely to give the fiscal and monetary authorities unquestioned authority and responsibility to vary the intensity of the controls in accord with the economic condition, leaving it to their good judgment as to precisely how this is to be done.

It cannot be denied that this is a meaningful interpretation of the idea of the rules of countercyclical adaptation. Rules

[3] In fact, the initial descent may be sharper for a minor recession than in the case of a severe and protracted slump. This is demonstrated by the 1937-1938 recession whose initial descent was much steeper than that of the previous depression (1929-1933) although it was of a less basic character. See *National Income: A Supplement to the Survey of Current Business*; United States Department of Commerce (1951 edition), p. 14.

of this general sort could do a great deal to make certain that agencies like the Federal Reserve Board which possess *de facto* power to affect the overall performance of the economy are given explicit responsibility commensurate with such power, and that such power is to be used for well-defined goals. This certainty might do much to inspire public confidence that something will be done to fight economic fluctuations.

But it should be obvious that such general rules imply the element of administrative discretion as to the specific ways in which the authority and responsibility are to be exercised. Such rules do not establish a case of automatic management.

CHAPTER 7

A SUMMARY APPRAISAL OF ALL VARIATIONS
OF AUTOMATIC MANAGEMENT

BEFORE we leave the subject of automatic stabilizers, it will be well to give a summary appraisal of all variations of the notion of countercyclical automatic management. Starting from the existing examples of constant built-in devices, we proceeded to examine proposals which aim at new and presumably more powerful devices of this general type. From there, finally, we approached the subject of prescribed rules of countercyclical variation attached to compensatory means.

All variations are characterized by a dual tendency: on the one hand, emphasis on government; on the other, distrust of government. The emphasis is shown by the nature of the means; they are all centrally installed. The government, as monetary and fiscal authority, is looked upon as possessing what it takes to fight business fluctuations. But while the government thus appears in a strategic position, most painstaking care is taken to see to it that the power to stabilize is exercised in a prescribed fashion giving the appearance of passive government.

According to one version, this is best assured by arrangements which are so constructed that the basic lines of government—tax rates, terms of relief, expenditures on goods and services—are fixed except for secular adjustments. Fixity, here, is regarded as the best possible way for the public to become familiar with the workings of the government and its stabilizing machinery, and to gauge its likely effects during upswings and downswings. This view is most strongly expressed by Friedman, according to whom "the attempt to adapt the magnitude

of government operations to the requirements of stability may
. . . easily introduce more instability than it corrects."[1] Aside
from this economic argument, there is a political point: fixity
is held to be the best possible safeguard against legislative
tinkering and administrative authoritarianism.

The propounders of fixed schemes, although sometimes
driven by the desire for more powerful stabilizers than we
now have, appear to be characterized by a tendency to sacrifice, if necessary, the achievement of a satisfactory degree of
stability to the achievement of absolutely nondiscretionary
procedure (Friedman),[2] or at least to place discretionary
procedure outside the proposed stabilizing device (F. D. Graham's suggestion of supplementary public works programs).
In the event of results which are disappointing to the community, and which lead to public clamor for improvement, the
very evils which the fixed fiscal and monetary framework is to
avoid may make themselves felt most strongly. There may
have to be frequent revisions of the devices in force, or frequent introduction of novelties of this sort. Worst of all, however, is the fact that reliance on a fixed framework of governmental stabilizing machinery may create large undefined areas
of discretionary policy, particularly as regards the setting of
goals of stabilization policy. Nothing is gained if, as a result
of insufficient means, the nature of the goal remains uncertain
or has to undergo revisions. No confidence in stabilization can
be established under such circumstances.

The method of variable controls appears to adjust the desire
for automatic management more closely to the desire for effec-

---

[1] *Op.cit.*, p. 252.

[2] "In conclusion, I should like to emphasize the modest aim of the
proposal. It does not claim to provide full employment in the absence
of successful measures to make prices of final goods and of factors of
production flexible. It does not claim to eliminate entirely cyclical fluctuations in output and employment. Its claim to serious consideration is that
it provides a stable framework of fiscal and monetary action, that it
largely eliminates the uncertainty and undesirable political implications
of discretionary action by governmental authorities. . . ." (*Op.cit.*, p. 263.)

tive stabilization. But here, too, we had to come to fairly discouraging conclusions. To begin with, prescribed rules of acceleration and deceleration in the use of controls demand a distinct degree of flexibility of the controls. Only the money-stock controls appear to possess such flexibility. Among the important budgetary controls, the method of heavy public works fails to qualify, and so does the majority of our federal taxes, particularly the corporate income taxes. It does not matter that the causes of inflexibility are not always the same. Wherever there are either technical, administrative, or psychological (anticipations) obstacles to change, the method of continuous adaptations along prescribed formulae appears to be out of the question. The case of countercyclical variations in relief standards has such strange economic implications that it must be dismissed as a crank scheme. Secondly, the method of prescribed rules of change fails to do justice to the complexity of causes which underlie swings. The rate of increase in unemployment may be the same throughout comparable phases of different downswings, and yet in one historical case the causes of economic contraction may be relatively short-lived whereas in another they may be stubborn. Application of the same mode of income-supporting measures may produce success here and failure there.

What, then, is the final position which should be taken on the subject of automatic management as a design for stabilizing policy? The answer is not easy. It would be simple only if better methods were in sight. In this event the method of automatic stabilizers should be kept within the modest limits of purely incidental stabilizers which owe their existence to motives other than cycle control—such as the devices which we now have. Of course as time goes on, more of these incidental stabilizers may be introduced, or existing ones enlarged. Developments of this sort depend upon the extent to which such factors as unemployment compensation and guaranteed public relief become broadened. They would also be contingent upon a further increase in the progressiveness of our tax structure. Stronger countercyclical reactions emerging from social security and taxation would merely be a by-product of secular reform which is carried by humanitarian and equalitarian drives. It is well worth pointing out that if society succeeds in narrowing the width of swings with the aid of *other* means, the countercyclical potentialities of these incidental stabilizers might become partially dormant. The primary purpose of these devices would then stand out more clearly.

But if no better methods are in sight or, though in sight, are not acceptable to the public, one must choose between various alternatives, none of which are very satisfactory. The logical choices are as follows: exclusive reliance on automatic stabilizers; an attempt to improve and broaden built-in devices without going to the extreme of complete eradication of discretionary procedure; finally, acceptance of the present admixture of automatic and discretionary controls.

The first of these alternatives can be rationalized in terms of preference for politically "safe" machinery over the achievement of reliable standards of stability. Despite our foregoing criticism, this position may continue to have appeal for some specialists. Wherever thinking is strongly dominated by aversion to discretionary procedure, it may take more than a demonstration of technical insufficiencies in automatic management to bring about a change of mind. It must be granted that the method of complete reliance on built-in devices can be pursued without sponsoring crank schemes. The two proposals selected for appraisal—particularly the agreed-high-level budget—surely qualify from the viewpoint of analytic content. From the standpoint of policy-making, analytical respectability must be combined with feasibility. One cannot be so certain that the proposals in question satisfy this additional requisite. The far-reaching institutional changes and procedural difficulties of the Graham proposal are obvious. Even the agreed-high-level budget, despite Friedman's claim that it involves a minimum of reliance on uncertain and untested knowledge, is still far from being an easy device, especially in conjunction with the drastic reform of the banking system that is to go along with it.

The second alternative, i.e., a strengthening of the automatic part of the stabilizing machinery at the expense of current forms of discretionary procedure, is a compromise about method, apparently in the interest of coming closer to the aim of setting reliable limits for cycles. While this type of position does seem to indicate a preference for permanently installed and routinized compensatory devices, it also reveals some awareness of the inherent limitations of automatic management. Its proponents—like Hart—seem inclined to retain (and perhaps also to improve) discretionary controls as an indispensable supplement to the set of built-in controls, presumably because they can be adapted much more readily to the concrete circumstances of a slump or a boom—or some national emergency.[3] Furthermore—as is true in the case of most compromise positions on economic policy-making—regard for the political temperament of democratically inclined societies may easily enter into the choice of some admixture of controls. A proposal for somewhat greater emphasis on automatic stabilizers might well suit the tastes of the American public. Be that as it may, such a proposal, like all halfway positions, enjoys an air of realism. It can be presented in terms of an improvement over present arrangements without being radical. It is also noncommittal and vague so long as no concrete suggestions are made about the extent to which the automatic part is to be pushed. In the absence of such information, the proposal does not amount to much more than an indication of the general direction which, presumably, the reform of stabilization machinery should take. Yet even so it contains an effort to make a contribution to the problem on hand and hence is more stimulating than mere acceptance of the arrange-

[3] *Op.cit.*, p. 488.

ment now in force. The latter attitude merely reveals either unwarranted optimism about the effectiveness of existing countercyclical machinery or unwillingness to probe into the undoubtedly difficult subject of improvement.

Before we can say anything more about these issues we must present an approach to stabilization which, in this writer's judgment, promises to be superior to what we have seen so far.

PART III

THE METHOD OF BINDING TARGETS

CHAPTER 8

THE THEORY OF BINDING TARGETS

....

A Direct Route to Dependable Limits of Fluctuations

WE HAVE seen that the main weakness of centrally installed stabilizers is their inability to establish dependable limits for economic fluctuations. This fact suggests that we must turn our attention to discretionary machinery. However, discretionary use of countercyclical controls is by no means a guarantee of success. Experience proves this. To make progress in short-run stabilization, the discretionary method must be vastly improved. It will be the main purpose of the following discussion to show that this can be done. In the judgment of this writer, the principal source of weakness in past stabilizing efforts has been the absence of clearly formulated responsibilities and powers on the part of the authorities entrusted with cycle control. This source of weakness must be removed. It can be removed only through the adoption of binding targets for compensatory programs. The objectives must be clearly stated and—what is more important—the government must be charged with unequivocal responsibility to reach and defend them. To avoid unnecessary harshness, and for other reasons which will be dealt with later, the objectives should be stated in terms of a binding floor and ceiling making allowance for a liberal margin of fluctuations. Both floor and ceiling should be stated in terms of comprehensive indexes measuring total economic activity. The mandate which formulates goals must also contain instructions about means. The means must be adequate to achieve the end. Since the adoption of binding targets is expected eventually to exercise stabilizing effects in itself, overconfidence in the effectiveness of available compensatory controls must be avoided. The stipulated controls should reveal awareness that the defense of the targets might necessitate great compensatory effort for some time to come. The controls must, of course, conform with certain political standards set by democratic tradition. While this involves a narrowing of the choice of means, the limitations are bound to be less confining than in the case of automatic management, where technical handicaps are added to political restrictions. It has already been shown that certain budgetary controls can be handled better on the basis of delegated powers to administrative authorities than on the basis of a minutely detailed set of prescribed rules designed to meet all possible contingencies.

In one important respect does the method of binding targets rule out administrative discretion as well as legislative opportunism. This concerns the targets themselves. Once formulated and adopted in formal legislative action, the targets should stand, at least for specified periods of time. If there are to be revisions, they must be made subject to highly formal legislative procedure. Both politically and economically, arbitrary goal-setting is the truly alarming part of discretionary procedure. In this respect the method of binding targets promises decisive improvement, provided the targets are chosen reasonably so that their defense does not threaten to drown the economy in a sea of central regulation.

The Question of Gradual Self-enforcement of the Targets

The ultimate purpose of a binding norm for economic stabilization is to create a psychological climate conducive to favorable private response to central stabilizing efforts. The binding character of the norm is to establish public confidence in future stability of markets and job opportunities. Given such confidence, there is hope that producers and consumers will behave so as to simplify greatly the task of the stabilizing authorities. We may call this self-enforcement of binding procedure. The possibility of self-enforcement is not an immediate one. It will not come as a prompt and direct result of the adoption of binding targets. Confidence in stability of markets and jobs must be achieved through demonstrated ability of the government to reach and defend the targets, perhaps in the midst of initial public skepticism and unfavorable reaction on the part of strongly entrenched private interests. A combination of resourcefulness and adequate means is necessary at the administrative center. In the beginning, the central measures must work out well without the benefit of public confidence and its favorable implications. The establishment of such confidence may involve a period of considerable length, depending on how long it will take for the government to demonstrate to the people that the objectives to which it has been committed can be reached with the type of controls for which legislative provision has been made. As has already been pointed out in an earlier part of this study, there might be anxious moments of uncertainty and friction between government and private parties. The government would have to steer cautiously between the dangers of doing too much or too little. Too much bossism might either crush private initiative or cause revolt. This is no basis for cooperation. On the other hand, too much leniency would account for public skepticism as regards the willingness or power of government to live up to the terms of the mandate.

There are various steppingstones toward the achievement of a reasonable compromise between too much bossism and too much leniency. Each of these will be discussed in the following chapters. For the moment let us assume that the difficult launching period has been successfully negotiated, i.e., that one can afford to look at the method of binding targets as it would present itself in the event of public confidence in the validity of the program. Under such assumptions it is reasonable to expect that the binding limits would increasingly become self-implementary. The program would work largely on a persuasive basis, making it possible for the government to reduce the order of magnitude of its compensatory operations.

Many economists may regard this hope for self-implementation as farfetched, and even abstruse. They may be willing to accept the doctrine of self-enforcement of binding rules in an area such as criminal law, but deny its applicability in economic stabilization. They may point out that in the latter case the commitment applies to the government itself and that there are no criminal aspects for the citizens when their economic actions give rise to depressions and booms, as well as no immediate and tangible penalties and fines to punish them for such actions. Therefore it cannot be expected that binding overall targets could ever work on a persuasive (or threat) basis. They might add that the element of self-enforcement is valid for such a thing as anti-monopoly procedure where there are fines as well as, perhaps, public pressure, but that this element is out of place in the case of rules which can never be spelled out for every individual producer or consumer.

But the hope for eventual self-enforcement of binding overall targets is actually not farfetched. Establishment of confidence in the ability of the government to live up to its mandate is tantamount to the creation of private conviction that it does not pay to count on a deepening of swings beyond the stipulated marks. If on account of unavoidable delays in the effect of compensatory action either floor or ceiling should be punctured, it pays to expect restoration and, hence, to act in such a way as to bring about restoration prior to the government's going so.

The following example will illustrate this point. There has been considerable emphasis on the potential anti-inflationary effects of buying strikes. Such strikes clearly fall within the category of stabilizing efforts which are implemented by the actions of the private public. However, let us recognize that the general buyer's resistance is effective only under the conditions of either (a) an expected reversal of the general price movement toward deflation or (b) the prospect of a firm governmental anti-inflationary program.

The first of these occasions is not in keeping with a stabilization program; it belongs in a cyclically unstable world and may be exploited for purposes of explaining reversals from booms to depressions. The second occasion is the one which demonstrates the point in question. We know from experience that buying strikes are likely to produce merely sporadic results in the absence of public confidence that firm central steps will be taken to counteract a prevailing upward movement of prices. Those persons who temporarily refrain from buying are likely to scramble back into the market if prices continue to rise. The strike breaks down. This situation is likely to be changed drastically if the community brings itself to the point of authorizing its government to apply stern anti-inflationary action around some stipulated mark. Suppose that for some technical delay in the taking of action, or because of some lag between the application of controls and their effect on total demand, the inflation is not immediately stopped by the authorities in charge of the plan. Then, if the people know and have confidence that it is only a matter of time until prices in general will be forced down to a stipulated mark, it will be the most natural reaction for producers and consumers to cut down on their buying (within the limits of postponable purchases). This will break the inflationary price movement. The result might not be perfect; self-enforcement might end up with a somewhat changed structure of prices. But the broad purpose of stopping inflation would be achieved. Only some supplementary government action, designed to preserve the price-relationships from changing too much in the process, might be called for.

This is self-implementation of a binding target. Analogous reasoning holds for the case of fighting an incipient deflation. Given the resort to a binding price floor, the producers and consumers would diminish their cash balances (or borrow) in favor of goods and services until prices in general reached the level which is to be defended by the stabilizing agency. If we view the situation from the standpoint of the economy in which such binding limits for price-level fluctuations have been in operation for some time, we must conclude, indeed, that the scale of prices would acquire virtual stability within the stipulated limits, except for times of unusual stress and strain, such as wars.

A Return to the Traditional Concept of Automatism

Without wishing to make a fetish of automatism, we may point out that the ultimate goal of the method of binding targets is to come as closely as possible to an automatically stable economy. Ordinary commercial incentives of private parties are relied upon to achieve *dependable* stabilizing results. The character of the rules as well as the mode of enforcement by government are designed specifically for this ultimate purpose. In contrast to automatic management, the luxury of nondiscretionary operation of controls is sacrificed because of its limitations in regard to the establishment of a reliable floor and ceiling.

Obviously, the type of automatism which is to be achieved with the combination of binding targets and discretionary implementation is in line with traditional classical ideals. The classical theory of self-sustaining balance was developed primarily with respect to the allocation of resources between industries. Rules of competition were relied upon to furnish an inter-industry balance. Maintenance of this balance is only one aspect of the stability problem. In the absence of a framework of rules which direct private economic incentive toward maintaining a stable level of total activity, a system of competitively flexible prices permits violent cyclical fluctuations. Expounders of a monetary cycle theory have tried to close the gap by supplementing competition with control of the money supply in accordance with a stable-money norm. They were on the right track, but their approach was insufficient in that they failed to make this norm binding and proposed techniques of implementation which were highly inadequate. The gap was not actually closed until the appearance of the work of Henry C. Simons. To him goes the credit for systematic development of the idea of subjecting the government to firm responsibility for monetary stability, and for opening the road toward a theory of economic automatism in terms of self-enforcement of binding rules. As far as the principle of the matter is concerned, there remains nothing to add to Simons's work.[1] In the judgment of this writer, the only task left is to free Simons's approach of its narrow monetary reasoning from the standpoint of both goal and techniques of implementation.

A Reasonable View on Self-implementing Procedure

Nothing would be more detrimental to the theory of self-implementary stabilization procedure than exaggerated claims as to what a "must" can do. Provocative statements to the effect that in the long view binding procedure will allow the government to coast along on mere token operations had better be avoided. They expose the theory to nothing but criticism, and even ridicule. Let us be reasonable and say that one can hope for a gradually diminishing compensatory burden. In this form the theory should not give rise to serious objections. It should be possible to agree that as long as we cling to an economy in which the bulk of economic activity and decision-making is to be carried on by private individuals, there can be no stabilization without a substantial element of self-enforcement of binding norms. This is not saying that such a course should actually be followed. It does mean, however, that the only alternative choices are unstable capitalism or a drift toward collectivism.

Although it is impossible to tell, in advance, the extent to

[1] Henry C. Simons, "Rules versus Authorities in Monetary Policy," *Journal of Political Economy*, 1936; reprinted in *Economic Policy for a Free Society*, Chicago University Press, 1948, pp. 160-183.

which a binding commitment will serve to give us a steadier flow of private investment and consumers' outlay, it is possible to add to the theory of self-enforcement in some other vital respects.

First, no society can afford to provide room for a certain amount of ups and downs of total activity without leaving for itself a vital field for research on fluctuations. Presumably some of the beginning ups and downs within the margin of tolerable swings will be the preliminary phases of movements which threaten to break through floor and ceiling and to carry the economy far off-balance. Each incipient movement of activity and prices will have to be examined for underlying causes. One of the tasks would be to try to isolate reverberations from previous major cycles and to distinguish them from new developments. An attempt should be made to find out at what stage, and for what reasons, a beginning downturn threatens to gain momentum. As in the past, there would be sufficient reason to evaluate the potential destabilizing influence of various factors which either alone, or in conjunction with each other, might be capable of ushering in major spurts and slumps, such as broad and erratic changes in technology and the development of important new industries, widespread wage disputes and strikes, or substantial fiscal changes resulting from other than countercyclical measures (national defense measures, foreign lending, etc.). Generally speaking, the method of binding limits should not become an excuse for abandoning the theoretical work and statistical research done in the past, nor for failing to accomplish further progress in the knowledge of the economic process.

Secondly, it may not always be possible to evaluate properly incipient disturbances for underlying strength. Therefore the community should not dispense with an available set of highly flexible controls—a procedure which has come to be somewhat neglected due to the current preoccupation with powerful fiscal compensatory measures, i.e., the traditional set of central banking controls. The purpose of these flexible controls would be to test the strength of beginning movements, even while they still keep themselves within the stipulated margin of tolerable instability. The controls should be used in conjunction with highly sensitive barometers. This machinery must be sharply separated in the mind from the mandatory part of the program which is to be set in motion only when the movements begin to threaten to puncture floor or ceiling and to carry the economy far off-balance. Its value is primarily informative and experimental. The usefulness of test controls will prove to be the greater, the less progress we can make in deductive reasoning about cycle causation. Failure of the experimental control tests to make any impression on incipient movements should set the signal for the government to get ready for its mandatory defense of ceiling or floor. Changes in reserve requirements for member banks, open market operations, or changes in margin requirements for speculative and consumers' loans, may be ideally suited for test purposes. These as well as the remaining central banking controls could be intensified as the movements began to break through the binding limits. They belong both in the experimental as well as the compensatory parts of the stabilization program.

Thirdly, nothing of what has been said here about the hope for self-implementary procedure applies to times which are troubled by serious national emergencies such as war. It is better readily to suspend programs predicated on peacetime assumptions when such emergencies loom than to risk costly failure. Premature return to the program must also be avoided. Failure to stress this point is apt to lead to misunderstanding and unnecessary criticism.

CHAPTER 9

THE PROBLEM OF INDEXES

....

Indexes as Guides and Objectives of Compensatory Action

THE method of binding targets relies very heavily on indexes. A comprehensive index, or if necessary a combination of broad indexes, has to assume the dual role of furnishing guide and objective of countercyclical procedure. The underlying principle is simple. The nation should decide on certain "must" values of the selected indexes, for floor and ceiling. These values become binding targets. Deviations of the index from the established marks—in the sense of a rise above the ceiling or a fall below the floor—operate as guides for imperative central compensatory measures and, in the longer view, for the mobilization of private action (self-enforcement).

Despite the simplicity of the principle, there are several questions which demand careful attention. The approach will benefit greatly from judicious selection of indexes. Logically, the selection might be made from indexes expressing aggregate magnitudes or economic relationships. The word aggregates refers to such matters as total employment, total production, national income, total money demand, or to some price aggregate. Examples of relationships are the consumption-investment relationship, the relationships between sales and inventories, wages and profits, farm income and industrial income, income and taxes, etc. These examples relate to the composition of national product (income). In connection with the cyclical behavior of the system, the list must be extended to include such relationships as the rate of change in the money stock compared with that of production, the ratio between bank reserves and the volume of bank deposits, relationships between different price groups (raw materials, wholesale and retail prices, etc.), the marginal propensity to consume, the marginal efficiency of capital, and so forth.

In addition to the issue of aggregrates and relationships, there are other aspects of a proper choice of indexes, such as the technical and political requisites of the statistical measurements which are to serve as guide and objective. The purpose is to find measurements which combine economic significance with ease of statistical compilation of data and which enjoy public understanding as well as appeal. Finally, there arises a question of alternative ways of stating "must" values. Binding limits may be expressed in terms of a minimum and maximum figure of the selected index, for example, a minimum and maximum level of employment (corrected for secular growth), or minima and maxima for total product, expenditures, price levels. Another possible method is that of determining critical, i.e., intolerable, rates of change of the index in question. Both methods are supposed to lead to a margin of tolerable fluctuations. Their relative merits must be examined.

Aggregates and Relationships

Traditionally, the theory of compensatory stabilization procedure has been oriented around the use of indexes measuring national aggregates. Until the recent progress in national income accounting, more or less fractional measurements of production, employment, and sales have served as indexes. A good example of indexes of this limited type is the *Federal Reserve Board Index of Industrial Production* which has been available since 1919 and which contains a wide sample from representative industries in manufacturing and mining. Although this index may have served as a reasonably representative indicator of general economic conditions, it has defects in that it leaves out important areas. It omits the measurement of services and stresses the production of durable rather than nondurable goods. Because of the latter, it tends to overstate the fluctuations of general economic activity and must be corrected by judicious interpretation.

The progress in national income accounting has given considerable impetus and range to the use of indexes designed to measure the scale of national product. From the standpoint of comprehensiveness, consolidated figures like gross or net national product seem ideally suited to indicate overall economic performance and to furnish the material for stating goals of countercyclical policy. Nevertheless, even aggregates of this sort may conceal the development of significant maladjustments in the system. Over short periods of time they may suggest a fair degree of economic stability—and hence a policy of tolerance—despite the fact that the structure of production and prices is getting out of line. Equally disconcerting is the fact that compensatory action which merely defends broadly defined goals with equally broad and indirect controls might fail to remove production dislocations and price dispersions indicative of cyclical disturbance. In fact, it is possible that prevailing structural faults may not only be perpetuated under the cloak of stable aggregates but actually grow in size. Also, new dislocations might be introduced.

It has been suggested by proponents of cycle control predicated on the use of broad aggregates and indirect monetary-fiscal means that the community might rely upon the "spontaneous responses of the system" to allocate the resources at its disposal.[1] Even if it is understood that these responses as to resource allocation are to take place within the framework of competitive rules of the game, this approach is open to attack. Granted that such rules can be established effectively, and also granted that they are instrumental in checking production dislocations and price dispersions, there are areas of private economic decision-making into which the force of competition does not reach sufficiently. Reliance on competitive responses is

[1] Lloyd W. Mints, *Monetary Policy for a Competitive Society*, New York: McGraw-Hill Book Company, 1950, p. 14.

not adequate to secure a balanced growth between such highly divergent and—in the short view—fairly segregated sectors as agriculture, manufacturing, construction, transportation, and trade and services. Equally, the competitive formula does not effectively control the consumption-saving pattern. It does so only through whatever equalizing effects it has on the distribution of income. Furthermore, even in a comparatively monopoly-conscious nation like ours, existing legislative procedure against anticompetitive practices involves a set of important exceptions to the application of competitive ideals. Pertinent examples are the organization of the labor market and public utilities. Unless, therefore, the subject of reliance on spontaneous competitive response for purposes of efficient and balanced allocation of resources is discussed on highly abstract grounds and runs in terms of perfect degrees of competition and mobility of factors, all these limitations inherent in actual conditions must be taken into account; so must the fact that even a potent movement of competitive reform in our economy would most likely have to stay considerably short of the rigorous standards implied in the concept of a competitive order.

Consequently, the aforementioned suggestion must be rejected. Cycle control involves more than the defense of broad aggregates, such as a stable price level, with the aid of broadly applied (monetary) means. It would be a mistake, however, to think that the use of national aggregates for purposes of setting guides and objectives is identical with this narrowly reasoned proposition. Rather, the method is, in principle, perfectly compatible with supplementary use of indexes expressing economic relationships.

A Possible Reconciliation between the Use of Aggregates and Relationships

A possible procedure is to divide a stabilization program into two parts, one of which is directed toward the public, and the other toward the stabilizing authorities. The first part should run in simple terms. It should establish a broad objective of stabilization, stated in simple and generally understandable terms conducive to the eventual development of self-enforcing features. These qualifications are more likely to be met by some broad aggregate—such as total employment—than by measurements expressing relationships, unless it were possible to find some relationship of such general character and importance that the public could be taught to gauge cyclical performance of the economy in terms of this particular relationship. Short of this possibility—which will be examined presently—the use of indexes expressing relationships should be confined to that part of the program which concerns itself with the strategy of the central stabilizing agencies.

This second half of the program—the "internal" part—would probably have to be handled on the basis of a good deal of cautious experimentation. It relies on sound theories concerning the proper set of relations between the components of national product and other magnitudes. To a considerable extent, the establishment or maintenance of such proper relations might be done with the aid of monetary and fiscal controls. By directing their fiscal and monetary operations in certain ways, the stabilizing agencies might be able to obtain specific effects. The same type of controls, if used in a less pointed manner, can be applied to defend the selected broad objectives. In any event, there is bound to be interaction between the defense of relationships and aggregates. Specifically applied controls will normally affect total activity. On the other hand, broadly applied monetary and budgetary controls are bound to affect one particular part of the economy more strongly than other parts, at least initially. Generally speaking, action designed to keep the general level of activity within the stipulated floor and ceiling may have significant repercussions on the composition of national product and the distribution of income. These repercussions might be in the right direction, but they might also be undesirable and hence call for correction with the aid of more specifically applied controls. For this reason alone the establishment of proper relationships may have to become a permanent feature of a program which, for all intents and purposes, runs in terms of stabilizing national aggregates. An additional reason is the possibility of misdirected forms of self-enforcement. The stabilizing agencies should use their more specific fiscal and central banking controls to offset types of public reactions to binding overall targets which carry the indexes back to their "must" values, but not without producing some maladjustments in the allocation of resources and the structure of prices.

The question is not whether it is procedurally possible or desirable to supplement the defense of overall targets with specific action, but whether valid criteria for proper relationships can be found. This is an issue which involves the validity of the theories on the basis of which relationships are to be affected. It also involves the question of whether, or to what extent, the public is willing to accept specific (direct) controls. The aforementioned suggestion of Mints concerning complete reliance on spontaneous private response in regard to resource allocation stems from a profound skepticism in both respects. While such skepticism is understandable, one should not yield to it to the point of making policy proposals which leave important gaps. In some respects, actual experience will tell that there is something wrong in the structure of industry and prices, and that readjustments are necessary. If these readjustments cannot be entrusted to competitive forces because the latter are not applicable, or too slow and ineffectual to bring about substantial remedy, then it will be a matter of common sense for society to resort to certain substitutes for competition, i.e., a set of centrally administered specific controls, in order to restore balance. Examples of such situations are furnished by the increasingly speculative expansion of investment in housing, automobiles, radio, and the stock market during the later stages of the boom in the twenties. Such excessive developments, indicated by the accumulation of unplanned inventories, might successfully be counteracted by a system of selective controls, including flexible margin requirements for consumers' and speculative loans.

The pursuit of proper relationships by stabilizing agencies will be much more difficult and controversial if it is to be carried on prior to the experience of actual trouble. It involves correct theories, and also correct anticipation of market conditions, particularly of demand patterns. Forecasting of this sort is handicapped by the possibility of distinct instability of these patterns, a possibility which should not be neglected even under the assumption that overall activity is kept stable within fairly narrow limits. Erratic shifts in demand patterns are not ruled out by cycle control, despite the fact that firm prevention of major booms and slumps could be expected to exercise some steadying influence on technological change, the temporal pattern of replacement in industry and households, and on the consumption function in general. In view of this, the pursuit of proper relations will tend to be more remedial than forestalling, except for certain general precautionary measures such as permanently installed minimum requirements for long-term and short-term borrowing (securities and exchange regulations, minimum margin requirements for loans to speculators and consumers, etc.).

All in all, the subject of proper relationships is too complex to be seriously considered for purposes of concretely stated binding targets. Publicly announced goals about these matters should be stated in purely general terms, and so should legislative provisions for this part of the stabilization program. This entire area of control is, by its nature, based on a great deal of discretionary judgment on the part of experts at the administrative center, both in regard to goals and means.

For the ordinary variety of economic relationships, this proposition will probably be accepted without serious challenge. Yet there is one particular relationship which, on account of its broad and perhaps strategic character, deserves special attention, namely the consumption-investment relationship. This relationship has been the focal point of most cycle theories. Economic crises and depressions are widely attributed either to marked short-run fluctuations of this relationship or to protracted high-levels of investment as compared with consumption. These positions involve either the hypothesis that overall economic stability depends upon the avoidance of erratic changes in the composition of national product in terms of these two broad categories, or the theory that general economic stability requires maintenance of a certain specific rate of net investment in comparison to the rate of consumption (a high-consumption economy). In either case, the logical inference is that cycle control must be predicated upon a consumption-investment index, if not exclusively so at least in conjunction with other broad indexes. This raises the question of whether a proposal for economic stabilization embodying the expedient of binding targets should include mandatory provisions for the achievement and maintenance of some consumption-investment pattern.

An examination of this proposition involves several issues. First, it must be asked whether there exists such a thing as a specific investment-consumption relationship which promises balanced growth of the system. Second, to meet the more complex argument that cyclical slumps originate in sharp swings of the consumption-investment pattern, it must be asked whether there are any convincing criteria for distinguishing between harmless and dangerous degrees of fluctuation in this pattern. From what point on, if at all, do such fluctuations become incompatible with balanced growth? Third, even if the answer to either one or the other question had to be in the affirmative, does it follow that the subject of a proper consumption-investment relationship must be tackled directly, or could it be safely entrusted to the indirect method of stabilizing total output or employment?

The Consumption-Investment Relationship

A simple formula for a justified or safe consumption-investment relationship is available only from the viewpoint of short-run equilibrium. It is implied in the Keynesian proposition that the economy will be in a state of equilibrium if planned net investment equals planned saving. Short-run equilibrium arises whenever the decisions of the producers to increase or decrease the scale of their investments happen to coincide with the decisions of the community to increase or decrease the scale of their savings. An excess of planned saving over planned investment leads to an unplanned accumulation of stocks (unintentional investment), a process which cannot go on forever. Equally, an excess of planned investment over planned saving involves disequilibrium. The (*ex post*) equality of saving and investment will normally be established only through inflationary forced saving. The inherent cumulative tendencies of the process have been greatly stressed by expounders of monetary cycle theory, according to which an eventual economic collapse is inevitable either because the banking system will sooner or later reach the limit of lending capacity (Hawtrey), or because the conditions for extracting unintentional saving from the public will deteriorate because of progressively increasing money wages and consumers' demand, leaving the new investment projects stranded prior to completion or causing them to be out of line with the long-run pattern of saving (Hayek).

The short-run equilibrium formula that planned investment must equal planned saving refers to the consumption-investment relationship only indirectly. The contact is easily made. The marginal propensity to save which governs the investment needed to preserve equilibrium is equal to the fraction of one minus the marginal propensity to consume. Therefore, the lower the marginal propensity to consume, the greater the amount of planned net investment needed to offset savings, and vice versa.

This proposition is at variance with the view of those economists who are known for their emphasis on the consumption-investment relationship in connection with the subject of economic stabilization, i.e., the underconsumptionists. According to this view, the amount of safe or justified net investment stands in direct proportion to the amount of consumption. From the standpoint of short-run equilibrium analysis, this assertion makes sense only if investment is defined as total cost of output (total allocations) and consumption as total effective demand (total expenditures). Obviously, this is a mere tautology and does not throw any light on the problem in question. Intelligent discussion of the consumption-investment problem demands concepts which are differentiated enough to make allowance for the fact that in a growing system only a fraction of total demand stems from households, and that only a fraction of total production consists of goods designated for immediate consumption. The problem of short-run equilibrium centers around the missing parts which are properly referred to as net saving and net investment.

The short-run equilibrium formula of equality between planned net saving and planned net investment possesses an engaging simplicity which is treacherous. It is difficult to translate it into statistically measurable terms. Any index expressing the relationship between the two magnitudes could probably not be brought up to date to be available for intelligent countercyclical policy-making. This is one reason why a short-run stabilization program should not be saturated with this type of index and objective, despite the fact that the relationship itself is of fundamental importance and embraces the entire economy. Another reason is that any marked discrepancy between planned saving and investment will be indicated by either general price inflation (excess of planned investment over intentional saving) or by a fall in output and employment (excess of saving over investment). A program which employs twin aggregates like total product and employment as guides and objectives for compensatory action would, therefore, seem to be adequate. In the judgment of this writer, the relationship between saving (or consumption) and investment should be accorded the sort of treatment which has been suggested earlier for all matters of relationships. It should be kept in the background of the mandatory part of the program, in the sense of becoming a subject of continuous concern for the stabilizing authorities. On the basis of past experience with destabilizing influences of certain improper relationships or improperly chosen means to correct the situation, the authorities might be able to improve their current and future policy-making.

As regards the subject of *long-run* connections between consumption and investment, even the theoretical aspects are difficult. To begin with, there are conceptual complications. In order to be able to establish a meaningful functional relationship between consumption and investment, one has to postulate that all net investment is undertaken ultimately to satisfy consumer demand. That part of current investment which consists of investment for further investment must be translated into additions to productive capacity designated to satisfy consumption occurring at a distant future. In short, all investment for the present must be treated as being undertaken to realize higher and higher points along the aggregate consumption function, at increasingly distant times. This must be done despite the fact that investment for further investment relies on a continuous process of saving and further planned net investment.

Such conceptual procedure is merely a preliminary to the design of a consumption-investment relationship which is compatible with the objective of balanced growth. To arrive at a simple and regular pattern of relationship calls for highly simplified assumptions concerning the level and slope of the consumption function. A preconceived model of stable secular growth could probably be set up only on the basis of the supposition that both level and slope of the schedule remain fairly stable in the long view. The increase in aggregate consumption which follows the rise in total income produced by net investment must proceed in a precalculable fashion. Erratic changes in the distribution of income are out of the question; so are simultaneous changes in the marginal propensity to consume for a substantial number of individuals. In the interest of balanced growth, not only the consumption function but also the future pattern of consumers' outlay—that is, the way in which the public will divide its income on food, clothing, housing, automobiles, etc.—must be assumed to be anticipated correctly by the investors.

In addition to this, certain simplified assumptions about investment are of crucial significance. The model would have to be set up with the aid of preconceived patterns of obsolescence and technological progress, and with advance knowledge of that fraction of total net investment which is of a noncommercial character (for example, parks, monuments, armaments). It must be possible to associate current investment concretely with the consumption of distant times. This involves knowledge of the character of investment from the viewpoint of its average length of amortization.

In the face of a nonconforming reality, such a model is of very limited value. Over longer periods of time neither the level nor the slope of the consumption function can be anticipated with any degree of accuracy. Both may be subject to change by unpredictable forces, or by circumstances which might be foreseeable in their general contours but which nevertheless defy precise evaluation. For instance, the promise of greater economic stability may well be expected to raise the consumption function. But it is not possible to predict how much this will be the case, and how long the process will take. Equally, no one can predict the extent to which the market will continue to offer new and tempting outlets for spending, especially in the area of durable and relatively expensive items (such as, currently, television sets). Yet there can be no doubt that such outlets have a boosting effect on the consumption function. An additional complicating factor is the inability to make valid long-run forecasts of changes in the distribution of income, the level of taxation, the rate of population growth—all of which are matters that are bound to influence the consumption function.

Not only theoretical analysis but also factual observation discourage the notion of a simple consumption-investment relationship. As Fellner points out,[2] the findings of Kuznets[3] and others show that in the historical long run, investment was not geared to consumption, speaking in terms of the relationship between the amount of investment and the time rate of change in consumption, or of that between the amount of investment and the marginal propensity to consume. The findings also show no consistency in these relationships for comparable phases of the cycles in the twenties and thirties. Immediately before the downturn of 1937, the rate of increase in consumers' outlay was sharper than in the earlier parts of the recovery which started in 1933, in contrast to the situation of the twenties—so often the subject of unwarranted generalization on the part of economists leaning toward the underconsumption doctrine—in which the marginal propensity to consume declined toward the end of the boom (1928-1929). The fact that in the thirties the average propensity to consume was lower than in the twenties does not prove that in the thirties, in contrast to the earlier decade, investment was more closely geared to consumption. Owing to its high degree of sensitivity to general economic conditions, the low level of investment during the thirties is adequately explained by the depression itself. Investment always corresponds to a reduced share of national product when the level of activity is low.[4]

[2] *Op.cit.*, pp. 40-42.
[3] Simon Kuznets, *National Income and Its Composition, 1919-1938*, New York: National Bureau of Economic Research, 1941.
[4] Fellner, *op.cit.*, p. 36.

The Adequacy of Aggregates

As long as proper criteria for the right kind of long-run relationship between consumption and investment are lacking, little use can be made of the fact that this relationship actually fluctuates distinctly during business swings and that it is a good indicator of cyclical processes. To establish this type of relationship as guide and objective of compensatory action presupposes that we know precisely how much net investment the economy can stand in relation to consumption, from the viewpoint of the ideal of balanced growth. A cruder but workable procedure is to base stabilization on aggregates. It is important to bear in mind that a program embodying binding limits for business fluctuations in terms of such types of measurement can claim for itself the achievement of indirect stabilizing effects on the consumption-investment pattern. Under the assumption that total activity is kept at a high level, and that the public feels confident about the maintenance of such level, a reasonable degree of stability in consumers' outlay can be expected. A high and stable level of employment would support the purchasing power for consumption and create a reliable future for the industries producing such goods. Wages could not be depressed, and admittedly by far the greater part of the workers' disposable income would go into consumption. There might actually be a tendency toward a high-consumption economy, without any direct effort in this direction. Public confidence in future avoidance of depression might easily weaken the propensity to save. As a result, the total amount of savings to be offset by investment might be relatively small—that is, in comparison to past prosperity levels of savings. At the same time, net investment might stay closer to consumption. Slowness of such tendencies would be gratifying in the interest of general economic stability itself. An abrupt transition to a high-consumption economy would have disruptive effects. The prevailing balance between producers' and consumers' industries would be upset; severe production dislocations and unemployment would occur.

Desirable Qualities of Indexes Measuring Total Activity

The indexes which are to furnish guide and objective of cycle control must meet certain requirements.

To begin with, the indexes must be a representative measure of total activity in terms of which a stabilization program can be offered to the satisfaction of a voting majority. The behavior of the indexes must be accepted by the community as an adequate symptom of cyclical processes. This implies that deviations of the adopted indexes from adopted "must" values are interpreted by the public as a sure sign that the economy is significantly off-balance. The indexes and their movements must be free from political suspicion. They must be acceptable to all groups as an equitable and nondiscriminatory basis for action, be it management, labor, the farming population, or consumers.

Secondly, the use of indexes for short-run stabilization must be consistent with maintenance of high standards of economic efficiency and rising levels of income. They must not be empty boxes. They should be either a direct measure of total activity, or some monetary aggregate which clearly reflects activity. From this viewpoint any of the national income measurements would qualify. So would an employment index. For purposes of short-run policy, such as is exemplified by cycle control, a price-level index is useful. Although a monetary aggregate, its movements are closely related to swings in activity. The same is true of an index measuring total money demand. Less reliable, however, are indexes relating to the stock of available money.

Thirdly, the material covered by the indexes must be such as to facilitate prompt and comprehensive collection and computation of statistical data so that a running account of the performance of the economy in terms of these indexes can be given. This is important not merely from the standpoint of timely compensatory action, but also from that of the government's ability to inform the public frequently about economic conditions. The public should be able to know, at all times, what the current situation is. It should know what kind of government action to expect in the event that the current situation indicates a state of off-balance.

Finally, the indexes should be sufficiently sensitive to swings to permit timely compensatory measures. The demands on sensitivity can be relaxed, however, through the expedient of a margin of tolerable fluctuations. All that is needed are indexes which clearly start to move at the fringes of the margin. It is not necessary to select indexes which are so sensitive as to signal incipient cyclical processes, although such sensitivity is desirable. It would be undesirable only in the ideal situation that we could find an index which starts to move at points at which dangerous cumulative processes begin. In this case, the sensitivity of the index could become instrumental in determining what is to be ceiling and floor.

Some of the available indexes may begin to show change at a very early phase of business swings, while there might also be this or that particular type which fails to register trouble soon enough, i.e., from the viewpoint of the limits to which the public might wish to let business fluctuations go. It is not out of the question that some particular index might lend itself equally well for defending ceiling and floor. Upper and lower limits, then, can be stated in terms of this one index. Such an arrangement would be desirable from the viewpoint of simplicity, especially as far as the public is concerned. Complicated arrangements involving different measurements for ceiling and floor are detrimental to popular appeal and understanding. Before one can expect private parties to counteract swings at a certain stage, they must be given an opportunity to familiarize themselves thoroughly with that stage. A simple announced goal, expressed in terms of an easily understandable index, is what should be striven for.

The adoption of a liberal margin for swings materially improves the prospect for such a solution. Perhaps any of the available indexes may register change soon enough and hence be useful for all purposes. To the extent that varying degrees of sensitivity cease to be of major import, the choice of indexes should be made dependent, primarily, upon the remaining criteria, such as the relative degree of public appeal, simplicity, compatibility with the long-run objectives of efficiency and growth, and also the relative ease with which statistical data can be assembled and computed.

Two Ways of Stating "Must" Values

In the interest of intelligent use of compensatory weapons as well as intelligent private responses, society must clearly define what it means by general economic stability. This holds true regardless of whether cycle control is accompanied by governmental guarantees or is pursued merely on a hit-and-miss basis.

As has already been pointed out, there exist two different techniques of setting up concrete limits for fluctuations. One is to face the issue directly, in the form of selecting a specific level of activity at which the economy is to perform steadily. A popularized version of this has been the 60-million-jobs proposal of recent years. This type of procedure is still in evidence if society prefers a more relaxed program, by designating a floor and ceiling for cycles involving a margin of tolerable fluctuations rather than a tight level. For example, rather than speaking of 60 million jobs as a "must" goal, the program may designate a maximum of, perhaps, 60 million and a minimum of (say) 55 million jobs.

The other method is to concentrate on rates of change in overall employment or production, and to define stability indirectly, i.e., in terms of the absence of such change. A realistic modification of this type of procedure would consist of drawing some distinction between permissible and nonpermissible degress of fluctuations. For instance, the dividing line might be drawn at a 5 per cent annual rate of change in employment, output, or the level of prices. The counteraction of movements proceeding at the rate of 5 per cent and over would again establish a margin for tolerable ups and downs, but it would do so indirectly.

Each variation has its advantages and disadvantages. The method of setting absolute values for floor and ceiling might easily turn out to have greater public appeal than a program embodying critical rate changes in indexes measuring total activity. Thus, if the limits were stated in terms of a maximum and minimum level of total employment, the public could keep itself informed with relative ease about the nature of the program. But there is the drawback of having to make periodic revisions of the values on account of the factor of secular growth. This need for revision arises, at any rate, for limits which are stated in "real" terms, be it employment or gross or net national product. The revisions may not be conducive to public familiarity with the aim of the program and may deprive it somewhat of the chances of private implementation. If the limits were stated in terms of a maximum and minimum level of prices, however, the complications of secular revisions could be avoided, i.e., as far as the statement of the limits as such is concerned.

By contrast, the method of critical rate changes might get along successfully without periodic revision even if it runs in real terms. Probably the only serious cause of revision would be an unreasonable initial decision about tolerable and intolerable rates of change. The program might define permissible rates of expansion so narrowly as to kill the chances of secular growth. Past experience could not furnish a reliable basis for drawing a line between a rate of expansion which is compatible with balanced growth, and rates of expansion which indicate a cyclical process. Is a 3 per cent increase in total output in any given year compatible with stable growth, or does it suggest the beginning of a cyclical upswing? Fortunately, this problem becomes less important if a program deliberately leaves some leeway for cyclical spurts. For instance, if the dividing line between tolerable and intolerable rates of expansion were set as high as 5 per cent per annum, one would not have to worry about the danger of suppressing growth. Anything as high as that would clearly fall within the range of cyclical spurts, so that the decision revolves around the question of tolerable and intolerable degrees of cyclical upturns, and nothing else.[5]

Yet the technique of critical rate changes cannot stand by itself but rather needs to be combined with the rivaling method setting limits in absolute terms. At the inception of the program, some decision would have to be made concerning the level of output, employment, or prices from which the technique of critical rate changes is to start. It would be absurd to entrust short-run stabilization to this technique if the economy happened to be in a slump at the time. First the economy has to be in a condition of reasonably high employment. Only from then on might the defense of near stability be entrusted to the counteraction of nonpermissible rate changes in representative economic magnitudes.

There exists, however, a still further and even more embarrassing shortcoming of the method of rate changes. The economy might experience a relatively slow but persistent—and eventually very alarming—rate of change in one direction. For example, there might develop such a thing as a gradual but highly persistent rate of contraction in total activity. Under the assumption that the program tolerates not only slow rates of expansion but also slow rates of contraction (as a

---

[5] This statement is somewhat exaggerated. There is bound to prevail some form of interaction between cycles and secular growth, so that any policy which has to do with cycle control may have some repercussion on long-term economic development.

logical counterpart), the method of critical rate changes alone would be insufficient for guiding countervening measures. The same is true if, in the wake of a cyclical downswing, total activity tends to hover around some low mark. A still further source of embarrassment would be a comparatively slow but persistent (secular log-rolling) inflation.

It is not necessary to explain in detail that these are potentially serious sources of trouble for the method of critical rate changes. One might discount, for the visible future, the danger of chronic economic contraction. But the danger of secular inflation is highly acute. To cope with it, the procedure would have to include strong action against price-level increases and either counteract inflationary tendencies altogether, or at least merely tolerate such a slow rate of decline in the money value that even over longer periods of time the distribution of income and debtor-creditor relations remain sufficiently undisturbed to prevent economic and political unrest.

If this were done, however, the result would be the absence of a leeway for purely cyclical price-level movements. The merits of leaving such a leeway for price movements will be discussed later. For the moment it may suffice to point out that the reasons are not specifically related to price policy, but rather to the policy of yielding to desirable spurts and recessions in total output and employment due to such elements as periodic need for readjustment in industry, replacement cycles resulting from an unstable past, technological changes affecting total private investment, and so forth. The tolerance of such spurts and slumps implies the tolerance of some degree of price-level instability.

The technique of setting up absolute limits for fluctuations is better suited for the purposes on hand. By establishing a fixed maximum and minimum for the scale of prices, the community can afford to leave a margin for intermittent price-level movements without giving up the defense against secular inflation. It is true that the advantage which the method possesses in this respect must be regarded as purely academic as long as the community refuses to endorse a program embodying a binding upper limit for the scale of prices. The forces which make for secular inflation are deeply entrenched. They stem primarily from aggressive groupism. Therefore the proposal is tantamount to the proposition of forcing organized pressure groups to fight out their distributive battles without the convenient tool of increasing the supply price of their services, except in so far as the victors may squeeze the money and real income of the remainder of society (presumably a slower process). The unpopularity of this proposition should not lead to its abandonment by sincere proponents of stabilization. It provides at least a formula for proper policy-making, whereas the method of rate changes fails to yield even theoretically satisfactory answers.

Again theoretically, the method of absolute limits can handle the aforementioned problem of a slow but persistent contraction in output, by setting a definite floor under the economy. It thus affords an implicit defense against stagnation, and it would actually shift from a countercyclical to a counterstagnation device in the event that the floor would have to be actively defended with income-supporting measures most of the time. There is always a possibility, of course, that this might happen sometime in the future, especially if the floor is periodically adjusted to make allowance for secular growth-rates suggested by the population movement, aggregate saving and investment needed to offset such saving. Yet the method could easily stay within the dimensions of a primarily countercyclical device provided the floor is not pushed up too close to some ambitious full-employment mark, and also provided that the periodic upward adjustments of the aggregates measuring the floor are not in themselves so impatiently high as to provoke the need for continuous central income-supporting measures.

All in all, the foregoing discussion definitely suggests that the margin of tolerable fluctuations should be established in terms of absolutely defined limits.

CHAPTER 10

THE PROBLEM OF THE MOST SUITABLE CHOICE AMONG AVAILABLE INDEXES MEASURING TOTAL ECONOMIC ACTIVITY

....

ONE of the conclusions reached in the previous chapter is that the binding part of a program of short-run stabilization should proceed in terms of national aggregates for purposes of establishing guide and objective. The present chapter will concern itself exclusively with this binding part, from the viewpoint of the most suitable choice among available indexes measuring total economic activity.

We have already mentioned certain desirable qualities which an index should possess if it is to be used in the dual role of indicating the limits within which activity is to be allowed to fluctuate, and of acting as a guide for mandatory compensatory action if activity threatens to break through these limits. The available indexes will now be briefly projected against these requisites in the following order: ability adequately to register the state of total economic activity; consistency with the need for speedy assemblage of statistical data and presentation of computed results to the public; consistency with high standards of economic efficiency and rising levels of income; finally, simplicity and public appeal.

If any of the available indexes could qualify on all these scores, the situation would be ideal. Unfortunately, this is not the case. Each index tends to have its strong and its weak points, and the final choice depends a great deal on one's personal views as to how much weight should be given to the good and the bad qualities. One may believe, for example, that on the balance of considerations the elements of appeal and simplicity should receive dominant consideration, and that any index which excels in this respect is the one to choose. This may very well have to be the ultimate outcome of such discussions, but as long as the subject of cycle control involving imperative norms is still far from the stage of practical debate and actual policy-making, one might as well give weight to factors other than political appeal. Technical and theoretical aspects should receive proper emphasis.

The purpose of the following discussion is not so much to arrive at definite suggestions as it is to demonstrate some of the conflicts and difficulties to which each type of index gives rise. The account is by no means complete; only certain salient points will be dealt with.

Available for choice are three general types of indexes, namely national income measurements, national employment indexes, and national price averages. The national income measurements are commonly known as: gross national product, net national product, national income (total factor payments), total personal income, and total disposable income.[1] National employment will be taken here to refer to the total of human employment only. National price averages appear in different forms, but for the purposes of this discussion only a broad index composed of prices of raw materials as well as finished goods (producers' and consumers' goods) will be referred to.

Ability to Register Adequately the State of Economic Activity

All of the aforementioned indexes can pass, more or less, the test of comprehensiveness, but not the criterion of ability to register adequately the degree of prevailing off-balance in total production (presumably the decisive issue). On the latter grounds, two of the income measurements, namely personal income and disposable income, appear inferior. Personal income varies somewhat against the cycle of production and

[1] The relationship between these various measurements may be assumed to be familiar.

hence may furnish a treacherous index. It tends to understate the drop of production during a slump as well as the rise of production during an upswing. In the event of a downswing, the built-in central stabilizers keep supporting personal income. Also, corporations may continue to pay dividends from previously undistributed profits and thus, like social security, cause personal income to understate the drop in output and employment.

Disposable income, too, is subject to these as well as additional countercyclical influences (personal income tax). It is an even more treacherous ground for determining the proper magnitude of countercyclical operations. Because these two measurements understate fluctuations in activity, they might involve compensatory action which to the authorities proves a source of surprise and last-minute upward revisions in the order of magnitude of such action, i.e., before activity itself is restored to the proper level. As the authorities were engaged in fighting a slump, they would experience that the restoration of personal or disposable income is slowed down by the fact that the various central stabilizers, and corporate practice with respect to dividend payments, act as leakages. The dragging effect of these factors is the greater, the more a community has tried to entrust cycle control to them by making improvements and enlargements in this respect. Here a government might run into unpleasant experiences, unless it has learned to make allowance for the leakages.

Since what is wanted is primarily stability of production and employment, society should favor an index which adequately portrays stability or instability in these terms. An index which does not understate fluctuations in production diminishes the danger of insufficient compensatory action although, of course, the leakage effect of the built-in stabilizers is always present and must be taken into account in any event. A real index would tend to show directly whether enough, or too little, were being done to stem fluctuations.

The Test of Prompt Collection and Computation of Statistical Data

The test of prompt collection and computation of statistical data is hard on any of the national income measurements. Much of the material which goes into them becomes available only with a delay which is probably too long for the purposes on hand. Estimates on a sample basis might involve too much possible error to establish public confidence.

Given enough time and the proper statistical data, these measurements are the most satisfactory information about the state of economic conditions. Their introduction into a counter-cyclical program as guides and objectives would be a great step forward, i.e., speaking of gross product, net product, or national income. At least in one respect their use in connection with short-run stabilization is indispensable. This is the tracing of the effects of various types of compensatory action—for instance, tax policies—on the scale and composition of national production. But the tracing of such effects runs behind the actual work of checking prevailing swings. The knowledge obtained can be used to improve the future techniques of cycle control. This process of integrating information from detailed study of past procedures into current programs can be viewed as going on all the time until, perhaps, some phase is reached at which certain compensatory techniques are definitively established as superior and become standard practice for future use.

While this kind of use of national income measurements may be taken for granted, there still remains the question whether any of these aggregates could ever become suitable for furnishing guide and objective of compensatory action itself. The answer to this question depends, in part, on what progress can be made in regard to estimates obtained on a sample basis, and on the reaction of the public to indexes based on estimates. Instead of trying to discuss these matters any further, let us point out that it might be preferable for specialists to abandon the hope of using national income estimates in favor of actual measurements of less informative character, such as an employment index. For the purpose of indicating the presence of short-run fluctuations in total activity and the limits to which they are allowed to go, it is not really necessary to use such highly informative and theoretically refined items as gross product, net product, or national income.

Keeping in mind the need for quick compilation and dissemination of data, one is probably directed to some employment or price indexes. Today no serious objections could be raised against an employment-oriented stabilization program from the viewpoint of the government's ability to obtain fairly prompt and accurate factual information about fluctuations in total employment. The methods of securing employment figures are much improved over what they were not long ago. The present state of knowledge about separating cyclical from seasonal fluctuations, the improved and enlarged access to employment data, etc., rules out the possibility of serious error. On the whole, an employment index is now feasible for short-run policy.

The same applies to price indexes. In this area the collection and computation of data has a fairly long tradition. Aside from the selection of a price aggregate which would be well suited for the purposes on hand, there do not appear to be important problems.[2] A mere cost-of-living index would not seem to be broad enough since it is rather onesidedly oriented around consumers' interest. Equally, an index of wholesale prices may never have a chance to be accepted as a measure of the money value by the masses of consumers. An aggregate embodying prices of consumers' goods, raw materials, and

[2] It is true, however, that available price information tends to understate effective short-run fluctuations in prices, largely because of incomplete accounting of short-run changes in premiums, discounts, and bargain sales. See *National Income; A Supplement to the Survey of Current Business* (1951 edition), p. 142.

producers' goods would probably be preferable despite the customary short-run discrepancies which develop during a cycle. The possibility that such a broad index would fail to be meaningful to either producers or consumers as a measure of the money value must not be exaggerated. Producers, at any rate, look beyond the prices of raw materials and producers' goods when appraising the market for inflationary or deflationary tendencies. Moreover, in the event of guaranteed near stability of the economy some of the tendencies of price dispersions might become weakened. In the past the expectation of highly speculative booms or fast deflationary spirals might easily have accentuated price dispersions at a relatively early stage of business swings.

As compared with an index of raw material prices (the traditional choice in the stable-money school), a broad index including many fairly rigid prices (especially prices of consumers' goods) would account for a certain sluggishness in the presence of fluctuations in total effective demand. To this point we shall return later.

Consistency with Economic Efficiency

Since the previous tests suggest a narrowing down of the choice to employment and price-level indexes, the remaining tests will be considered only for these two types of indexes.

A stabilization program which runs in terms of employment is bound to raise an issue from the viewpoint of efficiency in the economy. There attaches a certain quality of onesidedness to an employment program. Granted that what the community wants is greater stability of its economic and social life, and granted also that a steady supply of job opportunities is an essential part of such stability, there is nevertheless reason to fear that a government which is directed to defend a high level of employment might be tempted to satisfy the letter of the mandate by providing jobs of doubtful quality. To be sure, this danger attaches to any compensatory stabilization program, no matter how it is worded, and even if it is not binding. But the particular wording of the program does seem to aggravate the danger somewhat. To phrase the plan in terms of employment enhances the almost inevitable tendency toward employment projects which are of relatively little value to the community and dictated mostly by the desire to remove unemployed persons from the scene. The incomes derived from these projects might be largely "quasi-doles." As one critic has pointed out, a democracy in which a significant part of the population lives on quasi-doles is socially less objectionable, and politically less unstable, than one with large unemployment, but quasi-doles would presumably fail to render the political life of a democracy stable in the long view.[8]

The importance of these misgivings about the employment criterion depends on how often and how long the government would be called upon to support employment, to what extent it were forced to stay away from projects which potentially interest private business (competing projects), and the extent to which the general public is willing to accept, or unable to resist, the method of quasi-doles. How often and how severely the government would be called upon to create jobs depends primarily on how high the level of employment were set. The danger of quasi-doles is much greater in the event of a full-employment objective than it would be if the community adopted an employment floor which is more nearly commensurable with a scale of employment that can be reached, most of the time, with private investment and privately generated income alone.

One of the reasons why the employment criterion has so often been criticized from the viewpoint of economic efficiency is that employment proposals are almost commonly identified with full employment. No adequate appraisal of the employment criterion is possible until we learn to divorce the criterion from the full-employment slogan. It will then become possible

[8] Fellner, *op.cit.*, p. 225.

to view an employment-oriented program without the continuous fear of undesirable forms of employment by government, as well of a *general* deterioration in the quality and quantity of productive services and goods.

Our comments about the relationship between the price-level criterion and maintenance of efficient resource allocation can be very brief. The price-level criterion can be used in such a way that it directly contributes to efficiency. As will be shown later, its most logical integration into a stabilization program is to set a ceiling for swings in terms of a tolerable maximum of the general price scale. In this fashion it serves to check the danger that a program which establishes an employment floor, but leaves a margin for spurts above this floor, would proceed without occasional violent price spirals in the upward direction. Violent inflationary spirals are not only detrimental to stability in activity, but they also very definitively indicate that resources are being used wastefully.

The Test of Public Appeal and Simplicity

In a program which asks no less than binding limits for fluctuations in total activity, a great deal of attention has to be paid to public appeal and, what is not quite the same, ability to understand the meaning of the program. Although each of the earlier mentioned indexes would lead to similar government action and results, the wording of the program counts heavily.

If we view the subject of choice from this angle, selection of the employment index might seem a foregone conclusion to many observers of the current scene. But the situation is not as simple as that. If we approach the subject of appeal from the angle of familiarity—in the sense that what has been generally associated for considerable lengths of time with stabilization must have appeal—then the outlook for a program worded in terms of stable prices is not bad. The relatively long history and persistence of stable-money proposals, both inside and outside the doctrine of imperative goals, is indeed a factor to consider. Even today there exists hardly a plan in which stable money does not appear at least as one of the objectives.

Appeal is not based on familiarity alone. As compared with other indexes, the price-level index has the advantage of being an item of direct and immediate interest for every producer and consumer. Increases or decreases in the general scale of prices affect him in a most personal way, whereas there is no such direct personal contact between him and the movements of total employment or total production. The closeness of the relationship between the individual and the money value enhances the persuasiveness of a program worded in terms of limits set against inflation and deflation. At any rate, it does so to people who are genuinely interested in economic stability.

What may somewhat diminish the appeal of the stable-money method is the perhaps widespread fear that a policy of stable money might not do enough toward establishing limits for fluctuations in employment and production. Although this fear may be exaggerated and can be reduced to proper dimensions in a sober debate of a stabilization program, many persons, especially workers, might wish to see a more direct commitment as to the maintenance of stable job opportunities. This seems to account for the prevailing tendency in current proposals, and actual policy statements of the government, to stress employment objectives in conjunction with stable money. To this subject of twin goals we shall turn presently.

The appeal of an employment program cannot be discussed intelligently without distinguishing between full-employment proposals and proposals operating with a less ambitious employment guarantee. If disconnected from the full mark, a program which operates with total employment as guide and goal would undoubtedly suffer in appeal among large parts of the population. But the outlook is by no means hopeless. A later chapter, dealing with the political problems of the suggestion of a margin of tolerable fluctuations, will deal with this matter in some detail.[4]

Some further pertinent observations about the choice of a proper index can be made in connection with the test of simplicity. This is a test which has importance for the public as well as for the stabilizing authorities. In fact one may venture to say that in some respects it is even of greater significance for the authorities than for the public. An index embodying complicated methods of computation can be presented to the public in simple terms. The work behind it does not show up in the result. But while none of the available indexes is devoid of laborious methods of construction, there appear to be outright perplexing *conceptual* difficulties in such a seemingly simple index as the employment index. It is this element of conceptual trouble rather than the amount of technical work behind an index which is under consideration.

Whoever thinks in terms of an employment-oriented stabilization procedure must concern himself with the thorny subject of involuntary and voluntary unemployment. In a liberal democratic system, stabilization policy has to concern itself merely with the involuntary type of unemployment. But what are the criteria of involuntary unemployment?

Traditional theory is inclined to regard all those persons as involuntarily unemployed who are without jobs although they are willing to adjust the supply price of their services sufficiently to be in line with what the market can pay. This is not satisfactory. In many lines of activity, the individual has no control over the terms at which he can offer his services in the market. Collective bargaining, or minimum wage laws, may often prevent him from adjusting his supply price to what the market is willing to pay. Under these circumstances it would be unfair to regard him as voluntarily unemployed. His membership in a union cannot be construed as proof that his personal attitude is always in line with the supply-price

[4] See below, pp. 163-167.

policy of the union. Access to employment may be closed if he fails to join, and this may be the reason for his being a member. Nor can he be made personally responsible for minimum wage laws which, in given circumstances, might cause him to be unemployed. Moreover, there are bound to be persons who would be willing to work longer hours than regulations permit. Again it would be artificial to treat such persons as voluntarily underemployed. Aside from difficulties created by lack of control over the terms of supply, there are other limitations of the abovementioned criterion.[5] In the absence of legal minimum standards the prevailing wages at which employment is obtainable may be so low as to cause income from such employment to fall below acceptable standards of living (or relief). In this event refusal to accept employment cannot reasonably be treated as a case of voluntary unemployment. Where wage rates are subject to unlimited downward flexibility the concept of prevailing wage rates may become practically meaningless because of uncertainty about the terms of employment for any relevant period of time.

Broadly speaking, efforts to separate voluntary and involuntary unemployment meet with the greatest obstacles in the case of *frictional* unemployment. It is a hybrid consisting of voluntary and involuntary elements. The personal will to work

[5] To avoid the conceptual difficulties provided by legal and institutional arrangements hampering personal control over the supply price of services, Keynes suggested that the definition of involuntary unemployment should be built around the distinction of money-wage rates and real wages, in the sense of calling those persons involuntarily unemployed who are actually without jobs despite the fact that they are willing to obtain employment at a lower real wage, provided the money-wage rates were not reduced at the same time. This method, while seemingly bringing the attitude of the individual into the foreground (a person who refuses employment at a reduced real wage acts independently of union policy), is not so helpful as it might appear at first glance. In cases of pronounced increases in the cost of living, a constant or even slightly rising money-wage rate may mean a level of living which is below reasonable standards. In circumstances of this sort, unwillingness to accept employment should not be treated as voluntary unemployment. Keynes's approach is subject to obvious political limitations; it pertains only to cases of mild increases in the cost of living.

is often limited by geographic and industrial immobility (in the objective sense) and by uncertainty as to the reliability and durability of job opportunities in different geographic areas or industries. From the point of view of *cyclical* mass unemployment, it is probably easier to proceed on the general assumption that unemployment is of the involuntary type. For this reason it may seem that stabilization procedure could be based upon some employment criterion since it deals with cyclical unemployment. But this is true only if the planned limits for economic fluctuations, stated in terms of an employment index, are set in a certain fashion. The floor must be considerably below the full-employment mark. In this event the distinction of voluntary and involuntary unemployment can be pursued with much less pressure and thoroughness. If in the United States the floor were set so as to permit a maximum unemployment of, say, five million workers, then the defense of such floor would undoubtedly be a defense against involuntary unemployment. In the five million there would be a substantial number of involuntarily unemployed persons. But the floor must not be confused with actual unemployment. The latter could be less than the floor permits, and the more often this were the case, the better. In view of this fact, and also because a less than full-employment floor recommends itself for a variety of other reasons, the suggested solution should not give rise to moral indignation.

There remains the test of sensitivity to fluctuations in total effective demand. For reasons which will become apparent presently, it is best to deal with this point in connection with the subject of twin goals.

The Possibility of Twin Guides and Objectives

The foregoing discussion draws attention to employment and price indexes as the most likely choice. This is in line with general thinking and far from original. Nevertheless, the habit of mentioning the two types of indexes jointly as guides and objectives of compensatory action should be accompanied by an effort to clarify the logical relationship between them. True concern about price-level fluctuations should lead to the proposition that a guarantee of near stability of employment must keep itself within the limits set by a reasonable degree of stability of the general scale of prices. This is tantamount to defining the margin of tolerable fluctuations of activity in terms of a ceiling and floor for prices alone. In defense of such a program it could be said that counteraction of price fluctuations is never an end in itself but merely a means to check fluctuations in employment (production).

Even so, this type of program would be open to attack. Under certain conditions, substantial changes in employment might conceal themselves behind a relatively calm price picture. The extreme would be a situation in which, on account of price-support systems, nonprice competition, and monopolistic pricing tactics, the prices in general became so rigid as to make a general price index fairly worthless as a criterion for cycle control. This is not the case now, but there might be a danger of this sort if society settled down to a mere stable-money program. The purpose of such a scheme might eventually become more and more threatened because both the government and private parties might learn to circumvent the program by increasingly preventing prices from registering general economic instability. Commodity prices and money wages might become administered prices all round, being held constant despite fluctuations in total money demand, shifts in demand, and changes in production costs. The use of twin criteria would seem to offer an escape from this dilemma, since it is impossible that both prices and employment could conceal the presence of fluctuations in production.

Even if we discount the danger of a hardening of the price scale and argue merely on the basis of the present scene, there is still some reason for concern about exclusive reliance on price indexes. The question is whether such *floor* for slumps as society might wish to set for its economy would be adequately protected by the price-level formula alone. This is a question which cannot be answered simply with yes or no. Much depends on what society would regard as a tolerable minimum of employment and output. It also depends on how much effort would be made to check pricing policies which tend to make prices impervious to a shrinkage in markets and jobs.

Prior to competitive reform, it might be found that the prevailing degree of downward sluggishness of a general price index is sufficient to cause apprehension. If so, it would indeed make sense to build the floor around an index which is more sensitive to depression than the price index. The purpose would be to improve the timing as well as the order of magnitude of income-supporting operations. This index might be total employment, on the theory that it is more sensitive to business contraction than the price index.

At the same time it might be found that the *ceiling* for activity could be set satisfactorily in terms of an upper limit for the scale of prices. Such procedure can be defended on the grounds that cyclical expansions in total money demand become increasingly abortive from the standpoint of adding to employment and output as cumulative inflationary spirals develop. It can also be justified in terms of checking the danger of secular inflation, i.e., the apparently continuous group pressure for higher supply prices. Some economists have suggested the use of a price-level ceiling, with the argument that many of our administered prices tend to respond to expansions in total money demand (more so than to contractions). The prevalence of such a one-way flexibility of administered prices would greatly add to the merits of the price-level criterion for ceiling purposes, since it establishes the price-level index as a fairly sensitive indicator of upswings in activity. A case for this theory of a one-way flexibility has been made primarily in regard to the money-wage rates of organized labor (Keynes). Since wage increases in excess of productivity per man-hour are usually accompanied by mark-ups in commodity prices (even if they belong themselves in the category of administered prices), the reference to the one-way tendency of wage rates appears to cover a sufficiently wide ground to make the argument impressive. However, it is not necessary to defend a price ceiling on the basis of this argument which, after all, still remains conjectural. The afore-mentioned reasons—particularly the reference to the increasingly abortive nature of inflationary expansions in total money demand—are sufficient to establish some price-level ceiling as a logical choice for setting an upper limit for cyclical upturns.

A program involving near stability of the money value is more difficult to set up than one which runs in terms of a rigorously constant price level. It becomes necessary to make a delicate decision as to how far prices should be allowed to rise above the floor (which latter is, of course, implicitly established by the limit set for unemployment). Theoretical analysis suggests that the danger of violent inflationary spirals arises with the approximation of full employment. In the long run, however, different degrees of resource utilization might be achievable before strong inflationary tendencies emerge. This means that one cannot simply consult the employment market for the sake of reaching a decision about a tolerable maximum of the price scale. One of the strongest arguments that can be made in favor of a price-level ceiling is that under the impact of such a ceiling labor unions and other monopolistically organized groups will gradually learn to give up the tactics which account for inflationary spirals before anything resembling full employment has been achieved. Therefore it is reasonable to expect that, as time goes on, the critical inflationary point coincides with progressively smaller floats of unemployment. This tendency would be reinforced by whatever direct attack could be launched against anticompetitive practices.

From a practical viewpoint, the best possible procedure in establishing a price-level maximum would probably be to compromise on the current price level and adopt it as the tolerable maximum. From then on, the scale of prices would be allowed to fluctuate between this upper limit and whatever price floor emerged indirectly from the adopted floor for unemployment. Since it may be taken for granted that the community would never be inclined to compromise on a price-level ceiling which does not happen to spell prosperity at the time in question, this kind of procedure might actually leave a fairly substantial leeway for changes in the scale of prices.

The envisaged combination of indexes is logical. Each index would have a definite and independent function. The two indexes would no longer be mentioned side by side without an effort to show what each factor is to achieve. The usefulness of the procedure rests on the degree of appeal and understanding which it would carry with the public. Given these elements, the program's anti-inflationary side might eventually be handled automatically by a slackening of total private outlay as price increases reached the critical mark, and also by the already mentioned factor of self-restraint on the part of organized groups. In this respect, nothing new could be added to the subject of self-enforcement. On the other hand, it does not seem farfetched to expect private producers to pay attention to a general employment index and to make decisions which support employment as the index started to break through the announced floor. It would be unwise for them to speculate on a further fall in the volume of employment. And however roundabout the influence of their individual decision-making and actions on total employment, the end result would be to make it easier for the government to fight slumps.

The purpose of this discussion is not so much to arrive at a concrete proposal as it is to show that if two indexes are to be used, each of them should be given a definite task. The general drift of our argument would not be affected by any proof that the particular arrangement suggested above rests on questionable assumptions as to the relative degree of cyclical sensitivity of the two indexes. In particular, it might be argued by critics that our point about the downward stickiness of the price index is exaggerated, not to mention the expressed fear of premature inflation on the upgrade. But while there may be some room for legitimate qualifications on this score, the assumptions made are basically in the right direction. Yet for the sake of argument let us assume that prices respond sooner to a contraction of total demand than employment but are relatively slow in registering a spurt in total activity. In this case it would still be true that the two indexes should be given separate tasks. Here the employment index would have to take the former place of the price index, in the sense of furnishing guide and objective of curbing measures, whereas the price index should be relied upon to indicate and defend the floor.

CHAPTER 11

A MARGIN OF TOLERABLE FLUCTUATIONS

....

A List of Margin-suggesting Factors

To MANY economists and men of public affairs, the tolerance of some degree of short-run instability may be a foregone conclusion. They might not even feel compelled to mention any specific reasons but merely point out that in a democratic system changes of great import are never made abruptly. The transition to a stable economy can only be made gradually, and such gradual procedure suggests the adoption of an initially liberal margin for swings which can eventually be narrowed as the economy acquires more and more inherent stability. While this observation is sound, it is nevertheless necessary, in a study of this sort, to consider all the reasons which speak for the adoption of a gradual program.

The wisdom of a margin of tolerable fluctuations can be defended on both short-term and long-term grounds. In the short-run, particularly for the launching period, the following factors are most relevant: (1) Avoidance of shock; (2) the absence of any factually observable stable equilibrium level or normal business; (3) the possible need for basic readjustment in the economy; (4) reverberations from previous swings; (5) the prevailing extent of built-in stabilizers or shock-absorbers. To these short-run factors must be added an important long-run consideration: the lack of any advance knowledge concerning the chances of secular progress and growth in the event of short-run stabilization.

Each of these factors must be examined.

Avoidance of Shock

This point can be dealt with very briefly. Producers, owners of wealth, labor unions, and so forth must be given the opportunity to adjust their decision-making to a changing environment. Such opportunity implies a policy which at no time is too radical to exceed comprehension and which allows the producer, investor, and worker to see the rewards for himself. The process of stabilization can be compared to that of the training of a horse. Here as well as there, one might feel inclined to deplore that the object of the discipline loses some freedom in the process. But the comparison also holds in another more salutary respect. As time goes on, the compulsory aspects of the process will diminish and give way to second nature. The comparison is also to the point in a third respect, namely, that the process should be slow and gradual for the sake of avoiding shock. The purpose of restrained freedoms must be understood, and that takes time.

No Factually Observable Equilibrium Level

It has already been pointed out in an earlier part of this study that there exists no factually observable level of activity which suggests a stable equilibrium. This fact makes it highly inadvisable to try to force the economy, in an abrupt manner, to operate on an even-keel basis. Such abruptness would introduce an unnecessary degree of arbitrariness and artificiality into a stabilization program. Again, it would be preferable from this viewpoint to begin with a liberal leeway for swings. True, the setting of a binding floor and ceiling would also be an arbitrary act, but since the level of activity would be allowed to fluctuate within the established limits the element of arbitrariness is weakened. Much would depend, however, on how high the floor were set. If it were set so high relative to available resources that its defense required more or less continuous income-supporting measures, the expedient of a margin would not amount to much. The situation would be virtually the same as in the event of an abrupt attempt at even-keel performance. To establish any reasonable leeway for ups and downs, the floor would have to be low enough to enable private investment and privately generated income to rise above it from time to time. Then, and only then, is there any point in talking about a margin of tolerable instability. It could not be known in advance whether, on the average of years, total activity would stay closer to the floor than to the ceiling. Even if it did, nothing drastic should be done about it. The answer to such a question depends, in part, on how high the ceiling were set. An ambitiously high ceiling—let us say a full-employment ceiling—is bound to show the actual scale of activity in a somewhat unfavorable light, namely closer to the floor than to the ceiling itself. At the moment, all of these questions must be left open. What counts is the fact that with a liberal margin no questionable decisions need be made concerning the level of activity at which, supposedly, the economy shows an inherent tendency toward a stable equilibrium.

Allowance for Readjustment

Short-run stabilization should never become an excuse for preventing or postponing readjustment in resource allocation and the price structure. Lasting stability cannot be achieved in an economy which suffers from severe production dislocations and from distorted price relations. Profound disturbances in resource allocation, such as those conditioned by war, forbid thinking in terms of immediate stabilization. Every expert operates with the idea of a transitional period of reconversion and restocking, a fact which is amply demonstrated by the postwar debate on stabilization. Another major occasion for economic distortion is a violent and protracted boom. The widespread tendency of stabilization experts to single out some intermediate level between the high and the low points of major swings for stabilization seems to result, in part, from the desire to see the economy first go through post-boom readjustments before the defense of a stable level is attempted. But a relatively short interval of falling demand and deflationary price movements is insufficient to do the work of readjustment. Some distortions in the price structure might be lessened (others perhaps increased); inefficient firms may be weeded out or undergo reorganization; inefficient production methods that crept in during the boom are apt to be replaced by better methods under increased sales pressure and competition. But basic production dislocations are bound to survive an intermittent slump. Propelled by the expectation of recurring peak demands and temporarily high prices, the normally dead weight of excess capacity hangs on in cyclically sensitive industries.

All in all, the hope for extended readjustment rests primarily on the following factors: (1) a thorough discouragement of the idea that from time to time total demand will be driven up to peaks for which one should be prepared with plant capacity which is in excess of sustainable levels of demand; (2) a reduction of monopolistic powers which make possible protracted malallocation of resources; (3) discontinuance of governmental policies which actively promote or support wasteful resource allocation (crop controls, tariffs, import quotas, and so forth). With respect to all of these policies, passage of considerable lengths of time is a foregone conclusion.

To discourage dreams about peak demands which invite maintenance of idle capacity, it is by no means necessary to have tight stabilization from the start, or even afterwards. An interim of less ambitious but nevertheless firm intervention with booms and slumps is sufficient, and in fact desirable. Here again it must be kept in mind that nothing is gained by unnecessary harshness. True, in order to have appeal at all, any stabilization program will have to contemplate a floor which promises operations above the break-even point for the average business firm. The interested parties must be given confidence in this important respect, and such confidence can be established through the experience of a *steadier* return on invested capital, as compared with the cyclically unstable past. This means demonstrated ability of the government to check the depth of slumps. It is reasonable to assume that under these conditions the scene will be prepared for a gradual adjustment of industrial capacity to a sustainable level of demand.

Readjustment through antitrust action and readjustment through stabilization of aggregate demand are mutually dependent methods. The success of monetary-fiscal controls hinges upon the degree of competitiveness which can be achieved. On the other hand, antitrust action will be facilitated, in some instances, by determined countercyclical measures. This is not saying that the fear of depression is the sole source of restrictive practices. In certain cases of aggressive disposition on the part of producers as well as trade unions, the promise of a more stable outlook for markets and jobs might actually give rise to added monopolistic pressure.

In a concrete situation it may be found that the need for readjustment in distorted price relations holds the center of attention. The restoration of a more balanced price structure could be entrusted, in part, to an initial deflationary policy. Before we can explain this point, it must first be emphasized that we are not speaking of an unchecked deflationary spiral. Remedial effects can be expected only when the producers have some tangible idea about the extent of the impending fall of prices. The proposed technique of setting up a binding floor could very definitely solve this problem.

On the theory that it is better to have some quick plan of action than to waste valuable time over what must inevitably be an arbitrary decision, the community might decide in a concrete case that prices in general should be allowed to fall as much as they had risen in the immediately preceding inflationary period. It will be understood that this is a crude procedure. But the procedure is crude mostly in the sense that it is inarticulate about what is to be achieved. The purpose would be twofold. On the one hand, the rise in the money value is to encourage spending. This purpose the method of a binding floor can achieve reliably.[1] On the other hand, the deflation is bound to end up with a healthier price structure. The mechanics of this process depend partly on the general degree of price flexibility. If most of the prices responded rather quickly to the drop in money demand, the deflationary interval would be short and hectic without much change in price relations. For a while, unemployment might assume highly alarming proportions, but the supporting influence of the new stable price-level—and of the increased value of cash balances and fixed securities—on spending would be felt quickly also. If large segments of the price structure are sticky relative to the remainder of prices, there will be greater room for the achievement of a healthy price structure. At the same time the deflationary interval might be more drawn out than in the former case, so that the favorable effects on spending would not materialize very soon. Let us concentrate on this case. The dragging downward movement of many prices might very well prevent precipitous decline in employment comparable to the first case.[2] But the need for readjustment in price relations would seem to be especially great. The progress of price readjustment would depend in large measure on the degree of tenacity with which administered prices (and wages) are defended by the respective parties in the presence of shrinking money demand. The worst possible thing that could happen is that the decline of the price average would be due solely, or primarily, to the fall of prices in the competitive sectors. In this case the distortions in the price structure would get worse rather than better. Only a direct attack on the monopolies (or, perhaps, a policy of reflation) could

[1] Protection against contraction of the money stock is an integral part of the method of a binding floor.

[2] A very interesting presentation of this (originally Keynesian) point can be found in K. Boulding's article entitled "In Defense of Monopoly," *The Quarterly Journal of Economics*, Vol. 59, 1944-1945, p. 524.

then help. However, this is not the last word spoken on the subject. It is most unlikely that we would have a price-level decline to an announced and guaranteed mark that would be due solely to the drop in competitive prices. There are various degrees of insensitivity of administered prices to shrinking total demand. Presumably, a considerable portion of our so-called sticky prices and wages could not withstand the influence of falling money demand for very long. From time to time, downward revisions would occur. As we came closer to the announced floor, the competitively sensitive prices would probably be the first ones to register the recuperative influence of increasing spending encouraged by the rise in the real value of the community's money stock and fixed securities, as well as by the general expectation that from now on the economy will stop falling. The economy, at this point, would operate considerably below the full-employment range. Consequently, there is little danger that the strengthening of total money demand would cause mark-ups in monopolistically controlled prices and money wages. This holds true even as far as the more aggressive producers' and labor monopolies are concerned. This segment of the economy would be characterized by a pricing policy which is dominated by a desire to hold on, as much as possible, to the prices carried over from the preceding inflation. Whether or not this policy would be successful might depend on the extent of the planned deflation. Given a more than perfunctory use of the technique of a planned price-level decline, it is far from hopeless to argue that the monopolistically controlled prices and wages might be caught in a process of delayed downward revision at a time when the competitive prices already have started to move up again. If so, the method of planned deflation is at its best. It would be a valuable, though perhaps only temporary, substitute for a direct attack on monopolies (or a system of direct price and wage controls). It would be valuable even if it did not work out with perfection, mixing instances of increased downward pressure by monopolists on competitive sources of supply with influences in the right direction.[3]

Allowance for Replacement Cycles

The reason for contemplating a margin of fluctuations in respect to replacement activity is that because of previous business fluctuations there will be years in which the need for replacement outlay, for the nation as a whole, is higher than in other years. A valid argument can be made to the effect that such replacement cycles should be tolerated. Suppression of such reverberations from past instability in investment through overly tight standards of cycle control would subject the community to hardship and inefficiency. After a severe and prolonged depression and its deteriorating effects on the age structure of much of a nation's durable wealth, a periodic concentration of replacement activity is a healthy and desirable phenomenon. Synchronization of replacement needs will be particularly strong if a very large portion of the durable wealth has about the same length of economic life and has been installed at about the same time in the past.

For the United States the area of durable consumers' goods is a particularly strong case in point, if only for the single factor of the automobile. As for industrial plant and equipment, one might proceed on the assumption of a more even temporal pattern of replacement needs, considering the greatly varying durability of the different parts of this type of wealth

[3] It is not intended here to argue that there is only one way of solving the problem on hand. Many economists seem inclined to think that removal of price disproportionalities requires inflationary rather than deflationary tactics, arguing that readjustments will be made more readily in an atmosphere of prosperity. The answer depends in part on where we start from. If we start from depression and severe deflation, the policy which is indicated should be inflation. This is not really at variance with the above view; in fact, it is a logical corollary.

There is no doubt, furthermore, that a great deal more analysis could go into the matter, although, in the end, every specialist would have to struggle his way back to some simple formula as he tried to adapt his readjustment model to the plane on which policy decisions are made.

as well as the tendency in many financially secure firms to make replacements in times of depression. But here too a prolonged and severe depression may lead to a backlog of replacement demands awaiting an improved business outlook.

The question is how much of a tendency of this sort would prevail. The past furnishes only insufficient information for the simple reason that the temporal pattern of replacement must be assumed to have been strongly influenced by the cycle itself, in the sense of periodic accelerations (booms) and delays (slumps). Without the background of new booms and slumps, a steadying influence on replacement activity could be achieved. But even so a substantial replacement swing may be indicated for some time after the inception of a determined countercyclical program, especially if the inception comes right after a prolonged boom or depression.

The Prevailing Extent of Built-in Shock Absorbers

The prevailing extent of built-in shock absorbers should be regarded as essentially different from the previous factors in the sense of being merely a permissive element, whereas there is something very forceful about making allowance for readjustment and replacement cycles. How much determining influence on the width of the margin one should permit such factors as unemployment compensation, relief, and other guaranteed types of government outlay in times of depression, is an issue which involves moral as well as economic considerations. The moral issue may be resolved in different ways by different economists. All members of the profession will have to admit, however, that the extent to which a nation is prepared to guarantee relief might have to furnish an element in deciding about the tolerable width of the margin of business fluctuations. But the strength of the shock absorbers should become a ruling factor only in the event that one were unable to come to any dependable conclusions about the size of the leeway for ups and downs with reference to the other margin-determining factors, be it readjustment needs, replacement cycles, or the fear of bad effects of tight standards of short-run stabilization on technological progress and growth.

If one were forced into this position, one would, of course, have to accept something which has been rejected earlier, namely that stabilization should be entrusted to the built-in stabilizers. This is a procedure which should be regarded merely as a last, desperate resort. Perhaps it should be avoided even if no trustworthy estimate of the margin-determining influence of the other factors can be secured. None of these factors suggests a leeway for swings comparable to the loose standards of stabilization set by our shock absorbers. Unless a nation should learn to make unexpected progress with automatic stabilizers, one could not derive more comfort from this angle than the thought that if, on behalf of any of the other margin-determining factors, society should leave an unpleasantly wide leeway for swings, the prevailing shock absorbers would afford some personal protection for those who normally suffer most from slumps. This is tantamount to saying that the significance of shock absorbers should be appraised with reference to individual or group welfare rather than from the viewpoint of their overall stabilizing power—a statement which implies no more than the suggestion that our interest in shock absorbers should return to their original and primary purposes.

Short-run Stabilization and Secular Growth

In the absence of any experience with a stabilized economy, one is in the dark concerning the chances of growth in the event of energetic cycle control. Conflicting views are possible. Some contemporary economists allow themselves a logical shortcut. They are inclined to concentrate on secular growth and to treat short-run stabilization merely as an integral part of a program designed to facilitate balanced growth. Their objectives are essentially long-run objectives. National income models embodying certain assumptions about the probable rate of growth of the working population and average productivity per man-hour, and about the probable length of the working hours per month, etc., establish full-employment targets for years to come. Although these targets are usually not meant to become the object of a governmental guarantee, they are nevertheless presented as targets in regard to which the government should make the greatest possible effort toward achievement.

While we do not intend to go into the details of this school of thought, we must nevertheless concern ourselves with one of its characteristic features: the projection of past rates of economic growth of productivity into a future from which, presumably, the tradition of business cycles is to be removed. This feature is untenable. The interaction of cycles and trend factors makes it unlikely that past rates of growth in productivity prove anything for an economy in which cycles are to be absent. One must be prepared for surprise. It is conceivable that cycle prevention would be conducive to growth, i.e., that productivity and living levels would improve faster than in the past. But it is also quite conceivable that the opposite would happen.

In view of the fact that all conclusions must be conjecturable, our discussion can be brief.[4] Strictly speaking, one should exclude from consideration all specific measures purporting to facilitate growth in conjunction with the adoption of a stabilization program, unless it can be demonstrated that this or that particular growth-promoting policy is an integral part of stabilization. Only the isolated effects of cycle control on growth should be considered. The significance of this point

[4] The reader may feel that this subject should be given the greatest possible attention in any treatment of stabilization and that it should precede whatever an author has to say about the ends and means of cycle control. With such a view the present writer is basically in sympathy, but he cannot help feeling the awkwardness involved in giving prominence to a subject about which only conjecturable conclusions can be reached.

becomes clear when one realizes that frequently compensatory and developmental policies appear lumped together in one program. Although these developmental policies may be soundly conceived and desirable, they can be, and should be, thought of independently of cycle control. This applies to incentive taxation, developmental public investment such as slum clearance, flood control, reforestation, canal and harbor projects, promotion of private investment through governmentally financed and freely available research, guaranteed loans, and so forth. All these measures might be made to vary countercyclically, but this is the only genuine contact with the problem of cycle control. Besides, in most instances countercyclical variation will have to proceed at the expense of simplicity and—what is even more important—effectiveness. Incentive taxation, in particular, is a long-run device requiring substantial periods of constant tax abatement for success when it comes to the promotion of new investment in heavy plant and equipment. Of all the possible growth-promoting policies, there is only one which clearly forms an integral part of stabilization, namely the curbing of monopoly for the sake of securing greater mobility of resources and an improved interindustry balance.

The practice of presenting all sorts of growth-promoting schemes in conjunction with cycle control arouses suspicion that they are to be potential offsets for growth-*retarding* effects of stabilization that appear in the back of the mind. This impression will last until it is made clear in these compensatory-developmental proposals that the accompaniment of growth-promoting policies is merely for the sake of pressing all desirable reform into one large plan of action.[5]

[5] Another possible explanation for compensatory-developmental proposals is that the underlying assumption is secular stagnation. In this case, the debate shifts over to an entirely new plane. As was pointed out in the beginning of this study (Chapter 1), the importance of the problem of cyclical instability would be greatly reduced in the event of a stagnant system, in favor of that of lifting the level of activity through continuous income-supporting policies.

This much had to be said to discourage unfounded optimism about the relationship of cycle control and secular growth and to present the issue in its proper form. This issue is still untouched. Those who argue that effective countercyclical action would be detrimental to growth must prove that growth needs the "exhilaration" of high booms. If this meant no more than the statement that we must move into an era where the years of high prosperity tend always to outnumber those of depression, the argument would be a tautology. The decision to abstain from countercyclical action is no assurance that we shall have a preponderance of booms over depressions. Besides, a preponderance of boom years over the years of depression means only a high level of output for the average of years. A high level of output over the average of years has nothing to do with the rate of growth. A secularly underemployed economy could easily grow faster than a full-employment economy.[6] Finally, let us bear in mind that one is guilty of a most superficial interpretation of the conditions of growth when one expresses growth simply in terms of a preponderance of booms. This mechanical, arithmetic viewpoint fails to take cognizance of the fact that what happens during depressions may be most essential to growth.

In the widespread concern about cyclical mass unemployment and privation, it has almost been forgotten that depressions are also intervals of economic reorganization, cutting back inefficiency, correcting past mistakes, planning new production and technical improvements the fruition of which,

---

Those who argue that the cyclical instability of the past was conducive to growth, and who fear the effects of cycle control with respect to growth, have in mind an economy which is able to furnish vigorous swings. They would no longer be interested in the controversy about the effects of cycle control on the chances of growth if they had to accept the view that in the future the capitalist economy can furnish only short and weak booms.

[6] For example, if the full-employment economy were a distinct high-consumption economy calling for very little net investment to offset saving.

presumably, is to come in subsequent prosperity. From the standpoint of progress and growth, booms are significant, primarily, in the sense that they furnish the climate in which this preparatory and corrective work of depression can be translated into action. This is the core of the growth pattern in capitalism to which other elements must be added. Some of these elements can be related to the cycle, others not. The affluence of boom periods is instrumental in providing the means for financing technical research and the acquisition of know-how in private industry. Other specifically cyclical elements of growth are stressed by the innovation theory of economic swings. They are, on the whole, of controversial character. According to Schumpeter's well-known cycle model, prosperities are, first of all, periods of introduction of new combinations on the part of dynamic entrepreneurs who for some reason or another are said to appear on the scene in intermittent fashion and whose swarmlike appearance at certain times, together with a certain accumulation of new ideas, supposedly explains prosperity. Obviously this is the most conspicuous way in which cycles and growth have been related to each other. No such ambitious theory of cycle causation is needed to explain the fact that cyclical fluctuations are more than simple movements of output along given production functions.[7] Nor is there any valid reason for assuming that technological progress, in its entirety, follows the abovementioned cyclical pattern. Research, acquisition of know-how, and actual introduction of new processes and new products go on all the time. Population movements, the depletion of natural resources, the discovery of new resources, and shifts in relative demand may induce innovations and adaptive improvements, and these are surely noncyclical factors.

Granted that the cyclical movement contains genuine elements of progress and growth, there is no reason to fear, how-

[7] This is no attempt to criticize Schumpeter's cycle theory which, as a hypothesis of cycle causation, is at least as plausible as any of the known ventures into causal models.

ever, that determined countercyclical action would mean the end of growth. The introduction of new methods or new products is, in each case, typically a historical process of long duration, comprising several more or less discernible phases. Conceivably, a protracted recovery and boom might compress some of these phases into a time interval which is shorter than that which countercyclical policy could permit. But a temporizing influence of countercyclical policy is a far cry from suppression of technological progress. In fact, it is not too much to expect that in an economy which is free from entrepreneurial fear of slumps, the time pattern of technological changes would eventually change toward a more even rate without much interference from the stabilizing authority. Even those entrepreneurial decisions which concern the introduction of major new processes or products are bound to be influenced by the current and anticipated general status of the market (as well as, of course, by specific market factors related to the industries in question, such as shifts in relative demand, the depletion of certain specific resources, competition, and so forth). Autonomous or spontaneous investment is not normally of the kind which proceeds irrespective of the condition of the market. It proceeds on a basis more tangible and substantial than the mere hope that, as it moves along, it will generate the income and demand which justifies the outlay. On the basis of appearances, at any rate, the argument that autonomous investment *creates* recoveries and booms is no more justified than the view that it takes a rise in total demand to start investment of this type, if only in the sense that some tangible evidence of the end of depression is in sight.

Those in sympathy with the drift of this argument will agree that there is no *inevitable* conflict between short-run stabilization and technological progress. It is no foregone conclusion that countercyclical action kills progress or that progress kills short-run stability. The two values may very well prove to be compatible. There might be times at which a co-incidence of major improvements causes general expansionary pressure. If so, the problem could most probably be handled in a satisfactory way as long as the community maintained a certain leeway for ups and downs in total activity. A co-incidence of major technological developments is more likely to occur, however, in an economy which from time to time goes through deep and prolonged slumps. As society learns to prevent such slumps and succeeds in maintaining a com-fortably high level of activity at all times, at least one possible cause of such a coincidence would be removed. In other words, the community might be able gradually to tighten its stabiliza-tion program without harm as far as progress is concerned.

No appraisal of the relative chances of growth in a cyclically unstable and in a stabilized economy can afford to overlook the fact that unchecked booms involve a certain amount of careless and wasteful investment. For this reason alone the case of overall stabilization embodying a ceiling which rules out increasingly inflationary phases of upswings looks bright from the viewpoint of progress. But it is not really the purpose of this discussion to persuade the reader that effective cycle control will inevitably result in a faster rise of per capita in-come than that observed in the past. A suggestion of this sort would be as doctrinaire as the contention that the price of determined countercyclical action is technological stagnation. Both extremes must be avoided.

To summarize: it is not possible to make conclusive state-ments concerning the probability of future growth in the event of short-run stabilization. In the face of uncertainty, several positions can be taken. One is to suggest complete eradication of swings despite full awareness that this might seriously retard growth, but without letting this awareness result in giving up the goal of stability. This position is one of complete preoccupation with short-run stabilization. It involves, if neces-sary, a sacrifice of the chance for progressively higher living levels. A second position is to suggest complete eradication of swings but provide, at the same time, for a set of independent growth-promoting policies in the event that future experience concerning growth should prove to be unfavorable. A third position is to allow for a certain leeway for swings and thus to strike a compromise between the values of short-run stability and secular growth. This position can also be rationalized as one which *might* produce optimal results from the standpoint of growth.

The first of these positions appears to be so much at variance with American economic philosophy that it need not be considered (in fact, it would be unacceptable to all industrial societies including, of course, the modern socialist nations). The second position is difficult to evaluate. A combination of abrupt and complete eradication of cycles with a set of independent developmental policies might be technically successful. Yet even if one refutes the cliché about the inevitable antipathy (or inability) of governmental bureaucracy to tackle problems of efficiency and progress, the answer cannot be so simple as the assertion that there would be no cause for worry. If government is to assume responsibility for both short-run stability and secular progress, then one must ask how much would be left of the system of private enterprise. Action to enforce even-keel operations, and particularly action to promote progress and growth, would have to go on forever. There remains the distinct possibility that slowly but surely the initiative concerning the disposition of available resources would pass over into the hands of government, even assuming that private response to such a program were by and large fairly favorable.

In the opinion of this writer, the soundest position, from the viewpoint of preserving a virile system of private enterprise, is the third one. It promises reconciliation of a reasonable degree of short-run stability with judicious caution concerning secular growth, as implemented by private initiative. Maintenance of a liberal but firmly circumscribed margin for ups and downs would not only be useful for obtaining experience about the influence of short-run stabilization on the expansion of private industry, but it would also constitute a convenient safety measure in case anything actually went wrong with growth. Society would be spared the trouble of having to revise thoroughly its stabilization program in the interest of rising standards of living. Rather society might easily come to the conclusion that the higher degree of short-run stability achieved by the binding margin is so valuable for its social and economic peace that a certain amount of growth-retarding effects should be accepted in the bargain. Not only might it be able to refrain from relaxing its stabilization program toward a wider leeway for swings, but it might actually entertain a reasonable hope that in the long view the initially adopted margin can be gradually narrowed without doing damage to secular expansion. A slowly increasing familiarity of management, capital, and labor with the changed scene might substantiate such hope.

CHAPTER 12

THE PROBLEM OF THE SIZE OF THE MARGIN

....

An Essentially Political Decision

IN THE previous chapter we discussed some economic factors which are relevant for determining the size of the margin of tolerable fluctuations. But no concrete suggestions about the spread between the limits were made. This is a subject which every economist will approach with the greatest caution and reluctance. Since the circumstances are never the same for any length of time, quantitative decisions would have to be made at the particular time of the inception of the program. No generalized answers can be given.

Furthermore, any decision about the size of the margin is bound to be reached in the form of a political compromise. On this compromise the technically trained economists might have relatively little influence. Much depends on the spirit of the major interest groups, i.e., their degree of willingness to subordinate their particular prejudices and fears to policy standards which are worked out with as much detached reasoning about general economic interests as possible. The best that can be expected is that the atmosphere of the political debate would be such that the major groups are willing to listen to the technical advice of economic experts. If such an atmosphere should prevail, the aforementioned margin-determining factors might have a chance to enter into the decision.

Even for the time being, the pursuit of the margin problem need not stop here. The consideration of political circumstances yields additional insight into the subject of the margin.

The Height of the Floor

The crucial issue in the determination of the width of the

margin is likely to be the decision about the height of the floor. This is so because of the simple fact that popular interest with cycle control is virtually synonymous with control of depression. Where much is at stake, the issues are bound to be fought hard by each group. The question is whether our major interest groups, on the basis of known strategies and reasonable interpretation of self-interest, can be expected to reach an agreement on some floor which makes margin discussion meaningful. There would be no point in considering the margin problem if general insistence on nothing less than a full-employment floor were a foregone political conclusion. Fortunately, this is not the case. To prove this point, we must look into the attitude of various groups.

Offhand it might be suspected that anything below the full mark has no chance whatever among the rank and file of labor unions. But this suspicion is erroneous. Labor leaders know that the prevalence of unemployment yields certain strategic advantages from the standpoint of organized labor. As Hart points out, unemployment raises the responsiveness of government to labor influence, partly because it makes the public more inclined to view unions as "underdogs."[1] Taken by itself, this factor may not be sufficient to induce the rank and file of union leaders to accept a floor which permits reasonable unemployment. A seller's market for jobs speaks louder than anything else when it comes to opportunities for raising wages. But the force of this argument is greatly weakened by the following circumstances. First, a seller's market intensifies the union's fear of inflationary dissipation of wage increases embodied in existing contracts. Even for the most ambitious union leadership, there is a limit to the value of victories in renegotiation of wage contracts, since this often means costly strikes (excepting cases of escalator clauses). Second, a guaranteed seller's market for jobs diminishes the importance of unions for job protection. In the long view, it might lessen

[1] Hart, *Money, Debt, and Economic Activity*, op.cit., p. 236.

the interest of workers in unions. Union discipline, and the importance of union leadership, might decline. Third, reasonable unemployment is no barrier for strongly organized unions to boost wage rates faster than output per man-hour. Wage gains will probably be slower than in the event of full employment, but so also will any rise in living cost which may accompany wage increases. Fourth, intelligent labor leaders will not continue forever to take the risk that the government—however lenient—might finally be driven to the point of cracking down on labor. A slow inflationary process may be regarded as politically safe by labor strategists. There may never be enough public pressure in favor of central wage controls.

One would most likely be guilty of underestimating the intelligence and strategy of our national labor leaders if one assumed that all this is blindly ignored by them. Were it not for the fact that in general debates on proper goals for national economic policy they feel it politically expedient to speak from the viewpoint of labor interest in general, including the masses of unorganized workers, a truer impression of their strategy might be obtained from their statements. Politically there are strong odds against discrediting the full-employment slogan. The dilemma can probably be solved only through retaining the full-employment slogan, but by relaxing its meaning so as to make it compatible with union policy which promises to work out best for organized labor in the long view. Political difficulties in accepting a floor which permits reasonable unemployment can be weakened by the argument that the setting of a floor is not the same thing as determining the actual level of employment. The latter is free to rise above it, and the chances of its being above it will be the greater the less ambitious the floor itself. In addition, much can be made out of the argument that a binding floor, especially if stated in terms of an employment index, is assurance against a drastic fall in employment and wage rates.

Let us now look at the attitude of management. It is widely

recognized that management and labor do not see eye to eye when it comes to proposals for determined stabilization at the full-employment mark. In fact it may be surmised that even those proposals which raise their sights less high meet with considerably less enthusiasm among the ranks of business leaders than they do among labor. The difference in attitude involves a combination of economic and political factors. Economically it is quite true that labor, despite social security and relief, is less well-equipped than large-scale enterprise to weather the storm of depression. To this extent, labor has relatively more to gain from a program which would hold downswings to small proportions. Taken by itself, however, this fact explains very little. Depressions are far from welcome to business, and as long as a group can economically benefit from a program one should expect it to support such a program.

We must look for other factors. It is often said that management and capital are more afraid than is labor of programs which involve uncertain and untested knowledge, particularly if such programs bring government to the fore. This explains a preference on the part of the former groups for a more moderate program—one which does not mean a sharp change from the past. The method of imperative standards per se is feared. This is probably a valid appraisal of business attitude, despite the fact that organized labor in the United States is also known to be suspicious of government powers which might come into conflict with traditional union power.

Broadly speaking, business attitudes toward stabilization seem to be strongly influenced by political speculation which centers around the chances of curbing the power of organized labor. If necessary, management's defense against the rising tide of labor power would avail itself of the expedient of periodic slumps, as it seems to have done in the past. The degree of emphasis placed on this strategy depends on the character of prevailing labor legislation, and on the degree of government responsiveness to labor influence.[2] Each of these factors could be such as to suggest either a high or a low floor. Obviously, this sort of strategy is not translatable into permanent answers about the subject in question. It can be described only generally as an attempt to avoid any policy which is suspected of playing into the hands of the opposition. This is not to say that the modern employer and capitalist is callous about the consequences of unchecked slumps. He cannot afford to be callous, even if he wanted to be. At a minimum he is bound to support action before a depression gets completely out of hand. The question is how much farther he is willing to go. Certain considerations make it probable that a compromise with labor strategy can be reached. The two ends can meet if labor leadership learns fully to appreciate and exploit the political advantages of reasonable unemployment; and if, at the same time, managerial groups learn to balance their desire for maintaining the weapon of depression against the desire of avoiding alarming shifts of public opinion and government policy in the direction of union interest. The meeting ground will obviously be some reasonable degree of unemployment. It would be unsafe to go beyond this general conclusion. No-one knows precisely at which point the economic disadvantages of unemployment begin to outweigh its political advantages from labor's point of view. It is possible that the difference between two and five million unemployed has no net effect on the strength of wage-raising pressures,[3] and that some powerful unions could even afford to accept a floor which tolerates six or seven million unemployed before their chances of raising wages are seriously crippled by the general condition of the labor market. But all this is highly conjecturable, and so are any attempts to estimate the critical range at which managerial groups might find the strategic advantages of un-

[2] We are disregarding here additional elements such as the dictates of national defense or fear that depression in this country will be exploited politically by hostile nations.
[3] Hart, *op.cit.*, p. 236.

employment offset by unfavorable public reaction, and a pro-labor bias of government, in the settlement of wage disputes.

There is at least one more group whose political influence on the terms of stabilization is of great importance, namely, the farm bloc. On purely economic grounds, farm interest could most likely be reconciled with a program which embodies an underemployment floor. One reason for this is the existence of a farm support price system which promises to place farm income on a fairly secure basis except, probably, in the event of severe industrial depression. The combination of relatively stable farm prices and relatively stable prices of industrial products is bound to serve farm interest better than a log-rolling inflation in which industrial prices might win the upper hand for at least short periods of time. Many of the industrial products which the farmers buy come from industries in which labor organization is particularly strong and capable of leading the inflationary movement (machinery, trucks, automobiles, producers' goods in general). Upward adjustments in the prices of staple farm products cannot always exactly offset price increases in a selected group of industries into which a major part of farm outlay goes.

Current thinking on agricultural strategy in national economic policy must also take into account the disappearance of the former debtor position of the farm population as a whole. This factor should be expected to interfere with the traditional tendency of the farm bloc to favor inflationary policy. Debt liquidation and the accumulation of liquid assets by farmers point toward monetary conservatism. Even if one makes allowance for the fact that farmers share the money illusion and are strongly impressed by the swelling of money income as well as the money value of their land and other real assets, one is led to the conclusion that farm influence would be in favor of a stabilization program which promises escape from a fast pace of price inflation. This means the tolerance of an underemployment floor.

A more convincing political case for full employment can be made only as regards the interests of the masses of unorganized workers, and perhaps some professional groups. The benefits of a guaranteed seller's market are most clearly in evidence here. They are marred only by the fear of a mounting cost of living. But however great the appeal of a full-employment proposal for these groups, the fact remains that lack of economic and political organization greatly weakens the influence of these groups on the shaping of a stabilization program.

The Height of the Ceiling

Politically, the height of the ceiling will be regarded as a thankless issue. Concern about unsustainable rates of cyclical expansion appears to be the doubtful privilege of a minority of level-headed persons in business, government, and of course in the profession of economists. The general public appears inclined to prefer a policy of prolonging the life of peacetime booms to a policy of checking them, partly because it associates curbing measures with the outbreak of an economic downswing rather than with a mere damping of expansion. Prior to an actual collapse, there appears to be always sufficient fear of the consequences of curbing action so as to prevent such action, or cause it to be of halfhearted character. This point is demonstrated by the events of the late boom years of the twenties, during which curbing efforts were confined to the stock market, on the theory that the industrial apparatus itself was healthy and could stand further expansion. Today new impetus is given to public optimism about the high rates of expansion that can be achieved without the penalty of collapse. A tremendous spurt which started during the war and lasted through the first five postwar years, despite occasional difficulties, may leave an optimistic note for the years to come. The unusual conditions which sustained activity may not be sufficiently appreciated, or will be widely forgotten. A revival of public consciousness about economic crises might have to await actual experience of another major collapse.

Politically it is conceivable that within the visible future any campaign for the adoption of binding targets may have to omit proposals for a ceiling and concentrate entirely on the subject of a floor. This would still save an essential part of the suggested approach. There would still be a margin of tolerable fluctuations, although the upper limit would be ill-marked. Without curbing efforts, or at least without imperative standards for curbing action, sharp breaks from feverish activity to slumps might occur. This would make the defense of the floor more difficult than in the event of systematic interference with upswings at some intelligently chosen phase.

We now come to an argument about ceilings which is of considerable interest. Skeptics may say that if a community adopts a planned floor it will need no ceiling, on the theory that total activity will tend to settle around the floor, i.e., where the government is committed to come into the scene with income-supporting operations. This view would be justified only under the assumption that the floor were set so high for each economic group that it leaves no desire for economic improvement. It cannot be emphasized too much that no such floor is envisaged in this study. If one had to come to the conclusion that from the political viewpoint the floor could be nothing but a highly comfortable cushion for management and labor—to the point of destroying the ordinary commercial incentives—this writer would be prepared to discard the method of binding targets in favor of loosely handled stabilization procedure. But the gist of the foregoing observations about group strategy in regard to the subject of a floor is that there exists a good chance for a solution which involves some sacrifice for each group. Seeking an economic future which, over a stretch of years, promises to be better than one without a permanent floor, each group can be expected to agree to terms about the height of the planned floor which are calculated to safeguard its *long-range* interests, without giving other groups a strategic long-range advantage. In so doing, each group may very well think in terms of normal business or normal trends. Quite aside from these normal situations, each group may visualize the possibility of sporadic opportunities for improvement which can be exploited jointly without upsetting the long-range balance of power and interest between the groups. Such opportunities may be furnished by important technological developments, intermittent increases in replacement demand, exports, government outlay, and so forth. If the economy happened to operate along the floor as these occasions arose, the nature of the floor would leave an incentive for spurts in production and employment.

In view of this, the problem of a ceiling has a very definite meaning. For as the occasion for spurts arose, the incentive for increased activity would tend to spread from its points of origin into more and more parts of the economy. If it had its origin in the introduction of some new industries, the increased investment outlay from there would undoubtedly boost production and employment in producers' goods industries and, via increased payrolls, expand the activity of consumers' goods industries. If it started at the consumption end, it would spread from the retail sphere back into industry. Whichever way the movement started, it would cause manufacturers, labor unions, farmers, and merchants to abandon the positions reached at the floor—if only in terms of marking up their supply prices. Depending on the strength of the disturbance and the ensuing momentum, the expansion might reach unmanageable proportions in principally the same way as did movements in the past which started from the bottom of a major depression. There is nothing new in this respect. The question is merely the one which was raised at the beginning of this discussion, namely, whether the political climate will permit the adoption of a firm barrier to cyclical expansion.

Pessimism on this score, unfortunately, is still in order in the event that a reasonable floor is adopted. After removal of the danger that the bottom might drop out of economic life, public fear of the consequences of unchecked booms would be greatly diminished. The penalties for wildly speculative positions would be reduced. The inclination to see booms checked, in these circumstances, may be slight.

This dilemma must be openly faced. The only way to bring the public nearer to accepting a binding ceiling is for economic advisers and stabilizing authorities to make it clear in counter-cyclical debate that the ability of the government to defend the floor hinges upon the avoidance of grossly unhealthy booms. The ceiling should be presented as a logical counterpart of the floor.

Persistent and skillful presentation of this point might eventually be crowned by success. The campaign for a ceiling should not dwell merely on the difficulties of defending the floor in the absence of a firm upper limit for fluctuations, but should also stress the futility of highly inflationary boom ranges from the standpoint of real income and resource allocation. While the most logical aim is that of a rigorously defined price-level ceiling, it would be unwise to jeopardize the campaign's success by insisting on this type of solution in the event of decided public resistance. If it became clear that a permanently fixed upper limit of the price index were absolutely unacceptable to the rank and file of union leaders, or conflicted also with the long-range strategy of the farm bloc, then the campaign should switch to some objective which has more appeal for these broad groups. Despite our earlier misgivings about the method of critical rate changes in an atmosphere characterized by secular inflationary pressure, it would be advisable to fall back on this method and to try to make the best of it by tolerating only very gradual increases in the scale of money wages and prices. The price level which happened to prevail at the inception of the program might form the basis for policy-making. If in the future the scale of prices tended to rise above this mark, only slow rates of increase should be tolerated—slow enough to prevent serious destabilizing effects on entrepreneurial expectations and wage contracts. Income distribution and creditor-debtor relations should not be alarmingly affected even if the tolerated degree of inflation continued over long stretches of time. The suggested procedure would leave room for possibly sharp reflationary price movements up to the stipulated mark, i.e., as activity recovered from one of the slumps permitted by the nature of the established floor.

PART IV

THE MEANS OF STABILIZATION

CHAPTER 13

ADEQUATE CONTROLS FOR THE LAUNCHING PERIOD

....

Proper Emphasis on Stabilizing Means

IT MIGHT seem paradoxical for an exponent of the theory of
self-enforcing potentialities of binding stability objectives to
devote a substantial part of his study to the subject of centrally administered stabilizing means. But this impression is
unfounded, and the author will do everything in his power
to dispel it.

The chances of self-enforcement of a binding norm rest on
demonstrated validity of the norm. The road to validity is
ability to enforce. Ability to enforce, in turn, rests on the
effectiveness of the controls adopted to make the norm come
true. In fact, where firm commitments are made, the demands
on means are likely to be especially strong. Errors as to the
stamina of means are particularly costly in connection with
guarantees, because they are bound to undermine faith in the
method forever.

Once more it must be emphasized that during the first difficult years the adopted controls must work well *without* the
benefit of self-implementary effects. Since the order of magnitude of the demands which might be made on the compensatory machinery cannot be reliably estimated in advance,
it is better to err on the pessimistic rather than the optimistic
side and to look for correspondingly powerful machinery.[1]

---

[1] While the writer acknowledges the inspiration received from the writings of the late Henry C. Simons for this study of binding norms and
their self-implementary implications, he has to take exception to Simons'
pioneering work when it comes to the question of allowing for adequate
compensatory machinery. Simons' observations on this subject indicate
a bias for rather lightly implemented controls. All in all, cycle control
is to be entrusted to (1) the adoption of a binding stable-money rule,

[175]

The demands on the means are likely to be strong even if no abrupt transition to a fully stable level of activity is aspired. The upper and lower limits for fluctuations have to be defended in principle with the same degree of determination as if an even-keel performance had been attempted. Only in this fashion can a nation make decided progress in cycle control. At the fringes of the established margin, certain cumulative processes might begin to operate, especially as long as the public is doubtful whether the government will be able to defend floor and ceiling. Inasmuch as these incipient cumulative movements may be hard to check, provision for particularly strong compensatory means is indicated. Also, of course, the need for proper timing would not be lessened by setting a leeway for ups and downs.

Emphasis on Monetary-Fiscal Controls

In short-run stabilization, budgetary and monetary controls hold the center of attention. This is true despite the fact that some specialists are getting tired of saying so, and also despite the fact that there is need for additional measures. Monetary-fiscal controls are the main line of defense against fluctuations because they are relatively variable and also sufficiently indirect to be acceptable in a private-enterprise minded community.

---

(2) open-market operations on the part of the Treasury, and (3) a system of countercyclically varying levels of exemption of the federal income tax (see his article entitled "On Debt Policy," *The Journal of Political Economy*, 1944, pp. 356).

The combination of open-market operations and varying exemption levels appears too weak, even on the background of a 100 per cent reserve system. A more pronounced use of open-market operations than in the past (Simons) does not remove the inherent limitations of this tool as a stabilizing weapon. The supplementary method of varying exemption levels does not leave much leeway for countercyclical budgetary operations. Ruled out in Simons' scheme are countercyclical variations in the total volume of government outlay on goods and services, and also variable tax rates. These confining features indicate a tendency to overestimate the stabilizing effect of public recognition of the stable-money guarantee itself.

For flexible firsthand action the central banking controls are a logical choice. As was pointed out earlier, they can be used for test purposes inside the margin and stepped up in intensity once activity threatens to break through floor or ceiling. The effectiveness of these controls might gradually grow in connection with public experience that more powerful controls will follow in the event that central banking controls fail to make a sufficient impression.

Discretionary Action

In the absence of reliably strong built-in stabilizers, very heavy demands will be made on either quick-action legislation or discretionary executive action within broad and permissive delegation of powers. It is fair to assume that on the background of binding targets some improvements would be made in regard to quick-action legislation. Once the community goes so far as to commit its government to guarantees, it would seem logical, at any rate, that the legislators are expected to support the executive arm of government with speedy instructions. Nevertheless, even if the legislators did act more quickly, the outlook is not such as to inspire confidence that the defense of the targets could be left entirely to a set of detailed legislative instructions about implementation of policy. Since there might be many unforeseen complications and contingencies, legislative instructions would have to be supplemented by grants of discretionary powers to the officials at the administrative center, enabling them to use their own judgment in the handling of budgetary controls. Even outside the doctrine of binding targets, the literature on stabilization is full of suggestions about possible ways of increasing executive initiative and power in regard to fiscal countercyclical measures. Of special interest is the proposal known as "executive action under legislative veto."[2] Here the President would be granted powers under which he must report to Congress what he in-

[2] Hart, *op.cit.*, p. 490.

tends to do about stabilization, within the limits of broad congressional instructions. The characteristic feature of this device is that it would shift the initiative of policy-making from Congress to the President and his staff of officials, and that the proposed action would go through unless Congress issued a veto. Propounders of the method of binding targets, such as this writer, must be prepared to accept this device as the most likely one to promise success. Its political aspects will be discussed later.

For the moment we must concentrate upon a technical point about discretionary procedure. It has become customary to associate discretionary stabilization programs with forecasting. Although this is understandable, one must nevertheless keep in mind that the association is by no means inevitable. Discretionary procedure does not necessitate the background of forecasting. A strong argument for the usefulness of broad discretionary powers in the handling of cycle controls can be forged from the previously discussed weaknesses of prescribed rules of countercyclical adaptations in built-in stabilizers. By contrast, discretionary procedure is superior, when in able hands, in the following respects: it facilitates action based on an appraisal of the character and strength of underlying forces; it permits, if necessary, a policy of throwing the full weight of available controls against swings in their early stages; finally, it permits the best possible adjustment of compensatory techniques to concrete circumstances, such as the selection of powerful but relatively unwieldy controls in the event of persistent tendencies toward off-balance. In all these respects it will not always be possible to draw a sharp line between the "current" situation, as indicated by an index, and the immediate future. This is to say, prevailing disturbances will be appraised from the viewpoint of the severity and tenacity of underlying factors. Such appraisals cannot usually be made without reference to the future. One type of disturbance may be of purely momentary significance, whereas another may have more lasting qualities. Nevertheless, between a mere diagnosis of *manifest* disturbances and their likely duration and repercussions (for purposes of remedial action), and efforts at predicting *future* events, there lies a significant difference. What is commonly known as forecasting belongs primarily in the latter category. It concerns attempts at predicting new events or the probable effects of events which are known to be coming. For example, a true forecaster tries to predict a new round of wage increases. Or, he tries to predict the effects of a coming act of legislation, such as a new agricultural law or a labor law. Accurate forecasts of this type would be highly desirable and would no doubt improve the timing and order of magnitude of compensatory action, but this is beside the point in question.

Psychological Aspects of the Magnitude of Stabilizing Operations

It is no secret that a capitalistically inclined society, when faced with the need for strong government action, will always tend toward programs which are designed to conceal the true magnitude of government operations. We are familiar with this fact from taxation, but it also holds true in the case of cycle control. There is nothing wrong with this tendency, provided the means are adequate to achieve the task on hand. Since the launching phase of the suggested countercyclical procedure might require strong central measures, and since the political fate of the program might depend very heavily on whether or not its sponsors can find techniques of implementation which somehow understate the extent of the government's operations, it is necessary to examine various types of control from the viewpoint of their psychological impact.

Public impressions about the extent of the government's stabilizing effort are influenced by how well the operations blend with the world of private transactions. Good blending is bound to have deceptive effects. For example, the method of government outlay on goods and services can be given a somewhat capitalistic slant by using private firms for carrying out public works programs. But this does not go very deep as long as the government decides what is to be done, and when it is to be done. It is not difficult to conceive of an arrangement whereby some additional room might be created for private influence. What comes to mind is the establishment of mixed planning agencies, or mixed producing units, in which membership is partly governmental and partly private. Although the funds used might be outright public funds, private interests could enter into the determination of the character of investments. Under these circumstances, a program involving a certain government deficit might not look as large as in the event of complete central determination of outlay.

To some extent these tendencies can be at work, and have been at work, even without the expedient of mixed or semi-public agencies. How much they are at work depends on the character and background of the officials in government. It is one thing if, by former experience or otherwise, the officials are close to the hearts of businessmen and see the affairs of the nation in the manner of business; it is quite another if they are motivated by concern about general economic welfare or, for that matter, by the interests of the economically under-privileged groups of people. In the former case, business acts through government sufficiently to obtain results which are similar to those of a formally recognized cooperation between government officials and private management. Indeed, it is conceivable that business influence on government is stronger than it could afford to be in the event of mixed enterprises. But from the standpoint of outward appearances, the story is different.

The public works' program of the thirties aroused consciousness in the business community far beyond the quantitative significance of the operations. This was probably the result of the fact that these programs were handled by a

President not recognized as being close to the interests of private management and capital. Under different circumstances as regards the personnel at the administrative center, the relationship between the magnitude of the operations and the degree of attention which these operations received at the time might have been the reverse.

It would be unduly onesided, however, to consider only the interests of employers and investors when discussing the subject of public reactions. An equally impressive case for the importance of the character of implementation can be made with respect to labor. Recently, the interest in blending government policy with private initiative has shifted toward our large labor unions and collective bargaining. Awareness of the potential usefulness of broad private organizations for the purpose of stabilization has indeed received a fresh impetus by the formation of large industrial unions. Frequently the student of current stabilization literature meets with the notion that the government, instead of burdening itself with the entire task of cycle control through tax management and variable public expenditures, might rely on the labor front to do at least part of the job. For example, instead of trying to raise the consumption function taxwise, the same goal might be achieved through a combination of aggressive wage policy and stable commodity prices. The exponents of this method (and its underlying theory of underconsumption) could not, of course, afford to leave government entirely out of the picture. But in their desire for a relatively inconspicuous government they would be—and actually are—greatly aided by the fact that organized labor does press for higher wages. Initiative is so firmly rooted on labor's side that no encouragement on the part of government is needed. If the government happens to be sympathetic with labor's drive for higher wages, and if it is willing to use labor as a vehicle for redistribution of income, then its role will be confined to an attempt to contain wage demands within the limits prescribed by existing excess profits available for distribution in the form of additional wages. This rules out wage demands which would be confiscatory or would necessitate markups in commodity prices. The task of the government would not be an easy one. But it must be admitted that in one respect the central authorities would find themselves in a relatively favorable position. Instead of being, so to speak, the aggressor, they can present themselves in the role of a mediator of conflicting private interests. Since it is likely that the producers would try to maintain profits by raising prices even if wage demands are within the limits just mentioned, the government could frustrate this attempt by using controls which bear down harder and more directly on commodity prices than on money wages. Examples of such controls are bank credit restrictions, such as increased margin requirements on loans to speculators and consumers. By employing its counterinflationary machinery in this way, government contributes in a rather inconspicuous manner to some degree of redistribution of income.

It is by no means intended here to belittle the tendency toward stabilizing machinery which relies on private group initiative or, for that matter, the tendency toward machinery which is deceptive as to the extent to which the government is involved in cycle control. These tendencies are sound provided they are used constructively and do not jeopardize the goals.[3] Nevertheless, there exists a grave danger of overstepping the limits within which they are useful. The limits are overstepped if any particular group is permitted to shape ends and means for its own advantage. Experience proves that group interest—be it business, labor, or farm interest—is usually pushed too far to permit an equitable, general-welfare minded program.

First a community should decide, in national debate embracing all interests, upon the objective and principal form of implementation of the stabilization program, and it should

---

[3] They are not to be confused with self-implementation of rules.

also make it clear beyond doubt that the responsibility for the program rests upon the government. Once these steps have been negotiated, the stage is set for thinking about politically expedient choices among available types of controls. The government should then try to defend the binding targets throughout the first difficult years with compensatory techniques which reveal a strong desire to avoid an unnecessary show of power. As a safety measure, however, the program itself should make explicit statutory provision for the ultimate resort to decidedly powerful means. The government could then fall back on the use of such means if its choice of palatable and mollifying policies should prove to be a failure, or if the situation on hand clearly indicated from the start that nothing but strong means will do.

All in all, the desire to avoid a show of power will express itself in a tendency to get along, as much as possible, with traditionally accepted controls; to examine relatively unfamiliar techniques for forms of application which are less shocking than others; to shun techniques which distribute private sacrifices and gains in arbitrary fashion or which force individuals to share a high portion of administrative burdens implied in the controls with the government (without or with sufficient compensation); and to make an effort to engage private initiative in the operation of controls wherever this can be done without endangering the success of the program. A detailed discussion of these points is beyond the scope of this study; only a few broad observations can be made.

Today it is no longer easy to distinguish sharply between familiar and unfamiliar controls. The times are gone when only central banking controls qualified as familiar ones. It becomes increasingly academic to treat fiscal controls as novel devices, despite the fact that they may not be as accepted as the former controls. Even so, fiscal controls are a suitable field for the exercise of caution. For example, it might be found wise to minimize countercyclical tax management in favor of variable public expenditures. The latter method might turn out to enjoy better private response because tax increases in times of inflationary pressure (high cost of living) are notoriously more irritable than reduced expenditures on public works, and because it may easily take a larger government deficit with tax abatement rather than increased public expenditures to support national income by a *given* amount. Equally, the tax method appears in a relatively unfavorable light from the viewpoint of private administrative burdens. The current-collection scheme for the income tax has improved the chances of proper timing of the major tax instrument, but it has also involved the employers in administrative work which is annoying, especially as regards the multitude of small business units equipped with comparatively inadequate bookkeeping methods and tax-trained personnel. While the percentage of erroneous payroll tax deductions is fairly high, even with stable rates, a system of countercyclically varying rates would add a most formidable amount of trouble to both employers and the government. In the case of variable taxes on business profits there are, among other things, specifically economic drawbacks of sufficient importance to be discussed separately in a later part of this study.

Controls which leave some leeway as to the timing and extent of private response are politically preferable to rigorously coercive controls. Hence an astute government will choose them, provided the leeway is not too large to secure response in the right direction. A harness of wartime controls should be regarded merely as a last resort, even if the program itself mentions them as eligible devices. As will be shown later, there might be need for some direct controls applied on a selective basis, to cope with maladjustments which cannot be reached with indirect devices. But the main body of the compensatory apparatus should reveal a desire to treat everyone as nearly alike as possible. While this points in the direction of broadly applied monetary-fiscal techniques, the fact remains that even here there will be some unavoidable minimum of arbitrary distributions of sacrifices and gains. However, some valid distinctions can be drawn in this respect between various types of income-supporting fiscal measures. For example, the method of subsidizing private producers will normally be handled on highly arbitrary grounds, unless a government were willing to go to the absurd extreme of subsidizing all industries long enough until employment were restored. Despite the fact that here we have a method which is truly deceptive as to the extent to which the government is involved in regulating the economy, it seems inconceivable that a capitalistically inclined society would welcome such policy even if it were administratively feasible. By comparison, a variable public investment program appears in a better light. True, such a program is not equally well suited to conceal the order of magnitude of governmental operations, nor is it free of arbitrary effects. But it has been pointed out with good reason that the "arbitrary effects are mainly the indirect ones, whereas the direct effects can usually be justified, in a more or less acceptable fashion, for periods of considerable length," since "countries obviously need highways, dams, and so on."[4] Among the fiscal techniques, tax management appears to offer the best possibilities of avoiding inequities, so that at least in this particular respect the method has something in its favor. Actually, a government may be tempted to concentrate on rate changes which promise fairly reliable control over aggregate private expenditures, i.e., rate changes which regulate the disposable income of the *nonsaving* income groups rather than that of persons who may respond to tax reductions primarily in terms of increased saving, and to tax increases with dissaving. One may therefore conclude that the minimization of arbitrary effects in the distribution of gains and sacrifices depends not only on the type of the technique but also on the political character of the government, and also on considera-

[4] Fellner, *op.cit.*, p. 219.

tions as to the most efficient ways of handling each type of control.

Finally, there is the question of the extent to which techniques of control rely on private rather than governmental initiative. A scheme may be set up at the administrative center, but the initiative in regard to its operations may not lie there. It may lie with private parties, and the more this is the case, the smaller the impression of government influence. But the possibility of discovering central controls which fit the bill is bound to be slim for anybody who does not favor the expedient of administratively routinized stabilizers, on the grounds of incompatibility with reliable defense of binding targets.

This study makes a plea for the use of discretionary powers on the part of the stabilizing authorities. This does not leave much room for the search of controls which are mapped out and operated primarily by private initiative. True, the discretionary powers of the agencies are to be limited by law, and they are to be projected on an economy in which the individuals are supposed to run their own affairs as much as possible. The discretion should consist largely of adapting the choice of compensatory techniques to such a public and its likely modes of response. Nevertheless, this task of adaptation should be performed entirely on the basis of the good judgment of the agencies themselves. The agencies should consult private parties for advice only to the extent that such cooperation furthers their task. Only in this fashion can they hope to pass successfully through the launching period. After the central controls have demonstrated their power to make the objectives come true, the stage is set for more emphatic reliance on private initiative. When this phase arrives, it will have nothing to do with the shaping of the controls. Rather, it will assume the altogether different form of entrusting stability to an economy in which it has become rational for private business to counteract fluctuations with its *own devices*. By that time the central controls should move into the background.

All in all, our examination of controls from the viewpoint of political expediency and public psychological reaction has failed to produce many tangible results. Considering the complexities of the subject, this is not surprising. Trustworthy findings are handicapped by the fluidity of the scene with respect to what may be called acceptable and nonacceptable types of control. They are also handicapped by the fact that the classification of controls into the categories of monetary devices, tax management, and variable government outlay is too broad for the purposes on hand. From the standpoint of public reaction, much depends on how well the government understands how to make politically astute uses of each type of instrument. Even direct controls can be sweetened. A further difficulty lies in the fact that different groups of people are bound to feel differently about any particular choice of controls, no matter how circumspect the government might wish to be in its effort to avoid trouble.

Of much greater significance in the opinion of this writer is the conclusion that a community should first agree on the nature of the objectives and their binding character before getting involved in the subject of finding forms of implementation which emphasize cooperation between the stabilizing authorities and private parties. The responsibility and power of these authorities to defend the goals must be established beyond any doubt prior to the invitation of advice and active support from private economic organizations, be it organizations of management, capital, labor, or farmers. Provided it is understood that the government will not permit any tinkering with the objectives, and that the ultimate power of decision about implementation rests with government, it may become safe to adjust policy-making to the idiosyncrasies and self-interest of private groups for the sake of favorable response. If an atmosphere of voluntarism could be achieved without endangering success, the negotiation of the launching period would proceed in ideal form.

CHAPTER 14

TECHNICAL REQUISITES OF MONETARY-FISCAL MACHINERY

....

Flexibility, Short Lags in Response, and Stamina

FLEXIBILITY, short lags in response, and stamina are essential qualities of compensatory machinery. To achieve this combination of qualities it is by no means necessary for each individual control to satisfy on all three scores. But there must be an array of controls which enables the authorities to choose so as to meet any possible situation. The agencies must be able to act quickly, without long or uncertain lags in response, and without fear that the applied tools will give out in cases of stubborn disturbances.

It is very unlikely that one type of control could do the entire work. This is not serious as long as we have controls of light caliber suitable for quick and highly flexible action, and controls of potentially heavy caliber suitable to offset persistent destabilizing forces.

Flexibility

The term flexibility of controls, here, refers to the ability of the authorities to use controls on short notice (including ability to reverse action). To evaluate the degree of flexibility of a controlling device properly, one must do so from the standpoint of action which takes its signals from the current situation rather than from forecasting.

There are two types of obstacles to flexibility. One concerns political impediments and delays, and the other rigidities in the controls themselves. Removal of the first type of obstacle depends upon the feasibility of institutional reform, the pur-

[188]

pose of which is to make sure that certain potential instruments of control are actually eligible and furthermore that they can be used with as little delay as possible. Eligibility means, as far as the United States is concerned, official acceptance of certain budgetary controls involving deliberate deficits or surpluses, either through countercyclical tax variations or through variations in the volume of public expenditures, or both. As long as this issue is not decided in a favorable sense, the only controls which at present qualify as flexible are the following: (1) the central banking controls; (2) the *unplanned* budgetary deficits or surpluses resulting from fluctuations in income in conjunction with our federal income tax, the corporate income taxes, and social security. In the case of the central banking controls, flexibility is assured through broad discretionary powers of the Federal Reserve authorities. In the case of the automatic countercyclical reactions of our constant budgetary stabilizers, the element of flexibility is not the result of central administrative alertness and ability to make quick decisions. But this does not matter as far as results are concerned.

Firm acceptance (either on a *de jure* or *de facto* basis) of deliberate countercyclical changes in taxes or expenditures would mean an important step toward making this method flexible. But eligibility is not enough. In addition it takes provision for speedy application of tax and expenditure changes. Also, speed must be in line with ability to make *intelligent* decisions. Tax management is an art no less than central banking. It requires a group of experts, and offices endowed with a wealth of information, to decide which of the taxes can be changed with the least amount of administrative difficulties for government and tax payers, and with the least amount of economic disturbance. Questions of how often tax rates can be lowered or raised, to what extent matters of administrative convenience must be sacrificed to the need for action, cannot be decided on general principles. The same applies to a host of related issues, such as the risks involved in recurrent tax rate changes in comparison to those involved in changes of exemption levels, the most suitable combination of tax deficits and deficits produced by additional expenditures, the choice between incidental and heavy work programs, and so forth.

While ability to make constructive decisions may be found in both arms of government, and while the initiative in handling budgetary controls will probably always be divided in some way between congressional and executive offices, it is nevertheless safe to say that the promise of effective budgetary cycle control involves an increase in executive discretionary powers as compared with actual practice. It will be recalled from our previous observations on automatic management that the method of prescribed rules of adaptation in tax rates, etc., is out of the question. But there is no need to go to the opposite extreme of leaving the choice of means, their timing and order of magnitude, entirely within the hands of the President and his advisers. Suitable compromises range from the already indicated device of executive action under legislative veto to the more orthodox method of executive action limited by fairly specific legislative instructions.[1] However, even the most auspicious political arrangement cannot remove rigidities which attach to the controls themselves. Instead of trying to press every budgetary control into uses for which it is not suited, the purpose of making room for discretionary judgment on the part of highly trained personnel is to decide what each control can do and to propose policies which fit the needs of the time. Barring the possibility that roads, bridges, dams, etc., can be constructed in piecemeal fashion without waste or public criticism, the method of heavy public works must be discarded from the list of flexible controls even if there should be a set of blueprinted and authorized projects. The possibility of varying the rate of activity on actually

[1] Hart, *op.cit.*, pp. 490-491.

started projects is limited. Instead of making it a regular part of countercyclical machinery, the method of heavy public investment should be governed by long-run considerations (growth) and by the practice of keeping a set of postponable projects in reserve for cases of unusually severe forces of depression As far as flexibility is concerned, preference must be given to small projects which permit fairly quick starts and stops. In this category belong not only items of questionable value (quasi-doles) but also limited types of public works projects capable of absorbing specialized labor and machinery, such as governmental low-cost housing. While countercyclically adjusted government aid in low-cost housing has not yet progressed beyond the proposal stage, there exists in the United States a flexible type of public outlay on goods and services, namely, the agricultural price-support program. This system cannot be said to be confined to countercyclical purposes, but it is bound to work out in this fashion during swings.

The inherent rigidities in tax management are not as obvious as those confronting the public works method. Lack of flexibility is partly due to political factors. A reform aiming at avoidance of delays in the mapping out of rate changes could do much to improve flexibility. Remaining obstacles to frequent rate changes lie in factors which cannot be properly dealt with in terms of administrative inflexibilities. They have to do with disturbing effects of unstable tax rates on business psychology and cost calculations.

Short Lags in Response

How close a nation can come to keeping fluctuations within certain limits depends in part on the length of the time which elapses between the taking of action and its effects on total demand or activity. The shorter the lag, the better. The lag is largely determined by private decision-making. The government has control over it only in a limited sense. It can choose such types of controls which for their effect on total demand do not have to depend on private cooperation. This points toward highly coercive controls. But it applies also to the method of government purchases of goods and services which in the act of buying directly affects national product. It will be noticed that an intelligent treatment of the problem of lags in response demands a clear definition of what is meant by response or effects. If by effect we mean no more than changes in the available stock of money, every controlling device tends to have a negligible lag in response. The situation is quite different if the effect is measured in terms of, let us say, total private expenditure. Here the money-stock devices are bound to appear with a considerable lag in response. For budgetary controls which directly affect private income, the lag is probably much shorter in general. Much depends on the incidence of the control. For example, the lag can be expected to be short in the case of transfer payments (relief, unemployment compensation) and tax changes for the low income groups. The lag in response here becomes identical with the so-called household-expenditure lag for which some estimates have been made. For the United States the studies seem to show that on the average the lag of household expenditures behind income payments is less than three months.[2] For low income groups and persons on relief it must be assumed to be considerably shorter than that. Every fiscal compensatory device is apt to take, to some extent, the initial form of additions to or subtractions from income payments to wage earners. For a certain part of their action, therefore, the lag in response would be the same as above. Consequently, if government policy is dominated by the desire for fairly short and reliable lags in response, the choice of means should be in the direction of relief and work projects which employ a great deal of labor

[2] Lloyd A. Metzler, "Three Lags in the Circular Flow of Income," in *Employment and Public Policy*, essays in honor of Alvin H. Hansen, New York: W. W. Horton and Company, 1948, p. 22.

in comparison to materials and equipment. It could also be in the direction of variable taxation for the lower income groups.

For government purchases of commodities, the so-called output lag, i.e., the lag of output behind a change in the volume of sales, is relevant.[3] Changes in output may lag considerably behind a change in the volume of sales, be it sales to government or to private buyers. Sellers who find their sales increasing may fail to step up their orders immediately by a corresponding amount. In the case of rising government purchases, a considerable output lag may result from lack of confidence on the part of the sellers in the government's effort to boost general economic activity. But the lag may also be due to inertia or simply to the fact that it takes time to change production schedules.

The output lag of the method of government buying might be regarded as being observable in the movement of business stocks at the time of enlarged buying. However, such movement is no reliable basis for measuring the lag. A shrinkage of inventories during such time could easily be due to factors not related to government policy. Therefore erroneous conclusions may be drawn. Inventory practices are notoriously volatile; they are affected by many circumstances of the market.

The output lag will probably always defy reliable measurement. However desirable it may seem from the standpoint of government policy to measure this lag, the result of such efforts could easily fail to satisfy since the primary purpose would obviously be to ascertain a typical and hence predictable length of the lag. From the viewpoint of a program of variable government outlay on goods, the output lag is likely to depend on the degree of intensity with which this particular type of control is applied. It may become the shorter, the more de-

[3] If the method of government outlay on goods and services is appraised from the standpoint of its effects on the nation's economic budget, that is, the sum of private and public expenditures, then there is of course no lag between the taking of action and its effects.

termined the government's action. There are, however, possible qualifications. Whether we like it or not, the order of magnitude of changes in the government's buying program is bound to influence the sellers' opinion about the probable caliber of the disturbance which is in the making. Hence one must reckon with the unpleasant possibility that a sharp use of this control might have a certain paralyzing effect on business psychology and thus possibly defeat the purpose of strong use. For obvious reasons this sort of complication must be faced primarily during downswings, that is, in regard to income-supporting efforts. The danger of such complication is quite broad and attaches to all controls which either directly or indirectly aim at regulation of outlay by business units.

Secondly, the output lag probably depends upon the average businessman's *own* expectations about the probable severity of fluctuations. If in the past he expected a beginning downturn to develop into a long and severe depression, or was unable to come to any tangible conclusion about the immediate future of economic conditions, the lag of output behind changes in sales was bound to have been longer than in instances of greater optimism. At a minimum, therefore, the study in question would have to differentiate between light and major cycles and try to measure lags for comparable cases of instability. Yet in view of possible discrepancies between the producers' expectations and actual subsequent experience, the statistician may find no close correlation between the severity of swings and the length of lags in response.

Uncertainty about the length of the output lag is bound to attach to every stabilizing means which is not coercive in regard to producers' response. Since coercive means are out of the question in a predominantly private-enterprise economy, many specialists have tried to work their way toward controls which, though devoid of coercion, nevertheless seem to promise results as if they were coercive. This they do, of course, by designing stabilizing means whose incidence lies in areas of relatively predictable individual decision-making. Again and again the area of low income groups is singled out for this purpose. If the analysis of effects could stop at the consumption level, the problem of lags in response could be handled rather simply. But these consumption schemes are expected to exercise desirable influences on private investment. Therefore the problem of the output lag remains, in the form of the timing of leverage effects.[4] In other words, the difficulties presented by this lag cannot be avoided.

Let us carry this discussion a step farther. Ordinarily, in commenting on the subject of varying lags in response, economists stay clear of the complications which are occasioned by the development of self-enforcing effects of central stabilizing policy. Yet another obstacle to predictability of the output lag, and even the household expenditure lag, is bound to emerge from the development of persuasive effects of controls, especially in connection with binding targets. If there are such effects, their impact on aggregate demand and activity will be felt at once. The situation resembles what has often been described as pump-priming effects. There is no objection to applying this familiar term to the subject of self-enforcement of stabilizing machinery, provided it is understood that the momentum to which the pump-priming theory refers is not regarded as being confined to an economy which, after having been shoved off dead center with the aid of the government, is allowed to move freely from slumps to booms, and vice versa.[5]

[4] The problem of leverage effects of changes in consumption (acceleration principle) is often discussed without reference to the time element. But in connection with stabilization policy, the omission of lag problems is unsatisfactory.

[5] In other words, it must be understood that pump-priming effects can occur, and in fact are most likely to occur, in an economy which adopts a binding norm for stabilization, and that the range of these effects is prescribed by whatever it takes to restore total activity to the norm. However, no stubborn attempts will be made here to reconcile the notion of pump-priming with that of self-enforcement. One may reject reconciliation on the grounds that pump-priming definitively has become associated

The emergence of self-enforcing effects presents a problem to the stabilizing agencies only as long as there is no assurance about these effects. Presumably, the tendency toward self-enforcement would begin to make itself felt after the government has shown that it can successfully dampen swings with the available controls. But the transition to more stable patterns of private expectations may be slow. The nearest thing to reliability concerning the change in the psychological climate would be a steadily mounting public confidence in stability. This is quite possible. But one must also be prepared for a less regular development. It is conceivable that for years on end every inch of stabilization has to be achieved through alert and assiduous use of the controls on hand—evaluating each control as carefully as possible on the basis of past experience—only to find out that during some stage of the game the compensatory endeavors are being struck by a wave of favorable response which throws overboard all previous notions as to what this or that control can do. Even the much maligned central banking methods, then, might develop unsuspected strength, although this strength might amount largely to a case of borrowed power in the sense that it reflects the power of other means to follow—once the public has learned to regard the central banking methods as a signal for more to come if necessary.

Such a sudden thrust of confidence could temporarily upset the defense of planned objectives. Frantic reversals of action might become necessary. Moreover, the gale of confidence might not keep blowing with the same strength from then on, leaving those in charge of stabilization in anxious moments of uncertainty about proper intensity of countercyclical action.

But let us not paint the picture unnecessarily dark. Despite these possible initial complications, there is valid reason to

---

with a policy of letting the economy freely travel from slumps to booms and that the theory of pump-priming, after all, is more narrow in that it does not cover the subject of curbing operations.

expect that the expedient of binding targets would eventually simplify the problem of lags in response. In the past, cycle control was tried at greatly divergent degrees of off-balance, and without the benefit of public confidence that stabilizing operations would go on until some announced goal is reached. These circumstances are most instrumental in creating varying lags in response. Binding targets would closely define the degree of off-balance at which countercyclical action has to start. Therefore the reactions to be reckoned with would tend to be more uniform. In addition, the very fact that the government is committed to persist with its offsetting measures until the need disappeared is likely to make a deep impression. Surprises would tend to become less and less frequent as time went on. Quick reactions to the inception of compensatory controls could be relied upon more and more firmly, to the point of diminishing actual use in favor of persuasive effects.

Stamina

Without emulating those economists who in recent years have discussed stabilization machinery with primary emphasis on the need for *continuous* large-scale compensatory operations, one may insist that a countercyclical program should make provision for some controls which could be used heavily if the need arose—a distinct possibility during the infancy of the program. In some instances, provision for heavy-caliber controls spells preparedness for specific forms of intervention. This subject will be dealt with in the next chapter. For the moment only the monetary-fiscal controls will be briefly examined for possibilities of sustained operations.

The primary choice for handling tenacious off-balance situations below the floor appears to be the technique of spurts in heavy public investment (to achieve sustained stimulation of producers' goods industries which are likely to be the seat of the trouble). Several objections to this technique are substantially weakened on account of the particular mode of use suggested by the program contemplated in this study. This applies to the objection that large-scale public construction involves the danger of either wasteful projects or encroachment upon the area of private investment outlets. Also weakened is the argument that the method precludes properly timed starts and stops.

Apprehensions about wasteful or unduly competitive policies are not to the point because there would be no need for continuous large-scale use. The proposed floor would lie below the full-employment mark, and this fact greatly increases the chances that the method could be held in abeyance most of the time. The central institutions should be continuously *prepared* to launch upon large-scale operations, but this is far different from advocating uninterrupted application of the method. In a community which grows and which is apt to make demands for improved public services, an occasional spurt in heavy public construction may well be consistent with genuine long-run needs for roads, dams, etc. The long-term order of magnitude of governmental activity of this sort might not be greater than it would be without countercyclical use. A shelf of blueprinted and authorized projects would hold a true promise here. If most of the time such a shelf can be held untouched rather than being continuously depleted by heavy investment activity, the government will be saved from considerable embarrassment occasioned by frantic improvisation and the search for projects which may either be premature from the standpoint of actual need or of increasingly low marginal value to society at any time. Furthermore, in connection with the expedient of binding targets, the entire length of the period during which countercyclical adaptation of public investment would be relevant is bound to be comparatively short. We are, after all, concerned merely with the problems of the launching phase.

The suggested program also improves the chances of coping with the unwieldiness of the method. Presumably, actual operations would be postponed until it became evident that lighter methods fail to restore activity to the floor. Also, the timing of stops could be handled with greater ease. If completion necessitated operations subsequent to the restoration of the floor, the situation would be considerably less critical than in the case of full-employment policy. Since the floor makes room for reasonable unemployment, overlapping operations may not produce serious inflationary leakages. In fact, they might be a welcome means of shoving the economy above the floor.

Even so, there would be no need to place the entire burden of income-supporting action on public construction. Large-scale construction could be combined with the method of tax abatement which also profits in various respects from the fact that only infrequent steps would have to be taken. Since tax rates would hardly have to be lowered before credit controls had failed to make the necessary impression, the government might have sufficient time to get ready with well-planned tax reduction. The new rates could probably be maintained for a sufficient length of time to act as an incentive for producers and consumers. Both corporate and personal income taxes would seem to be logical choices for checking persistent slump tendencies. Again, there would seem to be no cause for alarm if the period for which the new rates are to go into effect should prove to be longer than needed for the restoration of the floor.

Overlapping effects are more serious in the event of action which is directed against persistent inflationary pressure. Owing to the fact that it would be desirable to have total activity stay close to the premeditated ceiling, any off-balance above the ceiling should always be checked with machinery which is not so rigid as to drag the economy down to unnecessarily low levels before action can be stopped. Therefore it might not be advisable to fight speculative booms with the same weapons as protracted slumps. Fortunately, our credit controls may suffice to cope with inflationary spells.[6] A tightening of credit controls is a broader and more forceful interference with the demand for loans than a depression-born relaxation of lending standards could ever hope to be. The tightening of bank credit catches many producers, speculators, and consumers who up to then have been active borrowers and who, consequently, have to take immediate and painful steps enabling them to pay back their loans. By contrast, an easy-money policy is essentially in the nature of a mere incentive or invitation as regards the majority of the individuals who under the circumstances may be relatively free from bank debt and can exercise discretion as to the extent to which their contact with the banks should be renewed.

The hope that credit controls may suffice to stop inflationary booms springs also from the presumption that it is easier to check a wave of optimism than waves of pessimism. Be that as it may, the greatest effort should be made to establish this instrument on a powerful plane. To be able to rely on it would be fortunate not only because it is a flexible instrument but also because it is politically less controversial than other curbing devices. Tax increases are always difficult to achieve. Contraction of public investment may be handicapped by the fact that in a growing community current needs suggest a fairly high minimum of urgent projects (for example, replacements, increased educational and health facilities to cope with population growth). If so, cutbacks in public investment would have to proceed with caution.

We may sum up this discussion on stamina by saying that persistent depression forces should be counteracted primarily with heavy works projects for which there is secularly increased demand in a growing community. To adjust the timing of such construction to countercyclical needs may fail to cause

[6] This statement refers merely to cyclical inflationary spells, but not to secular inflation for which some specific controls may be necessary (see the following chapter).

the long-run total of public investment to be higher than it would be if such investment were not used at all for purposes of cycle control. Besides, most of the time—even during the launching phase—it might be possible to defend the floor with some combination of expansionary credit policies, incidental work projects, transfer payments, and other flexible light-caliber weapons. If so, the method of variation in heavy work projects could be kept in the background. The suggestion to confine this technique of income-supporting operations to the role of a last resort, and to use it only for the restoration of a floor which falls short of full utilization of resources, removes various objections pertaining to timing and size. The same holds true for supplementary tax reductions.

CHAPTER 15

NONMONETARY STABILIZATION POLICIES

THIS chapter will briefly discuss some of the nonmonetary measures which should supplement the budgetary and central banking controls. Attention will be focused upon possible improvements in the internal balance of the economy. It is generally admitted that the relatively indirect budgetary and central banking controls would work more satisfactorily in a reasonably competitive environment than in a system characterized by restrictive practices and by artificial barriers hampering the flow of resources. The automatic responses to central income-supporting or income-curbing operations will be improved, in the sense that the regulation of aggregate money demand promises to be accompanied by desirable resource allocation on the part of producers. The greater the chance to rely on private response for proper resource allocation, the less need there will be for using credit and fiscal controls in a pointed manner, or for backing up these devices with a set of highly direct controls.

As long as we do not have a reasonably competitive system, this is a fairly idle speculation. The stabilization program itself must include measures designed to establish gradually a reasonably competitive order. In the long view, these measures should constitute the major part of what is meant by the term nonmonetary stabilization policy. Because the progress of competitive reform is bound to be slow even if society is willing to endorse such reform in principle, the attack on restrictive practices would at first have to be flanked by a certain selection of direct controls. If past experience with American antitrust procedure proves anything for the future, any revival of the drive toward competitive arrangements in industry, agriculture, transportation, marketing, etc., will be subject to some important and quite deliberate exceptions. This suggests a long-run minimum of direct controls which are to be used, more or less openly, as substitutes for genuine antitrust procedure.

Before discussing the scope, standards, and limits of competitive reform as well as the assortment of direct controls which is to flank such reform, attention must be drawn to the fact that the emphasis on this part of the program will have to be the greater the more ambitious the nature of the premeditated floor. Our suggestion that the community should refrain from establishing a guaranteed seller's market is partly motivated by the fear that neither competitive reform nor the resort to direct controls might proceed with sufficient determination to minimize the danger of monopolistic abuse of the program. In fact, the safety device of an underemployment floor should suggest itself most forcefully to those economists who have lost faith in the political feasibility of determined competitive reform. The issue at stake is the protection of monetary-fiscal income-supporting machinery from the charge of inefficiency. It is not enough to show that under certain circumstances this machinery can be given the necessary degree of flexibility and stamina to control total money demand. There must also be reasonable assurance that stabilization of money demand will not perpetuate production dislocations and unhealthy price dispersions inherited from the unstable past, or create new maladjustments.

To forestall unwarranted inferences from the above statements, it must be pointed out that the proposal of an underemployment floor is not necessarily indicative of such lack of faith in the feasibility or desirability of competitive reform. As this study indicates, the proposal can be defended with arguments which have nothing to do with the point in question.

The Problem of Competitive Reform

Much of the current criticism against competitive reform is directed against the concept of atomistic competition and hence can be deflected by advocating some reasonably realistic standards of competitiveness. Ill effects of restrictive practices on the composition of national product (resource allocation) are still widely conceded.[1] By and large, the issue today is merely whether or not the prevalence of monopolistic powers accounts for general unemployment (underemployment).

For the purposes on hand, this issue can be formulated in such a way that less controversial conclusions may be obtained, namely, does the existence of anticompetitive arrangements account for inability to remove prevailing unemployment with the aid of monetary-fiscal income-supporting measures? If the issue is stated in this manner, one does not have to probe into the question of the nature of the causes which, originally, account for the loss of jobs. In fact, one could afford for the sake of argument to concede that the prevailing unemployment was not brought about by monopolistic forces. With respect to a certain portion among the total of idle persons or plant facilities, this is indeed a sound presumption. For to some extent inactivity is apt to result from frictional impediments not associated with deliberate restrictive supply tactics, but rather from ignorance concerning employment opportunities, immobility caused by a high degree of specialization, and also, of course, by cyclical contraction of demand. All in all, this may be a very substantial portion of unemployment. Be that as it may, the only thing that is at stake is the question of how well expansionary finance will work in the face of monopolistic organizations. If these organizations make it difficult to absorb the unemployed resources through raising the supply price of their services (in-

[1] See, for example, A. P. Lerner, "The Concept of Monopoly and the Measurements of Monopoly Power," *Review of Economic Studies*, June 1934, pp. 157-175.

flationary leakages), they deserve to be made responsible for the maintenance of unemployment although they might not have been the cause of the previous loss of jobs. Conceivably, the detrimental effects of monopoly would be slight if, in this context, one had to reckon only with monopolistic control of specific resources in specific industries. The situation would then be one of bottlenecks here and there, with isolated price increases and difficulties of balanced expansion. But the problem becomes more ominous in the face of groupism (monopoly in the wider sense of the word). We need cite only one example: the combination of alert and aggressive collective bargaining and the policy of compensatory increases in agricultural prices. This combination alone can set the stage for log-rolling inflation and crippling effects on expansionary finance, especially on the background of governmental responsiveness to the demands of farmers and organized labor. Experience with the hampering effects of prevailing power blocs upon monetary-fiscal controls is so well-established that those who deny the effects surely must be charged with the burden of proof.

While these simple facts furnish a sufficient basis for proposals to check restrictive practices in connection with programs of expansionary finance, it is nevertheless important to know whether, or to what extent, anticompetitive practices also account for some of the previous loss of employment. The logical point of departure for reaching a sound conclusion on this subject is still the question whether monopoly output is smaller than competitive output in each individual case. If this question has to be answered in the affirmative, then there is a strong presumption that an all-round tendency toward monopolistic practices leads to a restriction of total employment and output. A rejection of this proposition is difficult. There are, as a recent writer has pointed out, only two fairly remote possibilities of offsetting forces which may prevent individual monopoly output from being smaller than competitive output. One is that monopolization may be associated with a lowering of the cost functions in the specific industries in which it occurs. The other is that *expected* demand curves may shift to the right, as compared to their previous positions; and this, by leading to increased output, may shift *actual* demand curves to the right, thereby restoring aggregate output, even in the long view.[2]

Neither of these offsetting factors is dependable. They do not accompany monopolization by necessity. There may be instances in which the acquisition of monopolistic powers encourages innovation and a lowering of cost functions, i.e., where the transition to new products or production methods involves large capital outlay.[3] But possession of monopoly power is, on the whole, not conducive to adoption of new methods. Students of economics are familiar with the proposition that in competitive industry new methods will tend to be adopted if total costs per unit of output with the new method promise to be lower than total costs with the old, whereas under conditions of monopoly innovations will tend to be introduced only if total costs with the new method are lower than prime costs with the old.

Admittedly, the question of the relative progressiveness of competitive and monopolized industry cannot be decided exclusively from the viewpoint of who would be more ready to adopt a new method. The question also involves the relative rate at which the search for new methods goes on. Where monopoly power springs from bigness we must allow for the superiority of research facilities as compared with those which are normally available to competitive industry, so that the rate at which inventions are made would most likely fall if bigness were reduced. This factor must be weighed against

[2] Fellner, *Monetary Policies and Full Employment, op.cit.,* p. 87.
[3] This developmental capital refers to the funds necessary for carrying an invention from the blueprint stage to final installation of production process and marketing facilities. In between may lie various phases of experimentation and improvement of know-how.

the restrictive tendencies involved in monopolistic pricing and output policy. The speedier lowering of cost functions may frequently be less important than the restrictive output policy which follows progress.[4]

There exist some marketing factors which conceivably may cause a shift-to-the-right of expected demand curves in conjunction with the monopolization of formerly competitive industry. The nature of these factors—advertising, improved sales organization, etc.—need not be discussed here. Suffice it to say that expected shifts of demand to the right cannot materialize into an actual increase in the level of output unless the economy suffers from unemployment at the point of monopolization. This case does not prove anything against a competitive system which, aside from intermittent (cyclical) unemployment and some irreducible small float of frictional unemployment, tends toward full utilization of resources. It is something which has significance for an economy in which all-round monopolistic tendencies prevail. Moreover, as Fellner points out, the upward shift is self-defeating if inflationary developments are counteracted by the stabilizing authorities.[5]

On the whole, an analysis of the effects of monopoly on total employment (output) which ignores the two potential offsetting forces appears to be valid. Assuming that the individual demand curve faced by the monopolist is identical with the former market demand for the product of competitive industry, and that the cost curves are the same before and after monopolization, such analysis warrants the conclusion that monopolization does lead to a restriction of output. The degree of the restrictive tendency depends on the curvature of the demand curve and on that of the competitive supply curve (Robinson, Chamberlin).

We are now approaching the difficult if not exasperating subject of the proper mode and extent of monopoly control. Professional opinion varies between the extremes of thorough

[4] Fellner, *op.cit.*, p. 88.   [5] *Ibid.*

decentralization of private economic power and purely sporadic, selective procedure designed to meet only the most flagrant cases of socially harmful individual or group practice. Between these extremes lies a large range of intermediate positions. It covers such remedies as: (1) an appeal to the reasonableness and spirit of cooperation on the part of strongly organized groups and mammoth enterprise in regard to their attitude toward government and national economic policy; (2) contemplation of a partial but by no means clearly circumscribed policy of decentralization of private economic power (antitrust procedure); and (3), as an alternative to the foregoing, the resort to a set of central direct controls which, although not attacking the concentration of private power as such, would nevertheless curb the range of their restrictive and socially undesirable policies.

In the British as well as American postwar debate on full-employment methods the appeal to the spirit of cooperation and the suggestion of direct controls often appear in conjunction, usually in the sense that the voluntary procedure should be tried for all it is worth, and that it should be supplemented by the method of direct controls if necessary. The outstanding area for both methods is that of collective bargaining. Its chief forms range from voluntary to compulsory arbitration. The two methods are, of course, based on different sets of assumptions as to the probable behavior of unions and employers. The resort to direct controls over wages and prices is bound to be more urgent in the case of a government commitment for full-employment opportunities, but it cannot be regarded as confined to this case. It is impossible to obtain any clear impression from the debate as to how much faith is placed on the voluntary method alone.

The second method, i.e., antitrust procedure, appears to live a life of its own, not only because of its classical roots but primarily because it is recognized, even by its contemporary advocates, as being very slow. Even with ultimately modest objectives, decentralization of private economic power, or at least a direct attack on unfair practices, has to proceed gradually. Since it is the slowest part of a stabilization program, the launching period makes the resort to some direct controls indispensable. About this point more will be said later.

What should be the objectives of antitrust procedure? This question can be answered in two different ways: what *should* be done or what *can* be done on the basis of available laws and administrative machinery. Even if one abstains from the idealized regime of perfect competition and attempts to concentrate on a reasonable degree of competition, the two questions are unlikely to lead to the same answer. For example, one may hold that reasonable competitiveness in industry requires some effort to limit the size of individual business enterprise. But neither the antitrust laws nor any other legislation affords a basis for action along this line. Moreover, the problem of what should be the objectives is under any circumstances less difficult to solve than the problem of a workable program. Reasonable goals have been spelled out by specialists independently of the question of available or procurable legislative and administrative machinery, i.e., solely from the viewpoint of a reasonable compromise between the economic and political advantages of maintaining rivalry among traders and a variety of sources of supply for buyers, on the one hand, and the potential advantages of economic concentration in terms of modern mass-production technology, access to capital, marketing facilities etc., on the other.

The subject of what could actually be done must be left untouched here. Its proportions are such that it requires too much space even for reproduction of conclusions reached by experts.[6] But a brief account of reasonable goals, however sketchy and unoriginal, is in order.

[6] See especially the recent study by Corwin D. Edwards, *Maintaining Competition, Requisites of a Governmental Policy*, New York: McGraw-Hill Book Company, 1947.

Let us begin with prices. The curbing of monopolistic pricing practices should lead to prices which are reasonably sensitive to changes in operating costs and demand. "Reasonably sensitive" here means that permanent changes in operating costs and demand should go into pricing. Purely temporary changes in production costs caused by sporadic factors such as strikes, weather conditions, etc. need not reflect themselves in price adjustments, and the same applies to sporadic shifts in demand schedules. A price system will be sufficiently flexible from the standpoint of efficient resource allocation and consumers' choice if it reflects technological progress, permanent changes in wage rates (as implemented by new wage agreements), and permanent shifts in demand resulting from the introduction of new products, population growth, and so forth. A moderate concept of competition should also make allowance for product differentiation, provided this practice does not go so far as to be confusing, i.e., in preventing intelligent buyer's choice on the basis of relative prices. The implied concessions to price differentiation and price rigidities are compatible with the desire to restore the price factor as a major vehicle of competition. They are a far cry from advocating private price fixing as a device for stabilizing price levels and for avoidance of deflationary spirals. True, as a by-product of even moderate attempts to secure greater flexibility of individual prices, the general level of prices will become more sensitive to fluctuations in total money demand (as compared with changes in relative demand). But this is no source for worry in conjunction with overall stabilization procedure which uses the money-value factor as guide and objective of compensatory operations. On the contrary, any improvement in the degree of sensitivity of the price index to fluctuations in total money demand is a gain for such a program. It is one thing to rely on price-level behavior as a guide and measure for income-supporting or curbing operations, and it is quite another to subscribe to the untenable view that the more we allow prices and money wages to fall in the face of unemployment, the sooner this unemployment will disappear.

Secondly, there should be an appreciable number of sources of supply as well as an appreciable number of potential buyers for substantially the same product or service. Reasonably competitive standards are satisfied if decentralization does not go to the extreme of eliminating individual influence on price. It suffices if buyers can turn away from any particular trader and find a variety of other alternatives.[7] Different degrees of decentralization of output are indicated for different types of industries, depending on the character of the technology and product. A uniform ceiling for the size of the business unit is undesirable and also impractical since it would be too large for industries in which there is a premium on small-scale operations, and too small for industries characterized by a large optimum size for the business unit. A set of differentiated standards for ceilings would be less objectionable but still unsatisfactory, since any absolute ceiling threatens to cripple the incentive for enterprises to seek more business after having reached the permitted maximum. Therefore the desire for rules would have to be abandoned here, at least in part, in favor of the familiar and actual method of discovering suitable criteria for determining whether or not excessive power is present or imminent in particular cases.

Thirdly, competitive reform should be directed toward maintaining opportunity for newcomers to enter into industry. There should be, in the apt words of one expert, no "handicap other than that which is automatically created by the fact that others are already well established there."[8] This means an attack on deliberate restrictions of opportunity, both private and governmental. More specifically, it means an attack on preemption of necessary facilities in the form of exclusive dealing arrangements, preemptory practices in regard to transportation facilities and satisfactory production sites, and pool-

[7] Edwards, *op.cit.*, p. 9.   [8] *Ibid.*

ing of technology confined to established members. It also means an attack on legal barriers or, as the case may be, their discriminatory abuse (exclusive franchise, laws against non-local business, patent laws, license requirements, etc.). Moreover, maintenance of opportunity for newcomers should also assume the positive form of diminishing automatic barriers in industries where size and technology make entry particularly hard. Here is a promising field for promotional government policy, such as tax reform designed to encourage new enterprise, incentives to move private industry into new geographic areas of potential comparative advantage, regional resource development, and so forth.

Finally, most proponents of competitive reform will agree that the curbing of restrictive *agreements* should be extended beyond present procedure. The American law shows a preoccupation with one particular aspect of restrictive agreements, namely, price fixing. Other types of restrictive accords, for example concerted action to limit output or marketing territories, have been neglected by the law despite the fact that economically they are at least as important as price fixing, and usually part of it. If they are prosecuted at all, they are apt to be prosecuted only upon the theory that their significance lies in raising prices.[9] Agreements concerning restrictions of output, marketing territories, and technology should be prosecuted as unreasonable per se.

All of the foregoing objectives suggest themselves not merely from the viewpoint of securing proper automatic response to monetary-fiscal controls. They emerge also from independent reasoning about the directions which a curbing of anticompetitive practices should take, i.e., the kind of reasoning which has always stood behind the opposition to practices which limit economic freedom and efficiency. They are predicated on the assumption that in most instances the reliance on competitive motives for determining resource allocation, and on individual

Ibid., p. 40.

reward for production and efficiency, is both economically and politically preferable to other types of economic organization. Within the limits set by ignorance, custom, inertia and immobilities caused by specialization, and within the limits of deliberate exceptions to the general rule of competition (such as collective bargaining, natural monopolies, including public utilities and monopolies predicated on patent privileges), competition is the most important regulator of economic life and corrective of maladjustment. It makes reliance on governmental controls over the *composition* of national product and distribution less necessary. At the same time, it increases the promise held by the predominantly indirect monetary-fiscal controls. On account of the exceptions and imperfections just indicated, it will always be necessary for the community to supplement competition with a selective set of direct controls. Some of this can be hidden in the broad category of monetary and budgetary controls which, aside from regulating total income (employment), can be used to influence resource allocation and inter-industry balance. But the order of magnitude of these direct or specific controls can gradually be lessened as competition is restored.

Direct Controls

The most important area of deliberate exception to the rule of competition is that of collective wage bargaining. Barring any unexpected removal of this exception, collective bargaining will always necessitate government intervention in the interest of economic peace and welfare. Such intervention requires standards for public wage policy for which the broad objectives of overall stabilization furnish limited answers. Certain currently popular ideas about proper wage standards become unacceptable if, as this study suggests, the ceiling for cyclical expansion is to be set in terms of a general price index. With this limit in mind, the government's policy should be to encourage wage increases only to the extent of increased productivity per man-hour. According to a familiar precept, proper policy calls for a different procedure in the cases of greater efficiency due to greater effort of the workers themselves, and greater efficiency resulting from the application of science to production. In the former instance, wage increases should be confined to the workers who are making the special effort, so that their money (and real) wages rise by a corresponding amount above the wages of those who do not make the effort. In the latter instance, the policy of price-level stability suggests a broad monetary expansion involving a rise in the *general* level of money incomes, including the level of money wages. This does not mean that all commodity prices will remain stable. Rather, it will mean a downward drift of the prices in the progressive industries, and an upward drift of prices in the remainder of industry commensurate with the rise in the money costs of production.

It is highly unlikely, however, that the problem of government wage policy can be solved in accordance with this simple theoretical precept. Only a competitively flexible system would operate in the above fashion, and the government would not be involved in the problem of individual wages. What calls for a government wage policy is the fact that wages are administered prices determined to a substantial degree by the relative strength of the labor organizations and the employers. Neither the groups involved nor the economic specialists on collective bargaining see eye to eye on what should be the nature of the government's policy. Even those economists and officials who support the idea of stable prices propose divergent directives for government influence in wage disputes. Within certain limits, price-level stability can be achieved with different patterns of the distribution of income between wage earners and owners of capital. This fact facilitates the introduction of more or less pronounced redistributional angles into the debate on proper government wage policy. A strong element of personal sympathy for either workers or employers enters into the proposals. There is also frequently a tendency to pass judgment along general lines rather than on the basis of the individual merits of the case. Frequently, either labor or management is subjected to one-sided and summary criticism. As a consequence, proposals often suggest one-sided controls, varying from one extreme of wage controls and "free" prices to the other extreme of price control and "free" wages.

In the face of broad and costly wage disputes and powerful pressures on both sides, it may simply be argued, of course, that it makes little difference whether the price or the wage area is singled out for direct government intervention. This is to say that if prices are controlled, trade unions will be subjected to fairly narrow limits within which they can successfully embark upon a wage-raising campaign, and if wages are controlled by government, one of the main potential causes of price inflation will be automatically removed.

But the problem is not so simple. Constructive and workable standards of wage policy suggest a differentiated procedure. Since it is prima facie unlikely that the threat of inflation invariably comes from the side of trade unions, or invariably from that of management, the government must be prepared to proceed from case to case in an effort to decide which side indulges in attitudes and demands that are unreasonable. Depending on the outcome of its investigations, the government should throw its weight against labor if that is where the unreasonable demands are made, and against the producers if they are the ones who cause the trouble.

This formula is only common sense and contains nothing that is new. But it is sometimes forgotten over the general excitement about costly strikes, the announcement of a new round of increased wage demands, or simply about the fact that unions time the inception of wage disputes in such a way as to maximize their bargaining power. The formula does not permit one-sided action even for relatively short periods of time. It is often claimed that during the postwar transition years there have been times in which the wage-raising campaign of trade unions furnished the chief momentum of inflation. This is questionable. To judge from statistical records concerning the relative movement of total wage income, corporate profits, farm income, and the income of retailers, the temptation to exploit a seller's market has not been confined to unions. Rather it is possible, and even likely, that at any time—and irrespective of the prevailing tenor of popular theories about the causes of inflation—the government will do well to refrain from one-sided action. The result will be a diversified program of specific directives against particular groups, perhaps to the point of formal selective price or wage controls.

Fortunately, there is hope that such a program can be operated on a relatively small scale subsequent to the disappearance of the abnormal conditions which characterize the postwar transition years. Provided the international scene becomes tranquil, there will be no general scarcity of commodities and services occasioned by a total change in the composition of national output which, in conjunction with the accumulation of enormous amounts of liquid balances, can be regarded as the chief cause of the recent atrophy of competitive standards in large parts of industry, labor, farming, and merchandising. Consequently there will hardly be need for a comprehensive program of price and wage controls. At any particular time in the future, probably only a handful of industries may necessitate direct government intervention as to prices or wages (or both) in order to supplement the broad monetary and fiscal stabilization techniques. If through direct operation at the danger spots the government succeeds in checking price inflation, there will be no fattening of profit figures through sales as well as through a rise in the value of goods in business inventories. Hence there will be less occasion for ambitious trade union leaders to stage rounds of wage increases. The atmosphere will be calmed down and will in no way resemble the restless postwar transition years. The consuming public will neither be starved for goods nor as amply equipped with accumulated savings as it was from 1945 to 1948. Consequently its pressure on the government to intervene in areas of potential inflationary pressure will be considerably stronger than it was in those years. Here, as elsewhere, the demonstration of the willingness and ability of the government to bear down on unreasonable groups will show its fruits in the longer view. It will take less and less effort to arbitrate labor disputes and to prevent major strikes. Given a narrow margin for cyclical ups and downs, one of the thorniest problems of wage policy, namely, cuts of money wages, will be avoided. This is one of the brightest implications of firm standards of countercyclical action.

Admittedly, price and wage controls are beset with difficulties. Especially in peacetime there exists an ever-present danger of evasion, and this danger can never be fully eliminated but only kept within certain bounds. To be effective, price control must be combined with quality control, particularly when it comes to finished goods. Branding and nonprice competition furnish a leeway for implicit price increases, through shifting quality labels. By the same token, there can be virtual wage increases through deterioration in the quality of work and slowdowns. But the danger of both explicit and implicit price and wage increases is a formidable one only at the full-employment level. The development of black markets, and other forms of evasion of price and wage controls, is bound to be much less important in conjunction with a stabilization program which does not pursue the full-employment mark.

A program of selective price and wage controls is not sufficient to supplement the monetary and fiscal controls. Certain areas such as housing, foreign trade, foreign investment exhibit a pronounced tendency toward instability or are subject to influences from abroad over which a domestic stabilization program implemented by broad means has insufficient control. It would be naïve to think that fluctuations in the income or capital part of the international balance of payments caused by foreign initiative could be completely offset by variable taxes or by a variable public works program at home. To stabilize the activity of export industries by way of purely domestic income-supporting or curbing operations of this sort would presuppose a degree of adaptability of these industries that cannot be expected. An analogous argument can be made for the housing industry, or any other highly specialized field of activity which happens to be subject to pronounced swings. Because of specialization and immobility of factors it is questionable whether fluctuations in private housing could be properly offset by countercyclical variation in the volume of government outlay for bridges, dams, office buildings, and other projects necessitating building materials and labor.

Yet there are latent possibilities of differentiated and direct action behind the general formula of monetary-fiscal controls. To bring these possibilities into the open, and to suggest them as valuable features, cannot be done without a change in the traditional meaning of these controls. This presents a problem to those who are inclined to accept government controls only so long as they fit the pattern of indirect controls or who argue, for example, that the method of public works should be confined to traditionally accepted types of projects which normally do not interest private enterprise. If this way of thinking should adequately portray general public opinion on the subject, then further discussion would be of purely academic interest. However, actual practice is far ahead of conservative notions about the proper range of government investment. While this fact is no final criterion for forming views on desirable procedure it nevertheless lends some support to detached reasoning about what it might take, in the way of direct controls, to carry the economy safely through the launching phase of stabilization.

To begin with it should be borne in mind that certain discriminatory implications attach to any monetary and fiscal control if such control is worked hard. Thus a community cannot practice heavy relief without favoring those particular industries which produce items of mass consumption. Heavy variations in discount rates will have a stronger effect on small producing and merchandising firms than on large corporations, since the former depend more heavily on bank-credit than the latter. It takes only relatively mild changes in margin requirements for consumers' and speculative loans to produce discriminatory effects. Changes in margin requirements for consumers' loans are felt strongly by those industries which are accustomed to sell a considerable fraction of their output on an installment basis. Countercyclical work programs, while not capable of completely offsetting fluctuations in private construction, nevertheless are bound to have a greater influence on the output of cement, bricks, and steel than on the output of, let us say, automobiles and clothes. In short, there is no such thing as a central banking or budgetary control which has truly general and nondiscriminatory effects. This point is sometimes forgotten.

If we follow the somewhat treacherous path of accepted practice, we can proceed to some more pointed cases. Direct government control is an established fact in the areas of agriculture, public utilities, foreign trade, and foreign lending. In all these instances government attempts at overall cycle control furnish one, though not the only, guiding motive of control. In regard to agriculture one may envisage future need for direct stabilizing policies without approving of the present type of price-support system. Current thinking on the subject of reform of federal farm policy is characterized by proposals to restore competitive farm pricing and to diminish permanent removal of supplies from the market (Brannan Plan). But this is to be done on the basis of compensatory subsidization of producers for discrepancies between market price and some hypothetical price—surely a highly specific and direct control —brought in through the back door. Moreover, the old feature of crop control would not vanish from the scene.[10]

A good many stabilization experts single out the area of public utilities for purposes of direct countercyclical controls. Owing to the fact that these industries already belong in the category of mixed enterprises, the exercise of governmental influence over investment is less likely to create a major political issue, even if resistance to such influence on the part of the utilities themselves would have to be circumvented by the drastic method of government construction of competing publicly owned facilities. The purpose of the latter type of action is sometimes described as a twofold one: on the one hand, it may be an effort to stabilize the scale of total investment in this area; on the other, it may be an effort to reduce private monopoly through the expedient of governmental yardstick enterprise. Since the balance of efficiency is not always in favor of private operations, the latter purpose is by no means farfetched. Despite this fact it would probably be more judicious for the government merely to prevail on the timing of private investment outlay rather than to pursue the yardstick notion. If possible, further socialization in this field should be relegated to the role of an ultimate policy device, in which case it might still be effective on a threat basis.

In recent years, a most prominent area of direct controls has been international trade and lending. Even if we discount the idea that the international balance of payments can be made the central field for a plan to stabilize total domestic employment, there is room for centralized efforts to influence the timing and scale of private lending abroad without exercising an undue destabilizing influence on the rest of the world and without inviting, therefore, bad repercussions on domestic stability. When left alone in the past, American private net investment abroad—as far as it resulted from the

[10] A critical discussion is beyond the scope of this study.

balance of the items on current account—exercised some automatic stabilizing influence on aggregate private investment and employment in this country. There was a tendency toward an active balance on current account in depression (capital export), and a tendency toward a passive balance in prosperity (capital import). Hence it might seem that the purpose of government control would be merely to strengthen an already existing tendency. But inasmuch as this automatic tendency is injurious to foreign interest, there is reason to exercise caution at this point. Such control should not follow the convenient pattern of discouraging imports of foreign commodities during downswings through increased protective tariffs, import quotas, exchange depreciation, and the like. Nor should American exports be boosted in depression through subsidization, government guarantees of private loans abroad, etc. Rather, it should seek forms devoid of the danger of increasing instability abroad. Such forms are available for long-term lending abroad which is not associated with the movements of the balance on current account (so-called autonomous capital movements). What comes to mind is the possibility of government incentive or pressure affecting the scale and timing of such loans in connection with foreign resource development. This might be done through a variety of techniques, for example, by having the government offer incentives to shift the delivery date of loan-financed exports ahead or backwards depending on the tendencies of total private domestic investment.[11] Another method would be for our government to control American long-term lending by way of using its influence on borrowing nations, in the sense of persuading them to attune their borrowing from this country more closely to the American stabilization program. Considering the prominence of the American economy as a source of international lending and commodity supplies—a feature which will probably survive the reconstruction of European industrial centers—efforts

[11] Hart, *op.cit.*, p. 410.

of this sort are by no means farfetched. The hope for success does not rest entirely on the discretion and skill of American officials. If the ceiling for activity in this country were set so as to prevent cumulative price inflation, public control of private lending abroad would have the benefit of a binding yardstick for determining the maximum of such lending. Together with foreign interest in delaying buying in our markets when prices are high and are promised restoration on a lower scale, this may help in preventing American autonomous lending from becoming a destabilizer. During the period of reconstruction and restocking in Europe and elsewhere, foreign buying proceeded on a large scale despite the fact that American prices were rising fast, and the quality of the goods not always equal to peacetime standards. But the reasons for this hasty exhaustion of American loans and accumulated dollar balances (Latin American countries) were unique. They are not likely to persist in the future. There may be some ability, and certainly desire, on the part of foreign buyers to adjust their imports in accordance with the prices they have to pay in this market.

Under any conceivable conditions it is safe to say that for the visible future American private investment abroad will be subject to strong control on the part of the federal government. The era of purely private decision-making in this particular field seems to have come to an end. Foreign lending, especially in the case of long-term loans to retarded areas for resource development, is perhaps the most conspicuous example of cooperation between private and public parties which we now have, not to mention the fact that a very high percentage of American loans abroad are outright government loans. At present the American government is making a considerable effort to direct private American capital into economically retarded countries. Involved in this program are many agencies, among them the United Nations Economic and Social Council. Obviously, a program of this sort is designed to make room for variations in the scale of American foreign lending without undermining the stabilization plans of other important industrial nations. It can be arranged eventually to enable all industrial nations to participate in countercyclically adjusted capital exports into the retarded areas of the world.

In the field of low-cost housing, direct control already assumes the very tangible form of government construction, as well as tax incentives and subsidies for construction carried on by private enterprise. As the present housing bill (Taft Housing Bill) indicates, there is room here for countercyclical flexibility of such construction. Deliberate countercyclical timing might be carried to the point of trying to offset not only fluctuations in private low-cost construction as such, but also the effect of fluctuations in housing of the upper income groups on the total outlay for new houses. Since the housing of the upper income groups, left to itself, is bound to vary with the general business cycle, and since presumably nothing would be done directly to change this feature, low-cost housing might have to be greatly accelerated during downswings. Aside from outright government construction of low-rent houses, the scheme could be handled in the form of countercyclically varying subsidies and tax concessions to private companies engaged in low-rent housing. The recent change in the population trend toward a high birthrate greatly intensifies the area of low-cost housing as a source of investment demand, but it also suggests that here activity will have to be high at all times so that the desire for countercyclical variation will have to be balanced against the steady pressure of population growth.

For a peacetime stabilization program, the aforementioned parts of the economy are probably the only ones which either strongly call for direct controls or, as the case may be, have somehow become accessible to the use of such controls. At the risk of unwarranted generalization, the remainder of the economy may be said to offer only politically remote possibilities of direct intervention. This covers the construction of industrial plant, office buildings, durable equipment, and investment in the form of inventories. By and large the unsteadiness of private investment in industrial plant and equipment would have to be checked with the aid of broadly applied monetary and budgetary policies. Suggestions which go beyond this measure are probably premature, and possibly unnecessary. In conjunction with binding overall targets, the method of indirect stabilization of private investment in plant and equipment through consistent fiscal and credit operations might yield satisfactory results. It has been proposed that business firms should enter into contracts with the government according to which the latter would pay them some subsidy, or make tax concessions, in the event that investments, notified in advance to the government, are actually carried out on schedule. Moreover, in those instances in which the firms allow the government to determine the schedule, a substantially larger subsidy should be paid.[12] Such a system of contracts is an outgrowth from the debate on forecasting. Forecasting of private investment is to be given a more reliable basis. But while the general purpose is obvious, the execution of the plan would be extremely difficult. Businessmen are notoriously reluctant to reveal their investment plans, and even more reluctant to subject themselves to any commitments concerning the timing of changes in production methods and capacity. To overcome the resistance, the government might have to be so liberal with its subsidies or tax concessions as to threaten the private nature of the investments. Most probably a scheme of this sort would be nipped in the bud by the community of financially independent and politically powerful corporations. It involves, after all, a penalty for private investment

[12] Morris A. Copeland, "Business Stabilization by Agreement," *The American Economic Review*, June 1944, pp. 328-339.

which is not channeled through the system of contracts with the government.

Business cycle theory emphasizes the volatile character of inventory policy. This would seem to suggest great difficulties in trying to stabilize this type of investment. In an environment characterized by wide swings in activity and prices, attempts to control fluctuations in inventories through central banking methods have not been very successful. Here, perhaps, is a type of investment whose control must be attempted in roundabout fashion. Inventory accumulation rises and falls sharply as businessmen expect price rises or increased volumes of sales or fear the reverse. More precisely speaking, business expectations serve to increase the amplitude of inventory cycles and to shorten their length. Hence if expectations concerning the general scale of prices and the volume of sales can be given greater stability, shifts from inventory accumulation to depletion, and vice versa, can be expected to become less violent; the same is true, of course, of changes in income produced by inventory cycles. Since the stabilization of prices and sales is to be entrusted to broadly applied budgetary and monetary countercyclical measures, the situation with respect to inventories can be characterized as a case of roundabout control. Moreover, the movement of inventories is one of the first fields in which the expedient of binding limits for fluctuations in income and prices should yield self-enforcing results. The movements of inventories are not as strongly governed by basic destabilizing forces such as technological change as is investment in terms of business plant and equipment. The comparatively greater influence of purely speculative forces justifies the hope that considerable stabilizing effects can be achieved by stabilizing final sales, especially to consumers. This holds true all the more if the government can handle the critical spheres of the economy—agriculture, housing, the balance of international payments, collective bargaining—with the aid of a set of direct controls. Ideally, inventory movements might be confined to shifts from accumulation to depletion which result from the lag of changes in the rate of production behind changes in demand. Since the margin of tolerable fluctuations leaves some leeway for ups and downs in total effective demand and prices, there would be an irreducible minimum of inventory cycles on account of this lag as well as mildly speculative motivations.

All statements about the way in which the community should mix indirect and direct controls are, of course, highly conjectural. Past experience—and even tendencies which are now discernible—cannot furnish a trustworthy basis for predicting the kind of mixture of controls which would be called for in the event of greatly intensified stabilization efforts. It is conceivable that the initial need for direct controls would be more widespread than indicated above. On the other hand, the opposite might be true under the assumption of substantial improvements in the design and mode of operation of budgetary and credit controls, as well as of improvements in the nature of private response to such controls. If society goes so far as to endorse a program which embodies binding objectives and competitive reform, then there is reasonable justification for expecting more favorable response than could otherwise be anticipated.

CHAPTER 16

BINDING TARGETS AND ECONOMIC FREEDOM

....

Conflict of Objectives

ECONOMISTS are aware of potential conflict between short-run
and long-run economic goals. Impetuous pursuit of short-run
objectives may jeopardize long-run goals, and vice versa. There
is always some danger that concentration on means and ways
to control cyclical movements may lead to a neglect of such
commonly accepted long-range objectives as the desire for
economic freedom, equality of opportunities, and secularly rising living levels. Any sharpening of the standards of cycle control should be held against the background of these objectives
and great care should be taken in making certain that such
sharpening is compatible with their pursuit. The guiding
principle should be to find some optimal compromise between
the two sets of values. The task is complicated by the fact
that there exists potential conflict between the long-range objectives themselves. Thus efficiency and equality of opportunities are potentially inconsistent, depending on how far each
principle is carried. If what we want, first of all, is efficient
resource allocation and rising levels of living, we must be
prepared to make some sacrifice in regard to equality of economic opportunity and power. Equally, there exist potential
conflicts between efficiency and personal freedoms.

The formulation of a compromise between the various long-
run goals is no direct issue of countercyclical debate. This
problem should be solved independently. Once there exist
clarified ideas on this subject, short-run stabilization can be
attuned to these ideas. Such attunement involves careful

scrutiny of those parts of the stabilization program which embody drastic institutional change.

In the case of the present study, the most critical part is the proposed method of binding overall targets. In connection with our previous discussion of the margin of tolerable fluctuations, we have already made an attempt to show that secular progress in technology and living levels is not necessarily hampered by rigorous cycle control. Reconciliation of short-run stability with these values can be effected through the expedient of a liberal but nevertheless sharply defined spread between ceiling and floor. This expedient makes allowance for the lack of trustworthy knowledge about the impact of countercyclical action on growth. In this respect one must wait and see what happens after the economy has been forced to perform on a more even keel. Pessimism is premature; only caution is indicated. Surely no one will argue that in order to have growth, we must allow the economy to experience the full momentum of slumps, and to squeeze the last drop out of a speculative and inflationary boom. It is agreed that from a certain point on, depressions become meaningless for purposes of readjustment, and that the final stages of a boom add little, if anything, to a nation's economic welfare. Somewhere there is a limit to the possible usefulness of swings which even the most skillful defense of instability cannot ignore. Conceivably the limit is uncomfortably wide. If so, the worst that can happen is that a community which is preoccupied with a desire for a sharp narrowing of swings might have built floor and ceiling somewhat too close together. If it refuses to correct the error, then we may safely conclude that here—as is so often the case—it makes a compromise between conflicting values.

The method of leaving some leeway for swings suggests itself also from the viewpoint of economic freedom. It has been pointed out in our margin discussion that a liberal leeway for fluctuations would not only reduce the shock which can be expected to result from the adoption of binding targets, but that it would also leave the economy entirely to private decision-making as long as total activity stayed within the margin. However, these considerations fail to reach the core of the problem of the relationship between binding targets and economic freedom. This important subject needs further exploration.

The Problem of Economic Freedom

It is no secret that in a country characterized by a strong traditional respect for personal freedoms the discussion of stabilizing procedure is dominated by the consideration of the prospective effects of such procedure upon the liberal fundamentals of social and economic organization. In such a country every novel approach to stabilization is subject to scrutiny and resistance on this score. The introduction of the freedom factor into the subject of proper economic policy is a source of great trouble. Interpretations of the concept of freedom vary and so do, of course, the theories about the type of economic and social organization which are conducive to a maximum of freedom. Whether we like it or not, the concept is surrounded by connotations which vary in different historical periods. Most of the discussion on freedoms has only this much in common: it centers around the question of how to maximize freedom. Otherwise, through the ages, discussion has moved from one particular aspect to some other, depending on what seemed to be the most important goal at the time. Thus for a considerable period the discussion was dominated by the problem of the relationship between the individual and the state. In the classical body of thought we find the state presented as the chief potential menace to personal liberty. Viewed as a sovereign agent equipped with powers potentially inimical to individual freedom and welfare, the emphasis was clearly upon how, in the face of this indispensable agent, the individual could live in such a way as to enjoy a maximum of personal initiative and freedom. The pursuit of this problem produced the doctrine of the Rule of Law, often misrepresented and misunderstood. It is not always sufficiently appreciated that the true purpose of imperative rules is to eliminate arbitrary acts of the sovereign power. The proposal to subject the state—relative to the individual—to rational and commonly understood principles of action, goes hand in hand with an effort to define the proper area of governmental activity and control.

The outspokenly individualistic and libertarian background of the doctrine accounts, of course, for the well-known tendency to make this area as small as possible. But it is advisable to distinguish this tendency sharply from a broader purpose of the doctrine: to establish a clear boundary line between the public and private sectors of the economy. Conceivably, the boundary line may become subject to revision as time goes on, but if it does, such revision—according to the propounders of the doctrine—must always be based on explicit legislative action, and the new line must be adhered to as long as the law which defines it stands.

The doctrine is concerned not only with the relationship between the individual and the state, but also with the relationship between individuals. Despite the preoccupation of the classics with the menace of the state, competent expounders of the Rule of Law have given ample demonstration that they are aware of the potential menace of *private* concentration of economic power. The system of private enterprise which they advocate and defend against other forms of economic organization is a system of equal economic opportunity. In other words, it is a highly competitive system. Theirs is a case of maximizing freedom through having everyone accorded a well-defined area of economic and social freedom, as against an arrangement in which a few enjoy all the freedom there is. In the presentation of this ideal, some have gone far beyond the recommendation of drastic reduction of monopolistic powers. Their equalitarian pursuits have led them to attack large inheritance of wealth, regarding it as inconsistent with equality of opportunity and freedom. In so doing, they have exposed themselves to the charge of radicalism— often more so than their "progressive" opponents who, as far as the concentration of private economic power and industrial bigness is concerned, speak a language which is less offensive to large-scale business and its laissez-faire notions of economic freedom.

More recently, the discussion of economic freedom in the Anglo-Saxon world has turned toward the subject of freedom from want and insecurity (as against the classical freedoms of economic self-determination and self-reliance). In this modern approach to freedom, the problem of the relationship between the individual and the state was placed on an unmistakably different basis. Largely as a reaction against the past economic defects of an *allegedly* automatic arrangement, the state now appears as the chief hope for freedom of the masses. The amount of freedom enjoyed by the masses is held to stand in a direct relationship to the extent of governmental participation in the economic process. The government is to become an ever-active, intervening, and planning agent—the champion of the broad economically underprivileged groups. It is to secure for them the freedom from want and insecurity which unstable capitalism could not achieve. In this development, so we are told, the community must make allowance for a distinct degree of flexibility as to the ends and means of economic policy. It must be made possible for the masses of voters to keep shaping ends and means, to define and redefine them continuously in the light of changing problems. Government policy and the determination of the boundary line between private and public initiative are to become matters which at all times are to be left to the immediate control of voting majorities.

The preoccupation with the new concepts of freedom goes

hand in hand with a diminished interest, and even scornful treatment, of the types of economic freedom which motivate the advocate of capitalism, past and present. The right of a man to engage in business is not regarded as a basic freedom, on the theory that it is a right which only about one in five of our working force finds himself able, or finds it worthwhile, to accept.[1] This habit of viewing freedom of enterprise as a privilege of a few, and the inclination to appraise its value coldly or with suspicion, is accompanied with a remarkable laxity and indifference about the meaning of free enterprise. Perhaps it will not be regarded as childish to point out that freedom of enterprise means not only the right to engage in business but, in general, the right to determine for oneself how one is going to make a living, be it as a businessman, or welder, taxi-driver, physician, manager, book clerk, and so forth. If we keep this in mind, we cannot very well regard freedom of enterprise as the right of a minority. Furthermore, free enterprise in the best tradition stands for a competitive order. But the progressive liberal is either unwilling or unable to think of capitalism in terms other than the highly monopolistic capitalism which we now have. Since he views capitalism as a system of mammoth corporations and effectively organized groups of businessmen, his interpretation of what economic freedom means to the working man, and how to get these freedoms, points necessarily toward the establishment of powerful labor unions and labor pressure groups.

Offhand, it may seem that the current emphasis on freedom from want and insecurity is apt to lend momentum to the notion of making the government firmly responsible for overall economic stability. But the situation is not so simple as that, even as far as the attitude of organized labor is concerned. True, there has been some labor-minded agitation

[1] Theodore Morgan, *Income and Employment*, New York: Prentice Hall, 1947, p. 175.

for a government guarantee of full employment. Labor leaders themselves (CIO) appear glad to accept the benefits for workers involved in such a guarantee. But there are strong reasons to believe that they refuse certain logical strings attached. They fear the authority and power of government implied in the guarantee. This is proved by their consistent opposition to central wage controls. In regard to various labor laws which have been under discussion in recent years, they have made it amply clear that they resent central regulation of the type that would interfere with union power and activities. Their behavior is essentially the same as that of any other group: regulation is acceptable, and even welcome, as long as it applies to the other fellow.

In short: maintenance of continuous, active, and flexible control over national economic policy on the part of organized groups is still regarded as the essence of progressive liberalism. It stands in contrast to the method of having the public decide, once and for all, upon the objectives and means of national economic policy, and from there on to leave the matter in the hands of administrative officials. The vast majority of the public seems to fear the authority and power which goes with imperative objectives. It is afraid of an arrangement which might leave stabilization procedure in the hands of a fairly remote and potentially ruthless administrative group. At best the public, having once formulated and initiated a program, might fear that in the course of time the people would sit back and leave the job of stabilization to a group of experts whose operations could become esoteric and devoid of any checks, except lack of proper results. At worst, the public might find itself confronted with an increasingly highhanded, self-perpetuating bureaucracy which it might find very difficult to control and dislodge.

It would be very unwise to say that such fears are without foundation. By contrast, a loosely defined stabilization program appears free from such worries. If a nation refrains from

[233]

charging its government with a binding responsibility to stabilize the economy, it will maintain for itself the appearance of a democratic process. Everything is left open to debate. There will be ample opportunity for the constituency to set marks and to change them, to express certain ideals and principles, to make allowance for the continuous struggle between groups, to make compromises, to adjust ends and means to the changing political trend. There is no denying the fact, furthermore, that as long as the central administration is not charged with responsibility and authority to do certain things, and to do them firmly and reliably, the occasion for a show of power is reduced. There will never be the problem of the first difficult years. It will never be necessary to resort to a combination of economic reforms and of possibly harsh and unfamiliar means. There will never be any particular period during which the nation could be said to go through the trying process of launching stability, since there is no attempt at a clean break with the unstable past in this sort of program. There would be no comparable degree of compulsion to produce success. Despite the expected and approved general advance of government along many lines (social security, public works programs, tax management, minimum wage legislation, etc.), no strenuous stabilization effort would be made except, of course, when things go definitely wrong, i.e., during unmistakable slumps. Under those circumstances, however, public pressure for government intervention will be strong, and few questions will be asked about the nature of the controls. The situation will have the character of an emergency, and everything that is done to remedy it is bound to benefit politically from this fact. No bridges will have to be crossed; no sober and cold resolutions concerning future and permanent prevention of trouble will have to be taken.

Both sides of the argument have now been presented, and the case against binding rules is admittedly strong. In fact it looks as if the policy of loosely defined goals and means, so wanting in respect to the technical requisites of stabilization, derives its value and strength from the angle of human freedom. But its appeal from this viewpoint is more emotional than reasoned. This easy and noncommittal approach is ultimately dangerous even for our cherished freedoms. Loose standards of countercyclical policy, and uncertainty about the timing and extent of governmental stabilizing efforts, provide no adequate foundation for the very freedoms which dominate current discussion, namely, the freedoms from insecurity and want. As long as a community allows slumps to occur and gets ready with countervening measures only after unemployment has reached alarming proportions, there can be no claim that fears of want and insecurity have vanished. Loose procedure is also indicative of unwillingness to offer resistance to increasingly intractable booms. The chances, then, are that each time severe production dislocations and price dispersions will be allowed to occur. These developments are bound to lend momentum to the ensuing downswings. Each time, large portions of the public would be subjected to apprehension about the probable extent of the deterioration of markets and jobs. Let us recall that there exists an unfortunate connection between ill-timed intervention and the effectiveness of compensatory controls. Frantic last-minute efforts to stem the tide of a swing are poison even to the best-conceived monetary and fiscal weapons. They may have to be overworked. The stage will be set for public clamor for new, more specific, and drastic controls. From the standpoint of freedoms little comfort could be derived from the thought that the change toward more coercive devices might proceed in a wave of revolutionary enthusiasm and hence could be construed as a perfectly democratic way of doing things. If we let ourselves get to the point of despair over previously tried methods and policies, our sense of values might become temporarily distorted, much to the detriment of our long-range interests, and perhaps irreparably so.

Even if society should refrain from endorsing radical institutional change, and should prefer to adhere to the controls which now are acceptable or within reach, the method of loose standards would eventually lead to a point at which our freedoms are in jeopardy. The economy would become top-heavy in the direction of government enterprise. Repeated efforts to build up the valleys with the help of relatively overworked means—extensive public works programs accompanied by secularly rising national debt—would push back the private sector of the economy and, therefore, the area within which the traditional economic freedoms prevail.

These observations contain the material from which a *conservative* interpretation of the method of mandatory stabilization procedure can be built. Adoption of a firm program *prior* to the "peril-point" of general public despair over previously tried methods of control, and over capitalism itself, furnishes an opportunity to concentrate on measures which are in harmony with the desire for preserving our old freedoms and giving our new ones a firm basis. Surely there can be no doubt about the ultimate intent of the method of binding rules. The method has been aptly described as "framework-incentive planning."[2] This term suggests a system of rules designed to direct the incentives for private decision-making toward overall stability and a proper balance between industries. Where there is room for private decision-making, there is room for freedom. The power to make decisions is almost synonymous with freedom, and a program which appeals to private initiative is freedom-oriented.

The only thing which is at all controversial about the expedient of rules is the launching period. In this respect it must be admitted that the approach amounts to a *calculated risk*. It is possible that over the fear of central regimentation the public would never endorse a system of imperative goals, or that initial experience under such a system would be such

---

[2] Hart, *Money, Debt, and Economic Activity*, *op.cit.*, p. 420.

that the effort will soon be given up or allowed to deteriorate. Awareness of these troubles can do much to avoid such a debacle. A tangible basis for alleviating public fear of loss of freedoms lies in the decision to abstain from imperative standards which would give the government an excuse for *uninterrupted* use of sharp controls. The floor must not be so high as to throw the initiative for maintaining it in the lap of government. It must be low enough to be sustainable, over the average of years, by private investment and privately generated income. Producers must be kept responsive to incentives of profit and loss. They must not be so dependent on government, so subsidized or so regimented, that their policies become indifferent to commercial incentives characteristic of private enterprise. In looking into the future, a generous leeway for unhampered private decision-making should be given, for the sake of keeping alive the spirit of personal responsibility for one's actions.

Nevertheless, the adoption of a margin of tolerable fluctuations fails to reach the heart of the problem of the relationship between binding targets and personal freedom. From the standpoint of our libertarian ideals, the expedient of a margin is merely a stopgap. It would serve to carry society through the difficult first few years without a risk of alarming loss of freedom in connection with the government's mandatory operations.

In the long view, a much more convincing case can be made about the protection of freedom in a community which resorts to imperative standards of stabilization. Ultimately, the subject of freedoms coincides with that of self-enforcement of the framework of rules. The stronger the development of persuasive effects, the more it will be true that scale and composition of national product are determined by rational economic choice on the part of producers and consumers.

In the judgment of the writer, this is the only logical approach to the subject of how to maximize our traditional economic freedoms. The political sobriety of the approach—the discipline and temperance which it imposes upon pressure groups and political parties in the form of lasting acceptance of a once formulated and adopted program—will undoubtedly be regarded as uncomfortable. But there is no other road to reconciling stabilization with capitalistic freedoms.

Moreover, it must not be forgotten that the approach necessitates merely a partial sacrifice of prevailing political prerogatives and practices of legislatively organized groups. Lasting acceptance of a once formulated and adopted program not only permits, but actually demands, active group support in Congress when it comes to mapping out a proper compensatory implementation. This holds true not only for the launching phase but also, to some extent, for subsequent times. The case of an eventually neutral government (complete self-enforcement of the framework of rules) must be dismissed as unrealistic.

Just as the compensatory action necessitates the active support and devotion of legislatively organized groups, so does eventual self-enforcement need the initiative of economic organizations which stand behind the broad legislative groups such as individual trade unions, trade associations, cooperatives, chambers of commerce, etc. It would be naïve to think that the self-sustaining stability should be predicated on purely individual economic motivation. Potentially, self-enforcement can be greatly aided by bodies which control substantial portions of industry, trade, and labor. Both breadth and timing of private action against depression will be improved. Wherever these bodies are relied upon for maintaining stable markets and job opportunities, economic freedom assumes the form of mildly collectivistic self-determination. There is nothing wrong with this, provided these organisms do not in themselves (i.e., even without their legislative superstructures or political parties) become so strong and willful that their policies prove to be an insuperable obstacle to achieving the goals embodied in the community's stabilization program. Public policy must find a way of securing the advantages which private control of substantial portions of the economy can give to self-enforcement, through a judicious mixture of competitive reform and selective specified controls.

Some issue of freedoms arises also in connection with the enforcement of competitive practices. In our discussion of this part of the program, it was duly emphasized that measures should be taken slowly. Together with the adoption of reasonably modest standards for competitive reform, slowness of action would serve to make this part less worrisome from the viewpoint of interference with deeply entrenched notions of freedom of enterprise. Despite the fact that competitive reform is precisely what it takes to accomplish the ideals of true freedom of enterprise and equality of opportunities, cautious procedure is indicated in the interest of the chance to make progress at all. The truth is that even the best conceived policy can become a failure if it is pressed too hard. If competitive reform were pressed into a short interval, the purpose of freedom would be served in such painful manner that few persons, if any, could see the advantage of the measure. Nothing should be done to add to the already precarious state of the types of freedoms which are involved here. To allow them to regain significance and public appreciation in a world which is preoccupied with the concepts of freedom from want and insecurity, they must be enforced in such a way that their virtues overshadow the discomfort of enforcement—and this means judicious procedure which begins with an attack on the most obnoxious monopolistic practices and arrangements.

The gap left by slowness (and by exceptions) creates, of course, a problem of substitute measures in the form of specific intervention. These controls may also come in conflict with accepted standards of economic freedom. But two things must be kept in mind. First, these controls will probably be among us even if no imperative stability targets are adopted. They will become necessary whenever the loosely defended goals permit the development of severe off-balances which can be handled only with drastic measures. Secondly, the gap must not be regarded as an excuse for introducing all sorts of freedom-restricting direct controls. Whereas the pursuit of competitive reform should go on at all times, an attempt should be made to confine the use of coercive wage, price, and production controls to intervals of extreme disturbance. The difference in procedure is suggested by the fact that direct controls cannot be brought in line with the drive toward individual economic initiative and self-reliance in contrast to competitive reform, whose function is to provide the minimum safeguards for freedom and equality of opportunities, and to economize the use of specified intervention.

There is always some danger that a slow attack on anticompetitive practices may lose some of its effectiveness since the direction of the attack is known beforehand by those against whom it is to be launched. Hence the frequent argument that the pursuit of libertarian and equalitarian goals should be entrusted not only to formalized antitrust procedure, but to a multiple set of incentives, pressures, and coercive forms of action covering all phases of governmental policy-making. It would be hopeless to deny that any particular device may to some extent become neutralized by private circumvention, so that shifts in the method of attack are indicated. For example, equalization of economic power might have to be entrusted not only to competitive reform but also to higher taxation of inherited wealth, or to any other suitable specific intervention with present inequality. Yet awareness of the ever-present danger of circumvention of any particular regulatory device should lead to something besides a multiple choice of means. It should also result in a steady improvement of this particular device itself. Thus the attack on anticompetitive practices should become the subject of continuous adaptive improvement and quick shifts in incidence of action so as to keep up with private ingenuity. Under these circumstances, there is hope that the danger of diminishing effectiveness can be avoided. It might then be possible to obtain progressively favorable results on a mere argumentative basis. Such development of voluntarism would be highly welcome from the viewpoint of economy in intervention.

To sum up: If we really want to know how a stabilization program promises to work out in regard to freedoms, it is always advisable to view the program primarily in the long run. Short-run appraisals are bound to furnish only very limited—and perhaps distorted—answers. The reason why the method of loose standards possesses libertarian appeal is that at no particular point in time the community makes an effort to break away from the unstable past with boldly conceived means. The government would not be forced to give definite priority to the stabilization issue. There would be no urgent problem of integrating public policies toward this formidable objective. Failure to make any decisive progress toward cycle control can always be given a somewhat benevolent interpretation by presenting it as a symptom of the free and easy way in which a democracy works, with all the diversity of interests and influences that goes into legislation and its interpretation at the administrative center. Since nothing decisive seems to happen at any particular interval of time, the subject of the fate of freedoms—both economic and political— normally fails to impress itself upon the mind of the community. Critics of the method are forced to refer to the gradual and perhaps insidious character of the threat to freedom, or to point to the possibility of sudden institutional change occasioned by failure to cope with major economic collapse.

CHAPTER 17

SUMMARY OF THE MAIN PROBLEMS AND CONCLUSIONS

....

For the reader who wishes to obtain a quick impression of the content of this study, the following summary of the main problems and conclusions is offered:

1. For some time now there has been an unfortunate tendency in certain circles to intermingle problems of economic stabilization with problems of economic stagnation. To avoid confusion, the subject of economic instability and of methods designed to overcome this instability has to be freed from the entanglements of the stagnation doctrine. It has to be presented as a problem of intermittent ups and downs of total business activity. In other words, it has to be focused on the so-called business cycle.

The stagnant economy offers only relatively unimportant problems of short-run instability. Its chief threat is that of a woefully low but comparatively stable level of activity. Measures designed to banish stagnation from the scene are not stabilization measures. Where they assume the form of a proposed direct onslaught on the forces of stagnation, the result, logically, would be a return to the dynamic pattern of capitalism associated by stagnationists with the nineteenth and beginning twentieth century. This intended result is precisely the point at which genuine discussion of instability and of countercyclical procedure starts. Where, on the other hand, the measures against stagnation are meant to be of the compensatory or offsetting type, we usually have nothing but proposals to lift activity from a low but fairly stable level to a higher and at the same time more precarious level. This, again, is not stabilization but perhaps a way of inviting a novel type of instability. It should be made clear whether or to what extent the possible instabilities involved in an attempt to lift activity to the full-employment level through more or less continuous income-supporting operations are the same type of instabilities which characterize the history of the private-enterprise system. In the opinion of the writer, an analysis of this problem cannot help but show that the character of the instability problem undergoes a remarkable change. Instead of being primarily concerned with the instability of the private-enterprise *economy*, the proponents of a program of perpetual income-supporting operations have to concentrate mainly upon the *political* infirmities of the governmental full-employment machinery. The mind of these writers is preoccupied with the question of how such a system of controls could be instituted in a way which minimizes the danger that the proposed controls will break down or be abandoned because of insufficient and lasting political support. We need only remind the reader of the issue of cumulative governmental deficits and a growing national debt. This issue does not arise, at least not with the same degree of seriousness, in regard to a cyclically dynamic economy where fiscal and other controls are meant to be reversible and where, for example, periods of deficit finance may be offset by periods of surplus finance and a reduction of debt.

2. Logically, countercyclical procedure should mean a direct attack on the forces of cyclical ups and downs. But policy-making along this line is hampered by the fact that we have no trustworthy knowledge about the nature of these forces. Only certain phases of the problem are sufficiently known to permit intelligent action of this type. Hence the chief formula for stabilization will inevitably have to be compensatory procedure. This implies stability in terms of the sum of private and public economic activity, rather than stability of total private activity alone.

If we aspire to such a thing as an essentially self-sustaining state of overall stability based on private investment and privately generated income, then the only hopeful avenue toward this state—in the eyes of this writer—is the resort to a binding objective for centrally administered stabilizing (compensatory) action. Such a mandatory objective may *eventually* tend to become self-enforcing so that the burden resting on the compensatory machinery can be diminished.

3. A program of this sort can embody whatever reliable knowledge we have about the nature of destabilizing forces. In at least two important respects the compensatory approach does involve a direct attack on causes. These causes are psychological factors (unstable expectations) and the presence of institutional conditions which facilitate cumulative monetary spirals.

4. The idea of reaching a state of self-sustaining balance through ultimately self-enforcing rigorous governmental commitments is not novel. It is known, especially, from the writings of Professor Henry C. Simons and his collaborators. But so far it has been presented in the rather narrow and one-sided terms of a proposal for a rigorous stable-money rule. A great deal of a priori reasoning about the true meaning of capitalism, as well as a predominantly monetary explanation of cycles, appears to enter into this particular choice. In the present study, no effort is made to emulate this procedure. There will be no a priori statements concerning the logical line of demarcation between the governmental and the private sectors of the economy. If the formula of a binding governmental objective of overall stabilizing procedure is hopeful from the standpoint of eventual self-enforcement, it is so not only for the case of a stable-money rule but also for such appealing and in some ways more forceful and comprehensive objectives as a stable total product, or stable employment (though not necessarily full employment).

5. In the United States as well as elsewhere, a great deal of intellectual effort has been poured into the design of so-called automatic stabilizing devices. In most instances, however, automatism appears synonymous with procedurally streamlined, mechanical, or fully routinized patterns of operations (governmental automatic management). In the writer's opinion this search for mechanical, built-in stabilizing gadgets is of only very limited value. Since these devices begin to operate only after the economy has gone off-balance, and since they are usually so weak as to wear out in the process of supporting total activity before the prevailing trend of activity is reversed, we shall probably never be able to obtain a tolerable degree of stability in this fashion. The devices should be considered only as a last resort, i.e., when it should become clear beyond any doubt that the method of a binding overall objective is not acceptable to the public.

Moreover, from the standpoint of a predominantly private system of enterprise, the ultimate meaning and surely the ultimate purpose of economic automatism is the achievement of an environment in which the decisions and actions of the private individuals themselves (as producers and consumers) are such that the result will be an essentially self-sustaining equilibrium. Hence, instead of interpreting automatism in the direction of governmental automatic management of centrally instituted controls, it is better to bring the concept of automatism back to the traditional theory of equilibrating market forces.

This proposition is likely to meet with fairly widespread sympathy as regards that one half of the stabilization problem which concerns proper allocation of resources and the achievement of an inter-industry balance. In this respect, it may be taken for granted that society must rely on the rules of competition which, if carefully defined and enforced, promise reliable, predictable, nonpolitical, and nondiscretionary—in a word, automatic—actions and results. But as regards the subject of overall stabilization—the other half of the problem—the theory of automatism remains relatively unexplored and highly controversial. Many contemporary advocates of automatism seem convinced that the achievement of overall stability (countercyclical policy) rests on the shoulders of government which, through continuous off-setting action, must try to force the economy to work on an even keel. But to make this proposition compatible with automatism, they attempt to design administratively routinized stabilizing devices. Yet it seems to this writer that the formula for automatic overall stability is fundamentally the same as it is for resource allocation and the achievement of an inter-industry balance. Here as well as there, the road to automatism is the setting of binding rules. Concretely speaking, the only hopeful approach to an essentially self-sustaining overall balance is the adoption of a clearcut, commonly understood and enforceable objective as to the level of total activity at which the economy is to operate. This, in itself, is not yet automatism. It is a preliminary step. Automatism enters if and when the adopted norm begins to work on an argumentative basis. The purpose of the mandatory target is to establish public confidence that fluctuations in total activity will not be tolerated. To establish such confidence, the government must be able to demonstrate ability to make the norm true. Hence the government must be given adequate powers to reach and defend the goal. Once such ability has been demonstrated, the producers and consumers will have a strong incentive to behave in such a way as materially to reduce the size of the government's compensatory measures.

It is this author's firm conviction that ability to make the norm come true necessitates skillful, essentially discretionary use of the controls which such a mandatory program provides. All we can do to prevent or minimize the element of discretion is to prevent discretionary *goal-setting* at the administrative center, and perpetual legislative opportunism concerning the goal. We can also minimize discretion through inclusion in the mandate of a section specifying eligible means. If we agree that what counts is confidence on the part of the public that a formally adopted goal will be effectively defended, then we must accept, in the bargain, the delegation of broad and permissive power to the executive arm of government in regard to the application (timing, etc.) of these means.

It is only fair to point out that the method of a binding objective of stability may involve, initially, such a show of power on the part of government as to arouse fears of collectivism. This possibility must not be dismissed lightly. To begin with, the method of binding norms is by no means logically confined to stabilization efforts concerning the system of private enterprise. It could be adopted in a system in which all ownership and control of resources is public. Everything depends on the nature and purpose of the rules, of course. Only if the rules are of a certain kind and purpose (such as, for example, competition) will it be possible to give the method a conservative interpretation. But since, in any event, the road to self-enforcement is an arduous one, great care should be taken to avoid the outcome that a program which is ultimately meant to emphasize private enterprise will arouse public consternation and fear. This study recommends the resort to gradual procedure. Gradual procedure here means primarily the adoption of an initially liberal (though well-defined) margin of tolerable fluctuations, and an attempt to slowly narrow it as the economy acquires increasing inherent stability. Analogous reasoning holds for the initial standards of competition.

The method clearly involves a calculated risk from the standpoint of the preservation of individual economic freedoms. By contrast, the aforementioned mechanical compensatory devices imply that the government will at all times be involved in the task of supporting or curbing private activity, no matter how much the element of governmental discretion is removed from the devices, and no matter how firmly they are built into the economy. There is little consolation in the fact that the role of government would be a passive one, in the sense that the government is made to buy something (or to make transfer payments) on stated terms open to all comers who qualify under the terms of the arrangement. Merely to make these gadgets work "on the level of a bank teller rather than on that of a bank president" is no formula for minimizing the area of government influence. In the extreme, a totally socialized system could be run in the fashion of automatic management. Only if the presence of these gadgets had an indirect stabilizing effect by creating a psychological climate favorable to stability—in the sense that they would lead to patterns of private expectations and actions conducive to even-keel performance of the economy—would there be such a thing as a chance for gradually reducing the size of central compensatory action. As it is, however, these devices are normally too weak to create confidence in their ability to break the momentum of swings.

6. All efforts at stabilization involve central planning. The planning aspect can only be concealed, or perhaps genuinely reduced, but not really removed. It can be concealed by statements to the effect that a true system of private enterprise must have a guaranteed stable value of money and that measures purporting to give us such stable money are merely in the nature of removing anomalies from the system. There is no such thing as establishing stable money without, *pari passu*, stabilizing total production and employment at some premeditated planned level.

The planning aspect can be *minimized*, however, through avoidance of a quick transition to strict even-keel performance of the economy. If society resorts to the expedient of a margin of tolerable fluctuations, it will still be necessary to make arbitrary decisions about the height of floor and ceiling, but within the margin the economy will be allowed to seek its own level of activity.

7. In all probability, the method of setting binding limits for swings will have to be implemented by indexes measuring national aggregates rather than complex relationships between the components of national product or income payments. These indexes, after all, must be relatively simple so as to be understood by the general public as a representative measure of overall activity, and must also facilitate quick assemblage and computation of statistical data so as to enable the authorities to inform the public frequently about economic conditions. Once such indexes are embodied in the mandate, a basis is laid for counteraction of swings by the business community itself. If the indexes show that total activity begins to break through the limits, then the general knowledge that the government is committed to offset these deviations will stimulate private action which, by itself, tends to restore activity at levels commensurable with the established ceiling and floor. It will be economically rational for private industry to scramble back to positions compatible with ceiling or floor.

The development of self-enforcing features of the method of binding limits is not likely to occur until the government has demonstrated its ability to defend the limits with compensatory action that proceeds without the benefit of argumentative effects of the guaranteed floor and ceiling. Therefore, ample provision for compensatory controls must be made for the first few difficult years. Even afterwards, the size of actual compensatory operations would probably be diminished rather than come down to the point of mere token operations.

8. The defense of binding limits with the aid of broadly applied (indirect) monetary and fiscal controls must not be construed to mean the entire program. It can be supplemented, if necessary, by more specific action. The stabilizing authorities, on the basis of tested theories concerning healthy

relationships between the components of national product (for example, investment and consumption), could combine their defense of overall targets with the establishment of such relationships for the purpose of maintaining internal balance of the economy. This they could do by pointed use of monetary and fiscal controls. In addition, a set of outright direct controls might be needed.

Generally speaking, the method of imperative overall norms need not, and should not, lead to a deterioration in our standards of knowledge about cycles and cycle control. There is no reason why the mandatory program—a mere minimum program—could not be accompanied and improved by continuous research about cycle causation and conditions of internal balance. On the basis of such research, future compensatory action could be improved.

National income measurements are probably too slow to furnish indexes for the defense of floor and ceiling. National income analysis, however, can furnish knowledge of how past compensatory policies have worked out. The knowledge gained should enter into the mapping out of future compensatory operations.

9. There is no such thing as pure compensatory action, or —on the other hand—pure cause removal. Compensatory action which is successful in the sense that the sum of private and government activity (employment) remains stable is bound to contribute heavily to cause removal. It can claim for itself removal of psychological destabilizing forces (particularly unstable expectations) as well as of institutional factors detrimental to stability (especially in the monetary field). The development of cumulative tendencies—the most serious aspect of cycles—promises to be substantially weakened by a determined compensatory program. Equally, the cause removal approach usually contains implicit elements of central planning of the equilibrium level, such as the determination of the level

of prices at which stable money (monetary cycle theory) is to be achieved.

10. Throughout the study an effort has been made to keep short-run stabilization in harmony with the pursuit of long-range objectives, especially the maintenance of economic freedoms, secular growth of living levels, and equalization of economic opportunity.

The currently emphasized freedoms from want and insecurity are sufficiently protected by the binding overall standards of stability suggested in this study. In the long view, the fate of the classical economic freedoms—private property, private power of decision-making as producers and consumers —is also closely linked with the method of binding rules. Eventual self-enforcement of the rules promises a workable maximum of private enterprise. The two things are almost synonymous. By contrast, the method of loose standards, permitting the development of severe states of slumps and calling for government action of the most desperate and gigantic dimensions, may gradually lead to collectivization of the economy.

There exists uncertainty about the impact of determined cycle control on secular progress and rising living levels. In this respect, the adoption of a liberal margin of tolerable fluctuations, rather than a program seeking strict even-keel performance, would make it possible for society to gain experience about the relationship between short-run stabilization and growth, without the need for costly revisions in cycle control. In addition, there exists a distinct possibility that gradually the business community will learn to free itself of the feverish pattern of unbridled booms and their contagious influence on venturesomeness so that we may enjoy, in the long view, as much improvement in our capacity to produce as we have had in the past, or perhaps more.

Inequality of economic opportunity and power would be substantially reduced beneath present proportions by a gradual attack on anticompetitive practices and arrangements, embodying reasonable standards of competition. Competition, also, is still indispensable for efficient resource allocation, as well as for the preservation of the traditional capitalistic ideals of freedom of enterprise and consumers' choice.

BIBLIOGRAPHY

Achinstein, Asher: *Introduction to Business Cycles*, Thomas Y. Crowell Co., New York, 1950

American Economic Association, Committee of: *Readings in Business Cycle Theory*, Blakiston, Philadelphia, 1944

Angell, James W.: *Investment and Business Cycles*, McGraw-Hill Book Co., 1941

Bach, George L.: "Monetary-Fiscal Policy, Debt Policy, and the Price Level," *The American Economic Review*, May, 1947

Beveridge, W. H.: *Full Employment in a Free Society*, W. W. Norton & Co., New York, 1945

Blough, Roy: "Political and Administrative Requisites for Achieving Economic Stability," *American Economic Review*, Papers and Proceedings, May 1950

Boulding, Kenneth: "In Defense of Monopoly," *The Quarterly Journal of Economics*, Vol. 59, 1944-1945

Clark, J. M.: *Strategic Factors in Business Cycles*, National Bureau of Economic Research, New York, 1934

————: *Economics of Planning Public Works: A Study Made for the National Planning Board*, Government Printing Office, Washington, 1935

————: *Social Control of Business*, rev. ed., University of Chicago Press, Chicago, 1939

————: "Financing High-Level Employment," *Financing American Prosperity*, Twentieth Century Fund, New York, 1945

Committee for Economic Development: *Taxes and the Budget*, November, 1947

————: *Monetary and Fiscal Policy for Greater Economic Stability*, December, 1948

Copeland, Morris A.: "Business Stabilization by Agreement," *American Economic Review*, June, 1944

Dillard, Dudley: *The Economics of John Maynard Keynes*, Prentice-Hall, New York, 1948

Domar, E. D.: "Expansion and Employment," *American Economic Review*, March, 1947

Economic Report of the President, together with the Annual Economic Review of the Council of Economic Advisers, Washington, D.C., 1948, 1949, 1950

Edwards, Corwin D.: *Maintaining Competition: Requisites of a Governmental Policy*, McGraw-Hill Book Company, New York, 1947

Ellis, Howard S.: "Economic Expansion through Competitive Markets," *Financing American Prosperity*, Twentieth Century Fund, New York, 1945

Estey, J. A.: *Business Cycles*, Prentice-Hall, Inc., New York, 1941

Fellner, William: *Monetary Policies and Full Employment*, University of California Press, Berkeley, 1946

Fisher, Irving: *Booms and Depressions*, Adelphi Co., New York, 1932

Gayer, A. D. (Ed.): *The Lessons of Monetary Experience: Essays in Honor of Irving Fisher*, Farrar & Rinehart, Inc., New York, 1937

Graham, Benjamin: *Storage and Stability*, McGraw-Hill Book Company, New York, 1937

————: *World Commodities and World Currency*, McGraw-Hill Book Company, New York, 1944

Graham, Frank D.: *Social Goals and Economic Institutions*, Princeton University Press, 1942

Haberler, Gottfried: *Prosperity and Depression*, League of Nations, Geneva, and Columbia University Press, New York, 1941

Hansen, Alvin H.: *Full Recovery or Stagnation?* W. W. Norton & Co., New York, 1938

————: *Fiscal Policy and Business Cycles*, W. W. Norton & Co., New York, 1941

————: *Monetary Theory and Fiscal Policy*, McGraw-Hill Book Company, New York, 1949

————: *Business Cycles and National Income*, W. W. Norton & Co., New York, 1951

————: "Stability and Expansion," *Financing American Prosperity*, Twentieth Century Fund, New York, 1945

Harris, Seymour E. (Ed.): *Postwar Economic Problems*, McGraw-Hill Book Company, New York, 1943

————: *Inflation and the American Economy*, McGraw-Hill Book Company, New York, 1945

Harrod, R. F.: *The Trade Cycle*, Clarendon Press, Oxford, England, 1936

————: *Towards a Dynamic Economics*, Macmillan and Co., Ltd., London, 1948

Hart, Albert G.: *Money, Debt, and Economic Activity*, Prentice-Hall, Inc., New York, 1948

————: "Model Building and Fiscal Policy," *American Economic Review*, September, 1945

Hawtrey, R. G.: *Good and Bad Trade*, Constable Co., Ltd., London, 1913

————: *Currency and Credit*, Longmans, Green & Co., New York, 1923

————: *Monetary Reconstruction*, Longmans, Green & Co., New York, 1923

————: *Capital and Employment*, Longmans, Green & Co., New York, 1947

————: *The Gold Standard in Theory and Practice*, Longmans, Green & Co., New York, 1947

Hayek, Frederick: *Prices and Production*, George Routledge & Sons, Ltd., London, 1931

————: *Monetary Theory and the Trade Cycle*, Harcourt, Brace & Co., New York, 1932

————: *Profits, Interest and Investment*, George Routledge & Sons, Ltd., London, 1939

————: "A Commodity Reserve Currency," *Economic Journal*, June-September, 1943

Hicks, J. R.: *Value and Capital*, Oxford University Press, Cambridge, England, 1939

————: *A Contribution to the Theory of the Trade Cycle*, Clarendon Press, Oxford, England, 1950

Hobson, John A.: *The Economics of Unemployment*, Allen & Unwin, Ltd., London, 1922

Homan, P. T., and Machlup, F. (Eds.): *Financing American Prosperity*, Twentieth Century Fund, New York, 1945

Income, Employment and Public Policy: Essays in Honor of Alvin H. Hansen, W. W. Norton & Company, Inc., New York, 1948

Kaldor, N.: "Stability and Full Employment," *Economic Journal*, December, 1938

————: "A Model of the Trade Cycle," *Economic Journal*, March, 1940

Kalecki, M.: *Economics of Full Employment*, Blackwell, Oxford, England, 1944

Keynes, J. M.: *Treatise on Money*, Harcourt, Brace & Co., New York, 1924

————: *General Theory of Employment, Interest and Money,* Harcourt, Brace & Co., New York, 1936

Kuznets, Simon: *National Income and Capital Formation,* 1919-1935, National Bureau of Economic Research, New York, 1937

————: *National Income and its Composition,* Vol. I, National Bureau of Economic Research, New York, 1941

————: *National Income, A Summary of Findings,* National Bureau of Economic Research, New York, 1946

League of Nations: *Economic Stability in the Post-War World,* Report of the Delegation on Economic Depressions, Geneva, 1945

Lerner, A. P.: *Economics of Control,* The Macmillan Company, New York, 1944

————: *Economics of Employment,* McGraw-Hill Book Company, New York, 1951

Metzler, Lloyd: "Business Cycles and the Modern Theory of Employment," *American Economic Review,* June, 1946

————: "Three Lags in the Circular Flow of Income," *Income, Employment and Public Policy: Essays in Honor of Alvin H. Hansen,* W. W. Norton & Co., Inc., New York, 1948

Mints, Lloyd W.: *Monetary Policy for a Competitive Society,* McGraw-Hill Book Company, New York, 1950

Mitchell, Wesley: *Business Cycles,* University of California Press, Berkeley, 1913

————: *Business Cycles, the Problem and its Setting,* National Bureau of Economic Research, New York, 1927

Monetary Credit and Fiscal Policies (Douglas Report), Senate Document No. 129, 81st Congress, 2nd Session, Washington, D.C., 1950

Morgan, Theodore: *Income and Employment,* Prentice-Hall, Inc., New York, 1947

Musgrave, Richard A.: Public Finance and Full Employment, *Postwar Economic Studies, Board of Governors, Federal Reserve System,* Washington, 1945

Myrdal, Gunnar: *Monetary Equilibrium,* W. Hodge & Co., Ltd., London, 1939

Ohlin, Bertil: *The Problem of Employment Stabilization,* Columbia University Press, New York, 1949

Oxford University, Institute of Statistics: *The Economics of Full Employment: Six Studies in Applied Economics,* Blackwell, Oxford, England, 1944

Pierson, J. H. G.: *Full Employment*, Yale University Press, New Haven, 1941

Pigou, A. C.: *Employment and Equilibrium*, Macmillan & Co., Ltd., London, 1941

———: "Employment Policy and Sir William Beveridge," *Agenda*, August, 1944

Robertson, D. H.: *Banking Policy and the Price Level*, P. S. King & Son, Ltd., Westminster, 1926

———: *Essays in Monetary Theory*, P. S. King & Son, Ltd., Westminster, 1940

Ruggles, Richard: *National Income and Income Analysis*, McGraw-Hill Book Company, New York, 1949

Samuelson, Paul A.: "Full Employment After the War," Chapter II in *Post-War Economic Problems*, McGraw-Hill Book Company, New York, 1943

Schultz, T. W.: *Agriculture in an Unstable Economy*, McGraw-Hill Book Company, New York, 1945

Schumpeter, J. A.: *Theory of Economic Development*, Harvard University Press, Cambridge, 1934

———: *Business Cycles*, McGraw-Hill Book Company, New York, 1939

Simons, Henry: *Economic Policy for a Free Society*, University of Chicago Press, Chicago, 1948

———: "On Debt Policy," *The Journal of Political Economy*, 1944

Slichter, S. H.: *Towards Stability*, Henry Holt & Co., New York, 1934

———: "Public Policies and Post-War Employment," *Financing American Prosperity*, Twentieth Century Fund, New York, 1945

Smithies, Arthur: "Full Employment in a Free Society," *American Economic Review*, June, 1945

Terborgh, George: *The Bogey of Economic Maturity*, Machinery and Allied Products Institute, Chicago, 1945

Wicksell, Knut: *Geldzins und Güterpreise*, Gustav Fisher, Jena, 1898

———: *Interest and Prices*, Macmillan & Co., Ltd., London, 1936

Williams, J. H.: "Free Enterprise and Full Employment," *Financing American Prosperity*, Twentieth Century Fund, New York, 1945

[257]

Wright, David M.: *The Creation of Purchasing Power*, Harvard University Press, Cambridge, 1942

————: *The Economics of Disturbance*, The Macmillan Company, New York, 1947

INDEX

acceleration of countercyclical controls, *see* Rules of adaptation of controls; *also* Flexibility of controls

administered prices: and cyclical price dispersions, 148-151; and cyclical sensitivity of general price index, 139-141

aggregates, national: as cyclical indexes, 106-107, 120-122, 127-142, 249; as targets of countercyclical procedure, 127-142; criteria for proper choice of, 120-122, 127-142

aggregates versus relationships as guides and goals of countercyclical action, 107-120

agreed high-level balance of budget, 58, 61-67

agricultural policy, 83, 219-220

ambiguity of the term antistagnation procedure, 8

anticyclical policy: cause-removal approach, 18-20, 30-32, 243-244; compensatory approach, 20-23; inevitable combination of cause-removal and compensatory action, 23-33, 250-251

antistagnation policy: cause-removal approach, 8-9, 10-12 (*see also* Reactivation of private enterprise); compensatory approach, 9-12, 13-16; relation to stabilization problem, 4-17

antitrust action: reasonable targets of, 207-213; relation to stabilization policy, 155, 202-203

attack on underlying causes of cycles, *see* Anticyclical policy

automatic stabilization:

in terms of automatic governmental stabilizers, 43-93; effectiveness of existing stabilizers, 52-55; improvements of existing stabilizers, 55-60; nature of countercyclical operations, 47-48; proposed new stabilizers, 61-77; tests of adequacy, 48-50

in terms of reliance upon stabilizing effects of market forces, 98-105; a matter of self-enforcement of binding stabilization targets, 98-105; demonstrated ability of government to enforce targets a prerequisite of self-enforcing effects, 99, 175, 186; degrees of self-enforcement, 103-104, 195-197; gradual nature of self-enforcement, 98-104, 186; misdirected self-enforcement, 111

Bach, G. L., 27

balanced economic growth, 113-120

binding overall targets: absolute limits versus intolerable rate changes, 107, 122-126; business climate and, 98; criteria for determining ceiling, 138-143, 168-172; criteria for determining floor, 138-143, 163-168; guarantee of full-employment opportunities, 133-134, 163-165; guarantee of high-employment floor, 138-142, 163-167; guarantee of stable money, 131-132, 139-142; requisites of suitable targets, 107, 120-122, 127-142; theory of, 38-40, 97-105

Blough, R., 33

Boulding, K. E., 149

Brannan Plan, 219-220

budgets, governmental: *see also* Fiscal policy; Taxes and Public expenditures; agreed high-level balance of, 58, 61-67; deficits, 47, 52-54, 61-63; size in relation to private economic sector, 63-64; surplus, 47

building industry, 223

built-in stabilizers, *see* Automatic stabilizers

business expectations: in the event of binding targets, 39-40, 100-101, 142; in the event of loosely

Lightning Source UK Ltd.
Milton Keynes UK
UKHW020014120422
401412UK00006B/574